MULTI-CLOUD
ADMINISTRATION GUIDE

MULTI-CLOUD ADMINISTRATION GUIDE

*Manage and Optimize Cloud Resources
Across Azure, AWS, GCP, and Alibaba Cloud*

JEROEN MULDER

MERCURY LEARNING AND INFORMATION
Boston, Massachusetts

Publisher: David Pallai
MERCURY LEARNING AND INFORMATION
121 High Street, 3rd Floor
Boston, MA 02110
info@merclearning.com
www.merclearning.com
800-232-0223

J. Mulder. *Multi-Cloud Administration Guide: Manage and Optimize Cloud Resources Across Azure, AWS, GCP, and Alibaba Cloud.*
ISBN: 978-1-50152-265-9

Library of Congress Control Number: 2024938177

242526321   This book is printed on acid-free paper in the United States of America.

TO

My wonderful wife, Judith
and
my girls, Rosalie and Noa

CONTENTS

PREFACE

Cloud-first is not a strategy, but a statement at best. For starters, the cloud does not say anything about your business strategy. It does not say anything about the goals you want to achieve by using cloud technology. Yet almost every company on earth is using the cloud in some form. And then the trouble starts: how do we manage our workloads in the cloud? Many companies find out the hard way that managing the cloud is something different from managing the more traditional IT. That is what this book is about: managing workloads in multi-cloud.

In this book, the reader will get guidance and hands-on instruction on operating multi-cloud environments. We will discuss all the various aspects that come with multi-cloud, such as interoperability between different cloud environments, networking configuration, data integration, and of course security requirements. There is no way of talking about cloud without addressing security and compliance.

This book provides new adopters of the multi-cloud approach with numerous frameworks and ideas for an efficient and sound multi-cloud infrastructure. Throughout the book, you will hopefully find solutions, techniques, designs, and administrative guidance for various types of multi-cloud environments, using AWS, Azure, GCP, and Alibaba Cloud. Why these? Because these are the most popular cloud platforms.

This book will hopefully help you in understanding the necessary steps in multi-cloud management. Let us now review the chapters in the book.

Chapter 1: Using the Cloud Adoption Frameworks – provides an overview of the various *Cloud Adoption Frameworks (CAF)* that help in setting up and manage environments in AWS, Azure, GCP, and Alibaba Cloud. CAFs contain pillars such as security, identity and access, cost, and governance. We will discuss the CAFs of the major providers and show readers how to use them to get maximum benefit.

Chapter 2: Virtualizing and Managing Connectivity – covers all aspects of connectivity in the cloud. Networking in the cloud is software based. In this chapter, you will learn what cloud networking is, with guidance to software building blocks, deployment models and operating networks in cloud computing. Concepts such as SD-WAN, SD-LAN and edge will be discussed. We will also introduce micro-services and how network virtualization can help with this.

Chapter 3: Virtualizing and Managing Storage – explains one of the major benefits of cloud: the almost limitless amount of storage that is available to us. But cloud is a shared resource model, so we need to understand how storage works in cloud, how to make sure that we get the right amount of storage and the right type, with the right performance. Cloud architects and admins should know about I/O, pooling, and the different storage types. All of that is covered in this chapter.

Chapter 4: Virtualizing and Managing Compute – covers the basics of compute, starting with virtual machines, but also discussing serverless and containers as cloud-native technologies. Public cloud providers offer a wide variety of compute power with different deployment models. We need to understand how compute in cloud works regarding for instance CPU and memory. In this chapter, we will also look at on premises offerings by major cloud providers.

Chapter 5: Creating Interoperability – explains why interoperability is one of the biggest challenges in multi-cloud. In this chapter, you will learn how to overcome these challenges between public clouds and between public and private clouds. The chapter discuss various solutions and frameworks such as Open Compute.

Chapter 6: Managing Data in Multi-Cloud – starts with defining a data strategy in multi-cloud. We need that strategy to determine where data is stored, who and what may access data, what the usage of data is as well as how to prevent events such as data-leaks and data loss. You will learn about data quality, security and integrity and data gravity.

Chapter 7: Build and Operate Cloud Native – further explores cloud-native technologies such as serverless and containers. Cloud native development offers solutions to create scalable applications using, for instance, micro-services, container and serverless concepts, and deploying declarative code. This chapter also contains an in-depth explanation of setting up micro-services architectures and how to manage these.

Chapter 8: Building Agnostic with Containers – covers all aspects of developing and managing containers in cloud platforms. Since Kubernetes has evolved to become the industry-standard, we will study setting up and managing Kubernetes clusters with Docker containers in more detail. Next, we will explore the requirements to monitor our containerized workloads.

Chapter 9: Building and Managing Serverless – helps in understanding the concept of serverless, providing guidance in developing and provisioning serverless functions. In this chapter, we will learn how to define our environments as functions, that we can deploy and manage as serverless environments.

Chapter 10: Managing Access Management – introduces the cornerstone of security in multi-cloud: access management. We do not want just anyone to be able to access data and applications in the cloud; we want to have control and thus, we need access management. The chapter provides an overview of various tools that we can use in multi-cloud, but also addresses concepts as privileged access management and Identity as a Service.

Chapter 11: Managing Security – discusses the principle of the single pane of glass view to monitor and manage security. With distributed environments, we must use frameworks that cover the various cloud technologies and tools that can manage various clouds.

Chapter 12: Automating Compliancy – starts with explaining why compliance in cloud might be more of a challenge than in traditional IT, where we have workloads mostly on premise. Governmental bodies, certification authorities and auditors are setting compliancy guardrails to allow usage of major cloud providers. In this chapter, we will learn how to use automation and even AI to ensure that our workloads in the cloud remain compliant.

Companion files with code samples and color figures from the book are available for downloading by writing to info@merclearning.com.

ACKNOWLEDGMENTS

First of all, I have to express my deepest gratitude to my beloved and wonderful wife, my girls, and my entire family and dearest friends. This has been a difficult year with health issues whilst planning for the move to a new house. Thank you for standing next to me, even when I have not been the best version of me. I am truly sorry.

Next, I also have to thank my employer Fujitsu for granting all the time I needed to get well again. And thank you all at my publisher for all your patience.

And of course: a big thank goes to you, dear followers and readers. You're making all the effort worthwhile.

ABOUT THE AUTHOR

After his study in journalism, Jeroen Mulder started his career as an editor for the economic pages of Dutch agricultural newspapers. From 1998, he got involved in internet projects for Reed Business Information, creating websites and digital platforms. Highly attracted by the possibilities of the new digital era and the booming business of the internet, Jeroen decided to pursue a career in digital technologies. In 2000, he joined the IT company *Origin*, as a communication specialist for a group designing and developing cross media platforms. Origin evolved to *AtoS* where he fulfilled many roles, lastly as principal architect. In 2017, he joined the Japanese IT services company Fujitsu as Senior Lead Architect, with a focus on cloud and cloud native technology. From May 2020, he held the position of Head of Applications and Multi-Cloud Services for Fujitsu Netherlands, leading a group of frontrunners in digital transformation. In 2021, he was assigned Principal Cloud Architect at Philips Precision Diagnosis. He returned to Fujitsu in the summer of 2022 as Principal Consultant for the Global Technology Solutions Business Group, focusing on hybrid IT.

ABOUT THE REVIEWER

Fouad Mulla is a seasoned Lead Consultant, Digital Leader, and Cloud Security Architect with 15 years of professional experience in the digital and software industry at global corporations. Fouad excels in designing and implementing comprehensive cloud solutions across multi-cloud platforms. He has assisted numerous businesses in effectively governing and safeguarding their information, proactively identifying cybersecurity risks, and enabling them to make informed and strategic business decisions. Fouad is CISSP, CISM, CASP+ certified.

USING THE CLOUD ADOPTION FRAMEWORKS

INTRODUCTION

Welcome to the cloud. Or better said: welcome to the multi-cloud. The major public cloud providers, such as Azure and AWS, offer *cloud adoption frameworks (CAF)* to help customers set up and manage environments in their clouds. Their usage should be secure and efficient. CAFs are good guidance for architects and engineers. These frameworks contain pillars such as security, identity and access, cost, and governance.

This chapter first discusses what multi-cloud is and next studies the CAFs of the major providers, showing how to use them to get maximum benefit. It also discusses monitoring, including keeping track of (business) *key performance indicators (KPIs)*. At the end of the day, value should be created from our cloud, and value needs to be measured.

STRUCTURE

This chapter discusses the following topics:

- Exploring the business challenges of multi-cloud
- Introducing CAFs: how to use them
- Deep dive in the CAFs of Azure and AWS
- Frameworks by GCP and Alibaba cloud
- Similarities and differences
- Monitoring multi-cloud and keeping track of value propositions

EXPLORING THE BUSINESS CHALLENGE OF MULTI-CLOUD

Before diving into the challenges of multi-cloud, multi-cloud must be defined. Multi-cloud refers to the practice of using multiple cloud service providers to distribute an organization's computing resources and applications. By leveraging the strengths of different cloud platforms such as Amazon Web Services (AWS), Microsoft Azure, Google Cloud Platform (GCP), and others, businesses can optimize their IT infrastructure for performance, cost, security, and scalability.

The rise of multi-cloud strategies has become an important topic in today's IT landscape for several reasons:

- *Flexibility and avoiding vendor lock-in*: Utilizing multiple cloud providers allows organizations to prevent reliance on a single vendor, offering them the flexibility to choose the best services and pricing structures for their specific needs.

- *Optimal resource allocation*: Each cloud provider has unique strengths and weaknesses. A multi-cloud approach enables organizations to allocate resources based on the specific capabilities of each platform, ensuring optimal performance and cost-effectiveness.

- *Enhanced security and compliance*: Distributing data and applications across multiple cloud environments can help organizations reduce the risk of data breaches, meet regulatory requirements, and adhere to industry standards.

- *Increased resilience and redundancy*: A multi-cloud strategy can improve business continuity by providing redundancy in case of outages or failures in a single cloud environment. This ensures that critical applications and data remain available and operational.

- *Innovation and competitive advantage*: Leveraging multiple cloud platforms allows organizations to access cutting-edge technologies and tools, fostering innovation and providing a competitive edge in the market.

Most companies are multi-cloud, even when they have a single cloud strategy. The staff will work with Office365 of Microsoft, store customer contacts in Salesforce, the book travels through SAP Concur, and have meetings through Zoom. At the same time, the backend systems of companies might be hosted on a public cloud such as AWS or Azure or on servers in a privately owned data center. Thus, companies use *software as a service (SaaS)*, *platform as a service (PaaS)*, and *infrastructure as a service (IaaS)*, and all these different environments must be managed. This is the IT challenge of multi-cloud.

Multi-cloud strategies are motivated by the desire to optimize IT infrastructure using different cloud platforms' unique strengths. Benefits include flexibility, optimal resource allocation, enhanced security and compliance, increased resilience and redundancy, and access to innovative technologies. These advantages make multi-cloud strategies relevant and valuable in today's competitive digital landscape.

But what is the business challenge of multi-cloud? Among others, there are the following:

- *Cloud sprawl:* Cloud sprawl is when a company lacks visibility into and control over the spread of its environments in various clouds, including instances, services, or providers across the company.

- *Lock-in, including data gravity:* A mistake that companies often make is assuming that multi-cloud decreases the risk of lock-in. That risk still exists, but now it is spread over multiple clouds. This risk is directly related to portability. It is not as easy as it seems to migrate native services across different clouds. Next, the issue of data gravity plays an important role. Applications often need to be close to the data. Having data sitting in a different cloud than the application may lead to issues such as latency. Moreover, rules for compliancy can cause issues. Think of laws that prohibit companies from having data outside country borders, limiting the choice of clouds.

- *Lack of multilingual knowledge:* If a company uses various clouds, it also means that it has to know how to use these clouds. Although the principles of public cloud are largely the same, clouds such as AWS and Azure still do differ in terms of operating workloads on these platforms. The company will need resources, engineers, and architects to cover the different technologies used.

- *Dynamics of changing cloud features:* Cloud is evolving fast. During the yearly large conferences such as Ignite for Azure and re: Invent for AWS, these providers launch hundreds of new services. Over the year, even more new features and services are added to the portfolio. Not everything might be of use to a company, but it needs to keep track of features and releases of new services to be able to improve its own cloud environments. This is not trivial, and certainly not when a company is operating multi-cloud. In most cases, cloud providers will help their customers in getting the best out of the cloud by adopting the right technologies.

- *Integration:* Using environments on different platforms might lead to integration issues simply because workloads cannot communicate with each other. This can be due to network issues such as bad routing and because technologies are not compatible.

Of course, there are many more challenges to overcome. Think of network performance and latency, security and compliance, governance, and policy management, not to mention controlling costs and the cloud vendor relationship as part of the governance. All these items are captured in the cloud adoption frameworks. During the course of this book, these items will be discussed in more detail.

Following best practices and guidelines from CAFs can help to at least address these issues and design solutions to overcome them.

INTRODUCING CAFs: HOW TO USE THEM

What is a cloud adoption framework, and how should it be used? Maybe a better first question would be: why use a CAF? The answer to that question is: because as long as the guidelines and guardrails as defined in the CAF are followed, it will be a lot easier to get support from the cloud providers when encountering issues. It is fair to say that the CAF provides a universal language between the cloud provider and the customer. The CAF is basically a set of documentation with guidelines and best practices on how to best design and operate the cloud.

Before we dive into the details of the CAF for Azure and AWS, which are the leading public clouds, we will study the generic pillars of the CAF. The six pillars of the CAF are as follows.

Strategy

Moving to the cloud just because you can is not a strategy. Cloud first, for that matter, is not a strategy. Using cloud technology should be valuable to a business. This means that there must be a business justification. This section discusses similarities and differences between the various CAFs. A business will have an ambition laid out in business goals. The next step is to define how the business can achieve those goals and, in the end, fulfill the ambition. The architecture will lay out what the ambition will look like (sometimes referred to as the North Star architecture), but more importantly, how to reach the goals. What steps must a business take, and in what order? That defines the business strategy.

Plan

Despite what a lot of people think, the cloud is not solely about technology. Of course, technology is an important part of the CAF and the forthcoming architecture, but cloud adoption is even more so about aligning business processes, people, and technology. In adopting the cloud, workloads such as applications will likely move to a cloud platform. Ask these questions in drafting the plan:

- What do we use?
- Why do we use it?
- Who uses it?
- When do we use it?

The answers will help in defining the strategy to migrate workloads and applications to the designated cloud platform. One essential question is: does it bring added value to move a workload to the cloud? Followed by the question: how will it bring that value? This is where the following five Rs is important:

- *Rehost*: This is lift and shift. Workloads such as applications are not modified but migrated as they are to the cloud platform.
- *Replatform*: This is lift and shift too, but this time some modifications are done. For instance, a business chooses to keep the application as it is, but some parts are shifted to managed services by the cloud provider. Think of having the databases managed through a managed service such as *Relational Database Service (RDS)* by AWS.
- *Refactor*: By refactoring an application, the application is modified. Services are replaced by cloud-native services, for instance using container technology or serverless functions. This often means a redesign of the application, such as from a monolith architecture to microservices.
- *Retire*: An outcome of the strategy or planning phase might be that an application is obsolete and can be retired.
- *Retain*: There might also be workloads and applications that cannot be migrated to the cloud for various reasons. The application must be close to the data source or the machine that it operates, which is typically the case in *operational technology (OT)*. Think of manufacturing or healthcare. There might be restrictions on using public clouds because of legal compliance, or an application is critical to the business but simply too old to move to the cloud. These might all be reasons to retain an application, meaning that they are not touched at all.

Prepare

The next step is to prepare the cloud platform that will host the workloads and applications. Typically, this starts with setting up the landing zone in the designated cloud. The landing zone is the foundation. If we are building a house, we need to know what the house looks like before we can lay out the foundation. It is the same for the cloud. We have to know what sort of workloads we will be migrating to the cloud to define and design the landing zone. During the course of this book, we will discuss the landing zone extensively.

Adopt

This is the phase where the workloads are migrated to the cloud according to the plan and the migration strategy that have been defined. We can either lift and shift workloads as-is or transform the workloads and adopt cloud-native services.

Govern

We need an organization that is able to manage the cloud and the workloads in the cloud. These are necessarily the same thing. In the govern phase, organizations might want to form a *cloud center of excellence (CCoE)* with a specific platform team, which manages the cloud, and application teams that manage the specific applications in the cloud.

Operate

This is the phase where organizations will monitor the workloads and make sure that these are performing in the optimal way, following the best practices of the cloud provider and fulfilling the business requirements.

Most CAFs have added two more pillars to these six: security and sustainability. These might be debatable since both security and sustainability should be intrinsic and taken into account for every workload that is migrated to a cloud platform. In other words, security and sustainability are part of all six stages in the CAF. Yet, both AWS and Azure have security as separate pillars in the CAF, as is explained in the next section.

DEEP DIVE IN THE CAFs OF AZURE AND AWS

First, take a look at the CAF of AWS. It includes the generic pillars of the CAF, but AWS calls these the foundational capabilities:

- *Business*: The business perspective helps to set the strategy for digital transformation. The AWS CAF takes the need for digital transformation as the starting point. In other words: it is not the question of whether a business must digitize but how. The business perspective helps define how cloud investments can accelerate this transformation.

- *People*: The people's perspective is mainly about transforming the culture of a business. Digital businesses need people with a growth mindset and people who are willing to learn continuously and change accordingly. One remarkable aspect of the people's perspective is *cloud fluency*. People need to understand the cloud, in this case, AWS. It might require a workforce transformation.

- *Governance*: The governance perspective is all about project and program management, guiding organizations in their journey to AWS, and making optimal use of AWS services. This includes risk management and cloud financial management or FinOps.

- *Platform*: This is, obviously, about the cloud platform itself and how to build it in AWS. There is one golden rule that applies here: AWS is responsible for the cloud, the customer for what is in the cloud. AWS provides its customers with a toolkit to build a virtual private cloud on their platform. It is up to the customer to use these tools and build a scalable, resilient environment to host applications and data. The CAF will help with best practices for platform, data, and application architecture, including *continuous integration and continuous delivery (CI/CD)* through (automated) pipelines that integrate with AWS.

- *Security*: As said in the previous section, AWS and Azure have separate pillars for implementing and managing security in the cloud. It includes *identity and access management (IAM)*; threat detection; protection of infrastructure, data, and applications; and the management of the security postures in the cloud.

- *Operations*: From the business, requirements will be set concerning performance and reliability. This must be monitored and managed. Typically, IT operators manage environments using IT service management frameworks such as ITIL, including incident, change, configuration, and problem management. Observability is key, next to fast detection and response. The AWS CAF specifically mentions AIOps, predictive management through *artificial intelligence (AI)*.

These capabilities are required to go through cloud transformation value chains. The value chains lead to the following business outcomes:

- Reduction of business risks
- Improved *environmental, social, and governance (ESG)* values
- Growth of revenue
- Increasing operational efficiency

To reach goals in business outcomes, businesses must go through a transformation. AWS specifies four transformation domains:

- Technology
- Process
- Organization
- Product

All these domains will continuously change and transform. But by using cloud technology, these transformations can become more agile: adaptable and scalable. If we put this all together, we get the CAF of AWS, as shown in the following Figure 1.1:

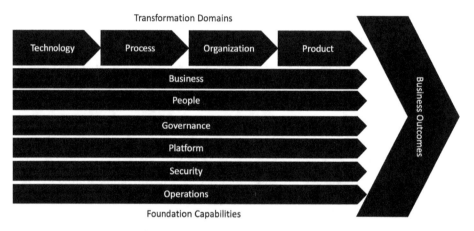

FIGURE 1.1 High-level representation of AWS Cloud Adoption Framework.

A whitepaper about AWS CAF can be found at: *https://aws.amazon.com/professional-services/CAF/*.

As we will see in Azure as well, the CAF is not a one-time exercise but more of a lifecycle. That makes sense if we realize that the business, and the cloud itself, constantly changes with updates and new features. AWS presents this as the cycle from envisioning to aligning, launching, and scaling. The business envisions how the cloud can help in achieving business goals, aligns this with the foundation capabilities, launches the new services and products as *minimal viable products (MVP)* or a pilot, and lastly, expands it to production. From there, the cycle starts over again.

Microsoft Azure presents the CAF as a cloud adoption lifecycle, too, starting with the definition of a strategy. The strategy is all about defining the desired business outcomes and the accurate justification to start the cloud journey. The Azure CAF is represented in the following Figure 1.2:

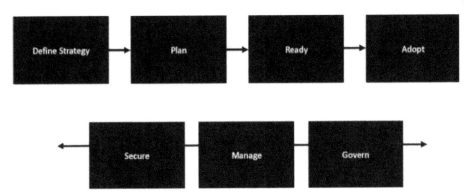

FIGURE 1.2 High-level representation of Azure Cloud Adoption Framework.

To get started with the Azure CAF, Microsoft recommends working from scenarios. These scenarios have been chosen from various business standpoints. Perhaps one remarkable scenario is the hybrid and multi-cloud scenario. It is remarkable since this scenario focuses on businesses that will have more than one cloud and even cloud combined with on-premises environments. Using the CAF, businesses can establish unified and centralized operations across these different clouds and their on-premises data center. The CCoE is an important element in this scenario, combining knowledge of various cloud solutions and integrating these into one unified set of processes and best practices for architecture.

One other special scenario is desktop virtualization, allowing customers to migrate to workplaces to *Azure Virtual Desktop (AVD)*. Using the CAF guidelines, businesses can implement AVD instances in Azure and integrate this with Windows and Office365, the latter being a SaaS proposition.

These scenarios all follow the same approach that is set out in the CAF: strategy, plan, migrate, manage (operate), and govern. The business will formulate the ambition and the goals that are worked out in a plan. Next, the workloads—for instance, the virtual desktops—are migrated. An organization centralized in the governing CCoE will manage the workloads compliant with the business requirements.

The Azure CAF pays extra attention to so-called antipatterns. There is a list of antipatterns to be found on *https://learn.microsoft.com/en-us/azure/cloud-adoption-framework/antipatterns/antipatterns-to-avoid*, but there are two in particular that we like to mention here:

- *IT as cloud provider*: This is the antipattern where the business treats its IT organization as the cloud provider. It is not the cloud provider; they are using technologies in the cloud. Keep in mind that the cloud provider is responsible for the cloud, the customer for what is in the cloud. For example, the failure of a region in Azure or any other cloud is not the responsibility of the IT organization. Monitoring and managing the resiliency of specific workloads, where these failover to another region, is the responsibility of IT. That, however, starts with business requirements and the forthcoming architecture to design the resiliency of that workload.

- *Inaccurate out-of-the-box security assumptions*: Again, cloud providers offer a massive number of tools that will help organizations to secure workloads in the cloud. Public clouds are likely the best-secured platforms in the world, but that doesn't mean that workloads are secured by default. That depends on how the customer applies security guardrails, guidelines, and usage of tools to protect applications and data in the cloud. The assumption that the cloud provider automatically takes care of that is wrong.

The appropriate use of the CAF will help avoid these pitfalls and antipatterns. The next section describes the CAFs of Google Cloud and Alibaba Cloud, which are a bit different from AWS and Azure.

FRAMEWORKS BY GCP AND ALIBABA CLOUD

Google Cloud Platform (GCP) and Alibaba Cloud also have versions of a CAF. These will be studied in this section. GCP defines its CAF in four themes and, with that, takes a completely different approach to cloud adoption.

Lead

This is about leadership from sponsors in the business, which supports the migration to the cloud. It also includes the teams themselves and how they collaborate and motivate one another in a successful transition and transformation to a cloud platform.

Learn

Cloud adoption is so much about technology but more about adopting a new way of working. Companies will have to learn how public clouds work. In other CAFs, this is typically gathered under people or as part of the operating model, including a center of excellence. Moreover, the staff needs to be trained and upskilled. This goes beyond technical skills.

A company and its employees also must learn to understand how, for instance, financing works in the cloud. What financial models are applicable in the cloud? Typically, organizations start with pay-as-you-go in the cloud, but there might be situations where reserved capacity might be a much better choice. Reserved capacity often means that a company still needs to invest or at least confirm and commit that it will use resources in the cloud for a longer period.

Migrating to the cloud is a learning process in many aspects. Not only is the technology different from traditional IT, but applications and data are managed differently in the cloud. Migrating to the cloud is a huge change and requires transformation and change management. Governance, security, development, operations, and financial management: these are all part of the transformation. This book focuses mainly on the technical management of cloud environments, but it is good to keep in mind that cloud adoption involves more than just technology.

Scale

One of the most important and obvious reasons for companies is that the cloud offers scalability. GCP focuses on limiting manual processes as much as possible. Hence, automation is a major topic in the adoption framework. Workloads and services in the cloud must scale automatically but are always triggered by business processes. This is referred to as event-driven. For example, an event can be a customer that places an order on a Web site. That will trigger the process of payment and delivery process of the product. When a company launches a new product, this might lead to a peak in orders. Using automation, the cloud services will automatically scale to facilitate the peak and make sure that the Web sites and associated applications keep performant. As soon as traffic decreases again, automation will also take care of scaling down, avoiding unnecessary costs.

Secure

Performance and cost control are important, but there is one more item that is at least equally important or perhaps even more important. The fourth pillar in the CAF of GCP is, therefore, security. Security starts with identity and access management but also includes several tactics and techniques to protect workloads and services in the cloud.

Next, the framework addresses three levels of adoption: tactical, strategic, and transformational. Simply put, tactical concerns the individual workloads in the cloud, but there is no plan to leverage cloud-native services, enhancing automation and scalability. It is a simple lift and shift of workloads to the cloud, causing no disruption to the company. Basically, the cloud is used as a traditional data center.

On a strategic level, there is a plan to automate individual workloads and start decreasing the manual efforts to manage these workloads. On the transformational level, organizations use the cloud to innovate, using automated development and deployment pipelines to enable regular releases of new features to products or new products as a whole. The cloud now has become essential in shortening time to market, decreasing the cost of sales, and, with that, increasing revenue. The cloud is adding value to the business and, with that, has become part of the digital transformation of the business. This is discussed in the final section of this chapter.

Putting the four pillars and the three stages together results in the cloud maturity scale that GCP uses. It can be seen in the following Figure 1.3:

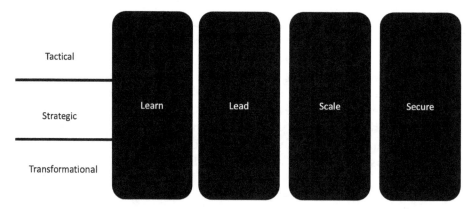

FIGURE 1.3 High-level representation of Google Cloud Adoption Framework.

This cloud maturity scale can be used to define where the organization stands and what the ambition should be. The following example makes this a bit clearer:

- Scale on a tactical level means that environments are hardly scalable. There is a lot of manual work involved in managing the workload.
- On a strategic level, an organization might already use automated templates to deploy workloads.
- On the transformational level, all workloads scale automatically, using blueprints from CI/CD pipelines, including automated deployment and scaling scripts. Manual work is very limited.

We can do the same for the three other pillars. This will help architects define what is needed to get the most out of the cloud and help businesses by adding value. A whitepaper with Google's approach to the CAF can be found at *https://cloud. google.com/adoption-framework*.

Like Azure, Alibaba Cloud presents the CAF as a journey and cloud lifecycle. The first step is setting the strategy. Essential in setting the strategy is answering the question of why the organization should move to the cloud; Alibaba calls this Cloud Adoption Motivation. Quite obviously, this starts with business requirements. Next, Alibaba Cloud provides examples of motivations such as:

- Speeding up global delivery of applications.
- *Reduction of costs*: Remarkably, Alibaba Cloud argues that most costs in the cloud are *operating expenditure (OPEX)*, where upfront investments are not needed in contrast to *capital expenditure (CAPEX)*. A characteristic of CAPEX is the need for upfront investments. This might be true for a lot of cloud services, but there are situations where upfront investments will be required, for instance, when reserving resources for a longer period in the cloud. The shift from CAPEX to OPEX in a cloud computing context has significant business impacts:
  - *Financial flexibility*: OPEX models allow organizations to pay for services as they use them, providing greater financial flexibility and reducing upfront investments typically associated with CAPEX.
  - *Scalability*: OPEX models enable businesses to scale resources up or down based on demand, improving cost efficiency, and reducing the risk of overprovisioning or underutilization.

- *Faster time-to-market*: Lower upfront investments and the ability to quickly deploy resources reduce the time-to-market for new products or services, offering a competitive advantage.
- *Focus on core business*: By moving to an OPEX model, organizations can allocate resources toward their core business functions, while cloud providers handle infrastructure management and maintenance.
- *Improved security*: In this case also, there is a trade-off. Public clouds are likely the best-secured platforms in the world since they serve millions of customers. Cloud providers offer extensive toolsets to protect workloads and data in their clouds. However, it is still the responsibility of the customer to use these tools.

Evaluating all these aspects is part of setting the strategy. The following step in Cloud Adoption Motivation is setting up the organization. Alibaba Cloud recommends having a Cloud Center of Excellence with cloud technologists, application owners, and security specialists. The application team works closely together with the business, responding to the business requirements. The cloud team is mainly responsible for the continuity of services. Lastly, the security team takes care of defining and controlling the security guardrails that must be followed in the cloud.

The next phase is cloud adoption preparation and management framework building. The first and main task in this phase is setting up the landing zone in the cloud. In the CAF, the landing zone refers to the foundation of cloud management, including:

- Financial management
- Security management
- Compliance and auditing
- Automation
- Network planning
- Resource planning

Once the landing zone has been defined, our cloud is ready to onboard applications, which is the following phase. The phase includes the migration of applications and data and development innovations to enhance applications and usage of data. In the case of the latter, an example is adding artificial intelligence to analyze data.

Now, we have a CCoE helping the business to start the digital transformation and setting up the landing zone to start adopting applications and data. This new cloud environment must be operated and managed from a cost and security perspective, identifying and quantifying risks that may impact the business in a timely manner and ensuring business continuity. This is done in the final phase of organization and governance. Reacting to events will lead to new insights and new motivations, taking us back to the first phase in the CAF, adjusting the cloud adoption strategy.

The complete CAF of Alibaba Cloud can be downloaded from: *https:// resource.al-ibabacloud.com/whitepaper/id_4303?spm=a3c0i.23458820.2359 477120.14.66667d3fFxjdMN.*

SIMILARITIES AND DIFFERENCES

If we compare the different CAFs with the generic principles, we will notice similarities. All CAFs start with defining the business strategy, which is absolutely a crucial step. There is no point in moving to the cloud just for the sake of being in the cloud: there has to be a business justification. A lift and shift of environments—applications—to a cloud platform will barely bring any benefit. The rationales for businesses to migrate and embrace cloud technology include business agility and scaling.

- *Business agility*: The ability of businesses to respond and adapt to changing customer demand or market circumstances swiftly. Since in the cloud, virtually everything is coded using infrastructure as code and configuration as code, it allows for applying fast changes and rapid development. One of the key elements in achieving business agility is scaling.
- *Scaling:* Remember that scaling can be both up and down, preferably automated. This way, a business will have the ability to use exactly what is required and also pay for the resources that are used. This is addressed by the CAFs from various angles: automation, financial management, and resource management.

Typically, we see a couple of common use cases for businesses to migrate to the cloud. Outsourcing is the number one reason why the existing data center is decommissioned. This is often financially driven, where data centers require a lot of upfront investments that must be depreciated over the years. These are CAPEX costs. By migrating to the cloud, companies can shift to OPEX.

Another reason is the lack of efficiency in the existing setup of IT. There might be technical debt slowing down development and increasing operational efforts. A lack of skilled resources to manage the legacy IT or skilled resources that cannot be utilized for innovations because of too many operational tasks will also be arguments to migrate to the cloud, including the adoption of automated, cloud-native services.

All CAFs emphasize the need for training and upskilling people. This includes technical staff but also other personnel, including financial specialists and senior management. Companies shifting to the cloud as part of digital transformation programs will encounter cultural changes. That requires sponsorship and teamwork. Management must endorse the adoption of the cloud; teams will need to learn to work with the cloud.

One other major similarity is the drive to set up specific governance. IT and business must be aligned, but in the cloud, this becomes even more important. The reason for this is that with the cloud, IT shifts closer to the business, meaning that the business gets more control over the development and deployment of products, whereas, in more traditional IT, the business is completely dependent on how fast IT can implement technology. In the cloud, this has become a much easier process. Every asset is turned into code, including the infrastructure. There is no need to define a long list of requirements for equipment; using the cloud, the infrastructure is a string of code that can be easily adapted to the exact needs of the application.

The cloud enables business agility and makes businesses really scalable, but the cloud must be managed. That is where the CAFs focus on governance and management, stressing the importance of:

- Cost management
- Security management
- Development and deployment of resources (starting with MVPs)

The outcome of the CAF should be business value. That is the central theme in all CAFs. To achieve this, organizations must agree on the strategy. All stakeholders must be involved and convinced that cloud migrations will add business value. The following step is to train the appropriate capabilities in the organization. People, processes, and technology must be aligned in a new way of working. Cloud adoption will bring significant changes to an organization, and this needs careful planning in a lot of domains. The CAFs will show where the organization stands and where and how it can grow those capabilities. This is where all discussed CAFs have the same focus.

Still, there are differences too. These differences can often be explained by the origin of a specific cloud provider. AWS is completely cloud-born and focuses primarily on cloud-native services. With that, AWS is set up in a more modular way, offering a lot of different, customizable building blocks, whereas Azure offers more out-of-box, complete services. Next, Azure also focuses more on hybrid clouds. Microsoft was already an established name in computing, with an operation system that could run on a variety of machines, from personal computers to servers. Microsoft is used to working in *hybrid* environments.

The Azure portfolio contains several services that enable hybrid strategy. Think of Azure Stack, which is basically an Azure extension on-premises, but also Azure Arc, which allows bringing non-Azure workloads under the control of the Azure console.

Note that customers could have AWS on-premises, too, via VMWare on AWS, allowing on-premises VMWare stacks to be stretched into the AWS cloud. This was later followed by native AWS on-premises, with AWS Outposts.

The bottom line is that a company that starts its journey in digital transformation and adopting cloud services must first set out its business strategy. From the business strategy, a solution and the right fit of cloud technology will follow. The CAFs are a great aid in defining the business strategy and how cloud technology can help in achieving the goals and ambition of that strategy.

MONITORING MULTI-CLOUD AND KEEPING TRACK OF VALUE PROPOSITIONS

So far, various CAFs have been discussed that will guide in setting up environments in the cloud. If workloads are running in Azure and AWS, just as an example, then a multi-cloud environment must be managed. However, the same is already true when a company uses SaaS, such as Office365 and Salesforce, next to having backend IT hosted in a hyperscale cloud (major cloud providers with a global presence, such as the providers that we discuss in this book: AWS, Azure, GCP, and Alibaba Cloud).

Alternatively, an organization might have workloads in public clouds and on-premises in privately owned data centers—this is typically referred to as a hybrid. To cut a long story short, the introduction of cloud technology has not made things easier or less complex. That is the reason why companies need to think about their cloud strategy before they start migrating workloads to any cloud. The CAFs are good guidance in defining that strategy, as discussed in the previous section.

But that is not all. Through the course of this book, it is shown that managing multi-cloud is not easy. There is a good reason why all CAFs mention the human factor in setting up and managing cloud environments. Professionals are needed: architects, engineers, and developers that have a thorough knowledge of the cloud.

Those are the hard skills, but soft skills are just as important. Cloud architects must be able to understand the business and translate business challenges into cloud solutions. It cannot be stressed enough: going to the cloud just because it is possible will not bring any value to the business. At the end of the day, it is about value propositions. How can cloud technology help businesses in digital transformation and move the business forward? Cloud architects need to understand business metrics.

Measuring Business Metrics

Measuring the performance of the business is done through business metrics that quantify that performance. Quantifying parameters can be defined in finance, marketing, operations, production, human resources, and IT. The following are examples:

- Sales revenue
- Cost of sales
- Conversion rate
- Web traffic
- Goods sold
- Time to delivery
- Payment cycle, including *days payable outstanding (DPO)*

Cloud technology can help in increasing revenue, lowering overall operating costs, reaching more customers, increasing the speed of innovation, releasing new products, and decreasing time to market. Is this part of the CAFs? The answer is yes. The CAFs are not as much about the technology itself. That is where concepts such as well-architected frameworks and reference architectures play a much bigger role. The CAF is really about business adoption and implementing value propositions. So, how can a business increase sales using the cloud? For instance, by providing webshops around the globe that automatically process orders, thus decreasing the cost of sales.

That is the key to digital transformation—companies adopting digital technologies to change the existing business or, even better, create new business. The cloud can help in this, but it likely requires a new operating model wherein digital expertise plays a much bigger role. First of all, the transformation must be data driven. Only through accurate, timely, and continuous analysis of data will a business be able to make the right decisions. What does the customer want? What is the competition doing? What is the best time to launch a new product? This is where the cloud brings real added value. In the cloud, data can be brought together, analyzed, and used to refine the strategy.

It has a major impact on a lot of aspects of a company. Does the company have the right skills? Has it chosen the right partners? Is the leadership supporting the changes? Does the company have a budget? Does it have access to the right data sources? Who should have access to data and resources? Before getting into the application, data, and technical architectures, these questions must be answered. It defines the level of adoption of the change that comes with digital transformation and the use of cloud technology.

Introducing Best Practices in Monitoring

Once solutions are deployed in the cloud, they must be managed. That is the core topic of this book. Managing starts with seeing what is going on; it starts with monitoring. Now, admins are likely not very fond of having to use multiple tools and consoles to monitor the various environments. Monitoring multi-cloud is best served with a single pane of glass view. Best practices in monitoring are as follows:

- Use monitoring tools that are capable of monitoring heterogeneous multi-cloud environments.
- Have a *configuration management database (CMDB)* that is truly responsive to the cloud. If an engineer spins up a VM in the cloud, it must be reflected as a new asset in the CMDB.
- Following the CMDB and the responsiveness: monitoring must support automation.
- Preferably, monitoring must be intelligent, supporting anomaly detection, self-healing, and automated remediation.

The next level is to have monitoring that can determine the impact of events on the business metrics. Full-stack visualization is needed for this: linking business processes to technical artifacts. This is the domain of AIOps, tooling that can determine the impact of events on business processes across multi-cloud. This is part of the operations phase in the CAFs. Operations typically contain:

- Operations fulfilling business commitments.
- Security ensuring business resilience.
- Governance limiting business risks.
- Monitoring with full-stack visibility is a must.

This concludes this first introductory chapter. The next chapters will explain how to manage environments in multi-cloud.

CONCLUSION

Before learning how to manage environments in the cloud, the cloud must first be reached. This starts with understanding why a company migrates its IT landscape to the cloud. There has to be a business justification to start a cloud migration. Moving to the cloud will have a major impact on the company: on the business, the operations, and the people. This book mainly focuses on the major hyperscalers AWS, Azure, GCP, and Alibaba Cloud. This chapter described the cloud adoption frameworks (CAF) of these providers. All CAFs start with the business justification and next provide best practices on how to transform a business by migrating to their respective cloud platforms. The CAFs focus on setting up a cloud management organization, obtaining cost control, and ensuring that environments in the cloud are protected and secured.

Migrating to the cloud, therefore, starts with studying the CAF and applying the best practices. The following chapters will explain how to manage the environments once they have been migrated to the cloud, starting with understanding the principles of virtualized compute resources.

KEY POINTS

- Cloud adoption frameworks are a good guide in setting a strategy to migrate workloads to the cloud.
- Every cloud provider—Azure, AWS, Google Cloud, and Alibaba Cloud—offers a CAF.

- It is very important to remember that every move to the cloud must have a business justification. Why is a business moving to the cloud, and what are the benefits to the business?
- CAFs cover important topics such as setting up governance, controlling costs, and operating security according to the best practices of the respective provider.

QUESTIONS

1. In what migration strategy is a workload simply lifted and shifted to the cloud without making changes to it?

2. What are the four stages in Google's CAF?

3. An important aspect of monitoring is having a CMDB. What is a CMDB?

Answers appear in the appendix.

2

VIRTUALIZING AND MANAGING CONNECTIVITY

INTRODUCTION

To understand connectivity in the cloud, the virtualization of networks must be understood, since networking in the cloud is also software based. This chapter explains what cloud networking is, with guidance on software building blocks, deployment models, and operating networks in the cloud. Concepts such as SD-WAN, SD-LAN, and Edge will be discussed. Microservices will also be discussed, as well as how network virtualization can help with this.

STRUCTURE

This chapter discusses the following topics:

- Building blocks in networks
- Cloud network operations
- Deployment concepts SD-WAN, Edge, and SASE
- Managing networks in multi-cloud

BUILDING BLOCKS IN NETWORKS

In the cloud, everything is coded, and with that, almost everything is virtualized. Public clouds use the concept of shared resources on which capacity can be reserved for one tenant. This includes computing, storage, and networks. The following chapters discuss computing and storage, but before building servers and developing applications on top of these servers, connectivity must be created. This section explains what the building blocks are for networks and how these are implemented in the cloud, discussing the various options in the major public clouds.

The three main building blocks for networks and connectivity are switches, routers, and firewalls. That applies to the cloud too. All of them take care of the following:

- Switch
- Router
- Firewall
- Load balancing
- Virtual network function (VNF)
- Network function virtualization (NFV)

The cloud has virtualized, software-defined versions of these building blocks. The first example is the virtual switch or vSwitch. In essence, this is software that allows a virtual machine to communicate with another machine to set up connections between machines. Virtual switches do the same thing as physical switches, but in the cloud, everything is transferred into code. So, a virtual switch is just software. That makes it easier to manage, as administrators will only have to look at some code and do not have to worry about hardware and network cabling. The software virtualizes the hardware and the cabling, so to speak.

Virtual Switching

Virtual switches are used in the cloud to connect to networks. Like physical switches, they use *network interface cards (NIC)* with virtual ports, which allow for traffic to the switch and to the network that it is attached to. The switch will detect data packets and allow it to travel to the packet's destination, as shown in Figure 2.1:

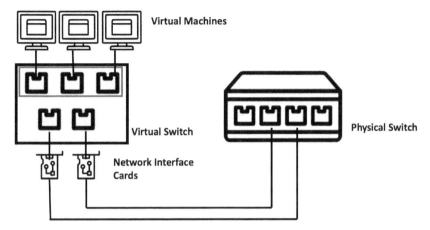

FIGURE 2.1 Working of a virtual switch.

Cloud providers offer various solutions for virtual switching. Azure uses vNets, virtual networks. vNets allow for traffic between virtual machines and other resources in Azure, and they look very much like the *virtual local area networks (vLAN)* in the traditional data center, allowing for segmentation in the data center network. Typically, every resource in a vNet will be able to communicate with each other. To enable communication between resources in different vNets, vNet peering must be set up in Azure. The basic setup of a vNet is shown in Figure 2.2:

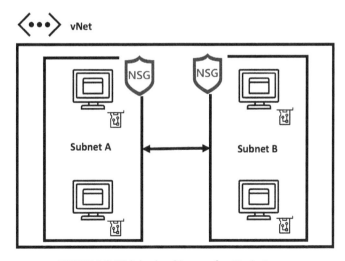

FIGURE 2.2 High-level architecture for vNet in Azure.

Network security groups (NSG) in Azure are used as *access control lists (ACL)* to determine what traffic is allowed or denied to resources in the network subnets. The principle of vNet peering is shown in Figure 2.3:

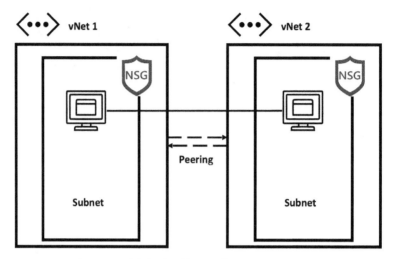

FIGURE 2.3 High-level architecture for vNet peering in Azure.

The principle of virtual networks and switching works the same in other clouds. AWS uses *virtual private networks (VPC)*. Just like in Azure, subnets can be defined in a VPC, allowing for more segmentation of networks. To allow resources in one VPC to communicate with resources in another VPC, use VPC peering connections. But what if there are multiple VPCs to connect to each other and route traffic? AWS offers *Transit Gateway* as a solution, acting as a central hub, also to the outside world over the Internet. The basic principle of the *Transit Gateway* is shown in Figure 2.4:

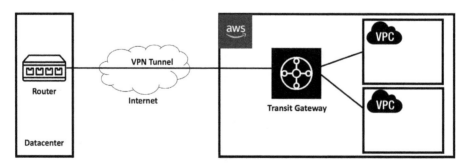

FIGURE 2.4 High-level architecture for Transit Gateway in AWS.

VPCs are also found in Google Cloud. As you may have concluded already, vNets and VPCs are not exactly the same as switches. They act on layer 2 of the *open systems interconnection (OSI)* model: the data link layer, which is the layer that only takes care of the transport of data.

Routing

Making sure that data reaches its destination requires more than just switching or, in the cloud, setting up vNets or VPCs. Data must be directed in the right direction. That is what routing is used for. Routing in the cloud is not quite like the traditional router in the traditional data center. Switching can be a task of a router, which supports the following functions: connecting different networks, receiving and sending data packets, and segmentizing network zones. Routers typically act on layer 3 of the OSI model: the network layer, connecting networks physically to each other.

Routing in cloud environments works differently. In that case, routing still takes care of connections between networks, either in the cloud or with on-premises networks, but it adapts dynamically to changing network conditions using the *border gateway protocol (BGP)*. Routing selects the optimal path for traffic in a network or between networks, and hence it is dynamic. All clouds use BGP as a routing protocol, allowing routers to quickly adapt to send packets over a different connection if an Internet route goes down, taking dynamic decisions based on paths, rules, or network policies.

Each BGP router maintains a standard routing table that is used to route packets to their destination. This table is used in conjunction with a separate routing table, the *routing information base (RIB)*, which is a data table stored on a server on the BGP router. This is at the level of routing tables in the cloud. In all clouds, these routing tables, or *user-defined routing (UDR)* as they are referred to in Azure, must be defined. The route table holds a set of rules that determine where network traffic will be directed, with preferred and secondary routes.

In addition to BGP, other routing protocols that could be used in cloud environments include *open shortest path first (OSPF)*, *enhanced interior gateway routing protocol (EIGRP)*, *routing information protocol (RIP)*, *intermediate system to intermediate system (IS-IS)*, and static routing. While BGP is the most common choice for public cloud providers due to its scalability and flexibility, private and hybrid cloud environments may use different protocols depending on network requirements and infrastructure.

Virtual Firewalls

Routing is essential for the next artifact in networking: firewalls. Firewalls are essential in allowing or rejecting network traffic coming in or going out of cloud environments. Since it is very hard to install physical firewalls (not impossible, though), the firewalls are virtualized, meaning that we have software fulfilling the function of a firewall. That function will be the same as in a physical data center. Firewalls help with intrusion prevention, filtering of Internet addresses such as *uniform resource locators (URL)*, IP, and blocking specific files or file types.

The big advantage of virtual firewalls is that they are scalable: they can be applied on various locations in the network and can protect specific resources, allowing for fine-grained protection of resources. For instance, *Web application firewalls (WAF)* can be used to protect a specific application or set of applications, filtering and monitoring HTTP traffic between a Web application and the Internet. Figure 2.5 shows a simple setup of a WAF:

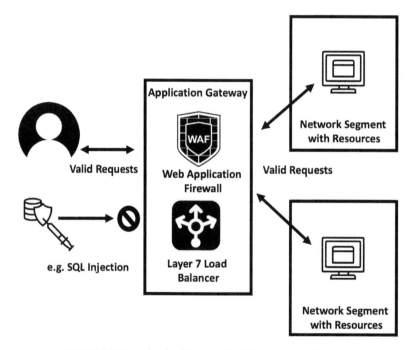

FIGURE 2.5 Example of architecture for Web Application Firewall.

Notice that the diagram also shows a load balancer. Load balancing will be discussed in a moment.

Cloud providers offer native firewalls, such as Azure Firewall, AWS Network Firewall, and Control Traffic, in Google Cloud and Alibaba Cloud Firewall. Yet, companies might want to use firewalls of companies that are specialized in designing these devices and that they use in their data centers. Cloud providers also have marketplaces where customers can find products and services of third-party companies, enabled for use in the cloud. Figure 2.6 shows the screen in AWS Marketplace, offering various types of firewalls that are supported by AWS. The following screenshot shows Palo Alto and Fortinet, but there are many other options:

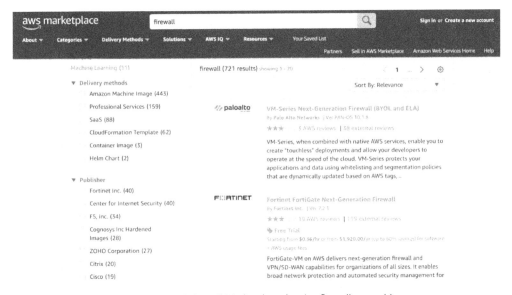

FIGURE 2.6 AWS Marketplace showing firewall propositions.

Note the left-hand side of the screen, where the various deployment methods are shown. A firewall can be deployed as an *Amazon Machine Image (AMI)*, a CloudFormation template, or a container image, among others. The AMI will deploy the firewall software as an image to a virtual machine. CloudFormation is the *infrastructure as code (IaC)* engine in AWS. One other possibility is to get the firewall as *software as a service (SaaS)*, completely managed by the vendor.

Native cloud provider firewalls and third-party firewalls or software as a service (SaaS) have some key differences that may affect which one is the best option for an organization:

- Native cloud provider firewalls are tightly integrated with the cloud platform they are provided by, such as AWS, Azure, or GCP. This can make them easier to set up and manage, as they are designed to work seamlessly with the cloud infrastructure. Third-party firewalls, on the other hand, may require more configuration to work with cloud platforms, although many of them now offer integrations with major cloud providers.

- Third-party firewalls and SaaS offerings may provide a wider range of features and greater customization options than native cloud provider firewalls. This can be particularly important for organizations with complex security needs, as third-party firewalls may offer more advanced threat detection and mitigation capabilities.

- Native cloud provider firewalls are often included in the pricing of the cloud platform, which can make them a more cost-effective option for organizations with simpler security requirements. Third-party firewalls and SaaS offerings may require additional licensing fees or subscription costs.

- Native cloud provider firewalls are typically supported by the cloud platform provider, which can provide a more seamless support experience. Third-party firewalls and SaaS offerings may have their own support teams, which can provide more specialized support but may require additional coordination with the cloud platform provider.

The decision between using native cloud provider firewalls and third-party firewalls or SaaS offerings will depend on the specific needs and requirements that have been defined.

Load Balancing

Load balancers do exactly what the name suggests: they balance the load across cloud resources, distributing the network traffic across resources so that resources do not get overloaded. Incoming traffic is routed across multiple resources, such as network segments and virtual machines in those segments. It is even possible to distribute network traffic load across different cloud regions.

There are different types of load balancing available, each with its own strengths and weaknesses:

- *Network-level load balancing* operates at the transport layer (layer 4) of the OSI model and distributes incoming traffic based on factors such as IP address, port number, and protocol. Network-level load balancing is ideal for environments with high traffic volumes and low processing requirements, such as simple Web applications.
- *Application-level load balancing* operates at the application layer (layer 7) of the OSI model and distributes traffic based on more granular factors such as HTTP headers, cookies, and URL paths. Application-level load balancing is ideal for complex Web applications with multiple components, such as microservices or API gateways.
- *DNS load balancing* uses DNS servers to distribute incoming traffic across multiple servers or instances based on geographic location or availability. DNS load balancing is ideal for global applications with distributed user bases and can help to improve performance and reduce latency.

Each type of load balancing has its own advantages and disadvantages, and the choice of load balancing strategy will depend on the specific requirements and characteristics of the workload. In general, application-level load balancing is best suited for complex Web applications with multiple components, while network-level load balancing is more suitable for simpler, low-resource applications. DNS load balancing, meanwhile, is ideal for global applications with distributed user bases.

Cloud providers offer a variety of load-balancing options that are designed to meet different needs and workloads. It's important for organizations to carefully evaluate these options and select the right load-balancing strategy for their specific use case to ensure optimal performance, availability, and scalability of their cloud-based applications.

In Azure, Azure Load Balancer is used, which operates on OSI layer 4, routing traffic between VMs. Azure also provides layer 7 load balancers, the layer for applications: both Azure Traffic Manager and Azure Application Gateway operate on that layer. Lastly, Azure Front Door is used for microservices. Azure Front Door acts as a global load balancer and *application delivery network (ADN)* that can route traffic to the closest available backend, providing low-latency, high-performance access to Web applications. Microservices will be discussed in the final part of this chapter.

In AWS, *elastic load balancing* is used to distribute and route traffic to resources such as EC2 instances. Elastic load balancing can operate on various layers, both on the network and on the application layer. Google Cloud offers *cloud load balancing* for internal and external load balancing. This is the same service that Google itself uses for its own services.

The most common load-balancing service in Alibaba Cloud is *server load balancing (SLB)*, which is fully managed by Alibaba Cloud. This section started by stating that public clouds use the concept of shared resources by reserving capacity for a specific customer, typically referred to as a tenant. Hence, there must be a means of separating networks in the cloud so that one tenant cannot reach the other and so resources are separated from each other in different network segments.

That is an important task of network operations: a task that is heavily changed due to the concept of *software-defined networks (SDN)*. The next section explores the concept of SDN in more detail and describes how to set up network operations in the cloud.

CLOUD NETWORK OPERATIONS

As covered in the first section of this chapter, in the cloud, there are virtualized networks, too, by translating network functionality into code. The concept is called software defined. But what exactly does that mean, and, more important, what does it mean to operate networks?

Software defined is all about the abstraction of layers. The term was launched by VMWare, which introduced the concept of a *software-defined data center (SDDC)* at the beginning of the millennium. With that, they shared a vision of how to build data centers with software and thus limit the use of hardware by virtualizing it as much as possible. The next couple of chapters will discuss the virtualization of storage and computing in more detail, but in essence, VMware introduced technology that could tell a server or any other device that it was more than just one server. That concept was later also applied to network appliances: creating multiple network segments on top of one stack of network appliances in the data center, instead of having to use dedicated network equipment for every network segment.

In fact, it is the technological cornerstone of any cloud. With virtualization and software-defined concepts, multitenancy can be created in the cloud. Look at the cloud this way: it is one big building where the owner of the building makes sure that everyone gets electricity, water, and heating. But every tenant still has their own apartment. The tenant is free to do with the apartment as it pleases if the shared services of the building are not compromised. Electricity, water, and heating are the software that serves multiple tenants—instead of each tenant having its own water supply and heating system.

This is what software defined does. Now the focus is on software-providing solutions instead of constantly having to bring in new hardware. Hence, the functionality of networking is abstracted from the actual devices, as shown in Figure 2.7:

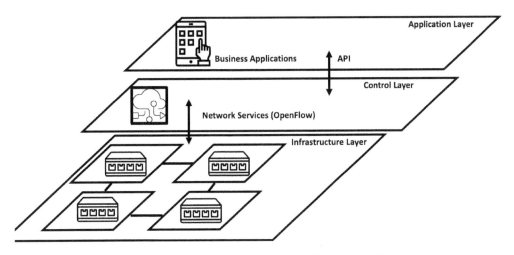

FIGURE 2.7 Abstracting layers in software-defined networking.

In a software-defined architecture, the network controls are decoupled from the underlying infrastructure: physical resources are abstracted, making networks programmable and very scalable. Applications can now treat the network as a logical or virtual unit. To abstract the control layer from the infrastructure, OpenFlow is used, a communications protocol that enables a server to communicate with a network device, instructing where traffic should go. The applications communicate with network services using an *application programming interface (API)*.

Obviously, this does have an impact on the operation of networks. Although this book is completely about the cloud, one must be conscious of the fact that a lot of enterprises and organizations will have legacy networks that they have to maintain as well, simply because only very few organizations will completely replace the existing infrastructure. Therefore, network operators will have to manage both the legacy infrastructure and the software-defined networks. It is good advice and best practice to explore the existing infrastructure—routers, switches, firewalls, proxies—to determine if these support SDN as well. For a start, it is strongly recommended to have tools that can monitor both stacks and preferably be used to manage the existing and the software-defined networks. Operators can use the existing tools and view the status of network components through dashboards that they are already familiar with.

Still, to understand networking operations in software-defined networks, the administrator will have to learn different skills. Be aware: there will still be hardware involved, but this hardware is now managed by the cloud provider. The network administrator—or cloud engineer—does not have to worry about the devices themselves anymore. The concept of SDN and networks in cloud computing does make life easier: there is no need to understand the operation details of hundreds of various network protocols. Still, understanding the concept of software-defined networking is essential. The concept contains three layers:

- Applications that handle resource requests and perform actions in the network.
- Controllers that route requests and actions through the network.
- Networking devices that receive the requests and process the actions.

Figure 2.8 shows how a software-defined network is configured:

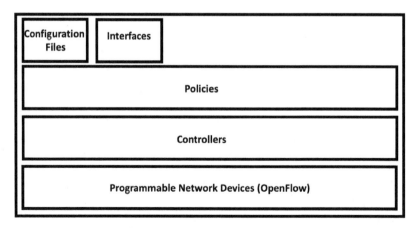

FIGURE 2.8 Layers in software-defined networking.

So, policies need to be defined and implemented to instruct the network controllers. The controller will eventually *program* the underlying infrastructure. For controllers, NOX, Floodlight, or Maestro can be used. NOX is the original OpenFlow controller. Floodlight and Maestro are open-source JAVA OpenFlow controllers and good, widely used alternatives.

This concept is applied in every cloud. In every cloud, the tenant must be defined by creating a virtual private cloud or virtual network. Next is to define who may access this tenant: the policies. Typically, this is done by an ACL. In Azure, NSG functions as an ACL. An ACL simply tells what traffic and from what sender the traffic is allowed. To control outgoing traffic and connections outside the tenant, the use of a virtual gateway is recommended, such as, for instance, if the tenant in the cloud needs to be connected to on-premises environments.

The cloud adoption frameworks (CAF) and *well-architected frameworks (WAF)* will help with best practices in setting up networks in the cloud. The benefits will be significant:

- *Enhanced network visibility*: Preferably through a single pane of glass view. SDN allows for centralized management and monitoring.

- *Scalability*: Since it is all software, networking through SDN is extremely scalable. No need to install new hardware to extend the network.

- *Enhanced security*: Since SDN is centrally managed, security policies can be propagated easily throughout the entire network, including all components and all devices.

- *Open source*: In theory, SDN uses open-source protocols and, with that, is agnostic to hardware. SDN abstracts the network functionality from the physical devices so that SDN is vendor neutral as long as the devices support the appliance of SDN.

- *Cost-effective*: SDN is less expensive to operate than physical networks, where engineers must be trained in specific equipment. Keep in mind that occasionally these engineers are still needed since, somewhere, SDN sits on physical machines.

Now that the concept of software defined networking is understood, take the next step and start deploying and managing *software defined wide area networks (SD-WAN), local area networks (SD-LAN),* and stretching networks to the Edge with edge computing. The next section discusses *secure access service edge (SASE).*

DEPLOYMENT CONCEPTS SD-WAN, EDGE, AND SASE

Enterprises will have a WAN that connects the offices with data centers and the cloud. It includes multiple locations of the enterprise, including the location it has in the cloud. A common technology to set up a WAN was by using *multi-protocol label switching (MPLS)* as a private network. MPLS takes care of connectivity on OSI layers 2 and 3, the data and the network layer. Before the cloud, MPLS was used in most WAN setups. The problem with MPLS, however, is that it is not very flexible. Typically, MPLS networks have fixed connections, providing secure tunnels to allow traffic between locations. With that, it is perceived as very reliable and secure. The problem is that MPLS is also complex to manage, costly to upgrade, and hard to scale.

In the cloud, flexibility and agility are needed. The network must be able to support this, and that is where SD-WAN comes in. As explained in the previous section, it abstracts the controls from the physical layer, offering much more flexibility. To put it simply, now only software represents the network. Managing the network is done by managing the software that can be configured and deployed to, in theory, any hardware stack.

SD-WAN allows for multiple types of connections and provides possibilities to route traffic in the most optimal way, choosing the best network path. This can be defined in the policies that were discussed earlier. With that, SD-WAN will offer better performance for applications and data transfer, regardless of where applications and data sit. It makes SD-WAN very suitable for creating networks that include cloud environments.

There is something that must be carefully considered, though, and that is security. MPLS is a private network, whereas SD-WAN is not. When we create an SD-WAN, we must apply security policies and implement tools, since security is not natively integrated. SASE will be examined in a moment.

Before getting into SASE, the concept of edge computing must be understood. The idea of the cloud is that there are centralized environments with shared services, preventing enterprises from having to build their own data centers. But the cloud is a data center too, and they have locations all over the globe. An example is Azure: Microsoft has Azure data centers in a lot of regions and countries. When looking for locations in Europe, the data centers are found in Ireland (Dublin) for Northern Europe and the Netherlands (Amsterdam) for Western Europe. There are also sites in France, Germany, Switzerland, Greece, Norway, and Sweden. Several other sites, for instance, in Finland, Denmark, and Spain, have been announced. European customers can host applications and store data in one of the Azure data centers.

There might be applications and data that have to be really close to the user to avoid latency. If the company is in Portugal with critical workloads that require very low latency, hosting applications and data in a data center in France might not be the best solution. Even with the fastest network connections, the latency might still be too high. For this, edge computing might be a solution. In most cases, edge computers are close to the customer, although managed from the cloud, even with the cloud services of a specific cloud provider. Examples are Azure Stack and AWS Outposts. Hence, a piece of the cloud is brought closer to the user. One remark: not all applications require low latency, and edge computing might not be suitable for every use case.

Edge networking allows bringing network segments closer to the user in a distributed network but is centrally managed. Cloud providers offer solutions for edge networking. Azure has private *multi-access edge compute (MEC)* and Private 5G Core. Indeed, 5G is typically used to set up edge connectivity for obvious reasons: 5G offers high speed, low latency, and immense capacity.

AWS offers Wavelength that connects AWS services to the edge using 5G. In Google Cloud, we use the Edge *point of presence (PoP)* that connects edge devices to the Google network. For this, Google uses Internet exchanges from *internet service providers (ISPs)* across the globe. To connect various clouds with each other, these Internet exchange services can be used. The well-known ones are *Equinix IX* and *Megaport*: they enable peering between different networks of network providers, ISPs, and cloud providers. The technology used for this is *multi-lateral peering exchange (MPLE)*: it uses BGP sessions to securely exchange routing information with connected networks.

All these connections must be secured, and for that, SASE is used. But what is SASE? It is an architecture concept combining SD-WAN, native cloud security, and zero-trust principles. A zero-trust network verifies user identities and establishes device trust before granting access to authorized applications, preventing unauthorized access and limiting security breaches. To set up a zero-trust network using SD-WAN, native cloud technologies must also be applied:

- *Cloud access security broker (CASB)*: Controlling traffic between cloud applications and services.
- *Secure Web gateway*: Prevents unsecured traffic from accessing the organization's internal network, also in the cloud.

- *Firewall as a service*: Also referred to as *next generation firewall (NGFW)*, it protects applications on layer 7, the application layer. Service includes URL filtering with black- and whitelisting, threat protection, and intrusion prevention.

- *Content delivery network*: This is a geographically distributed network of servers delivering content close to where the users are. The service is a solution to solve issues with latency but also enhances security, since the CDN servers can function as a shield to the servers where the original content is stored.

- *Domain name services (DNS) protection*: Authentication of DNS requests before communication with the systems of an organization is established.

Cloud providers offer native solutions to establish this, but as previously mentioned, a variety of third-party solutions are found in the respective marketplaces, including SaaS offerings that are completely managed by the vendor.

Solutions, concepts, and components have been explored to create networks. What follows is a discussion of how to manage the connectivity between clouds. That is the topic of the final section of this chapter.

MANAGING NETWORKS IN MULTI-CLOUD

There are multiple ways to connect to the cloud and to connect clouds with each other. This section discusses the various technologies to create and manage connectivity, starting with the one that is still commonly used, the VPN. Next, the different direct connections that cloud providers offer are explored. Connecting clouds with each other is typically done through brokerage, using a connectivity broker. That will be discussed in the final part of the section.

Setting Up VPN

A VPN uses the Internet as a carrier: a tunnel is defined over the Internet by only allowing traffic from a specific IP range to a destination IP range or address, typically the address of a gateway in a public cloud. Hence, the only thing to do is assign IP addresses or the IP range from which communication is allowed and to what destination.

Assuming that the destination is in the cloud, a point needs to be defined where the connection terminates. Traffic should not be able to reach every single resource in the cloud, so the VPN is terminated on one location in the cloud. From there, routing is defined inside the cloud. This implies that there is a zone where it is safe to have a VPN connecting before other cloud resources are accessed. This zone is referred to as a *demilitarized zone (DMZ)* or a transit zone.

A DMZ is a network segment that sits between a public network, such as the Internet, and a private network, such as a company's internal network. The DMZ acts as a buffer zone that provides an additional layer of security for the private network by isolating it from direct contact with the public network.

In a cloud-based DMZ architecture, virtual servers or instances are typically used to provide the necessary network segmentation and security. Traffic from the Internet enters the DMZ and is directed to these servers, which act as proxies or gateways, filtering and forwarding traffic to the appropriate destination in the private network.

This allows organizations to expose certain services or applications to the Internet while keeping sensitive data and resources protected behind the DMZ.

A basic architecture for VPN connectivity is shown in Figure 2.9:

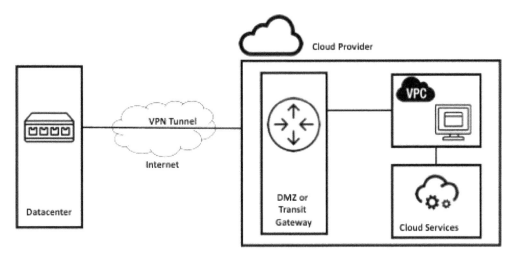

FIGURE 2.9 VPN connectivity to DMZ or transit gateway.

Cloud providers offer solutions to securely set up VPN connectivity to their clouds using VPN gateways:

- Azure VPN Gateway
- AWS *Virtual Private Gateway (VPG)* and Transit Gateway
- Google Cloud VPN
- VPN Gateway in Alibaba Cloud

These solutions commonly support the following standards:

- OpenVPN, based on *Secure Socket Layer (SSL)* and *Transport Layer Security (TLS)*
- IKEv2, based on IPsec
- Border Gateway Protocol (BGP): Used to establish routing between *autonomous systems (ASes)* on the Internet, such as cloud platforms and cloud services.

First, the private cloud must be defined in Azure, AWS, GCP, or Alibaba, and a segment must be defined to terminate the connection securely. Now, a gateway can be placed in that segment. This is a software-defined device that usually provides several features, such as authentication, authorization, encryption, firewalling, and routing. As with any service, a native service from the public cloud providers or a third-party vendor that is supported in that cloud can be used. Common brands are Juniper, Cisco, Palo Alto, Fortinet, and so on. Which traffic is allowed to communicate with the gateway and the resources in our cloud must be defined. From the gateway, the traffic will then be routed to the destination resources.

As said, VPNs use the public Internet as carriers. An alternative is setting up direct connectivity between the enterprise and the designated public cloud. These solutions will be explored in the following section.

Setting Up Direct Connections

Secured, encrypted tunnels are safe, yet a lot of enterprises will prefer an even more secure solution that is also more stable and really dedicated just to the enterprise. Direct connections provide that type of connectivity. Basically, with a private, dedicated connection, the corporate network is extended into the cloud, something that is enabled by software defined networking.

Direct connections have benefits over VPNs:

- *Faster connection speeds*: Direct connections often provide faster connection speeds compared to VPNs, as there's no overhead associated with encryption and decryption.
- *Simpler setup*: Direct connections are often easier to set up and maintain, as they don't require additional software or configurations.
- *No encryption overhead*: Direct connections do not incur the performance overhead associated with encrypting and decrypting traffic.

A drawback of direct connections might be limited network access, as some organizations restrict access to their internal network from outside their physical location. On the other hand, VPNs have their downsides too. Typically, VPNs have slower connection speeds due to the overhead associated with encryption and decryption. VPNs might also be more complex to set up since often this requires additional software and configurations.

There are various offerings that public clouds have for direct connections. In Azure, ExpressRoute can be used, deployed as point-to-point ethernet, any-to-any IPVPN, or using a cloud exchange colocation. The latter will be discussed a bit further in this section.

The point-to-point ethernet provides connectivity on layer 2, the network layer, or layer 3, the data layer. Another option is any-to-any IPVPN, where the Azure environment can be connected with an MPLS WAN network, which was discussed in the first section of this chapter. Connectivity will always be established over layer 3.

AWS uses *DirectConnect*, allowing enterprises to connect routers or firewalls that are on-premises directly to a VPG in an AWS VPC. DirectConnect also allows for direct connectivity to AWS services, such as storage in S3. AWS uses private *virtual interfaces (VIF)* to set up these connections. AWS uses colocations to establish these connections.

Google Dedicated Interconnect uses the same principles as AWS. In a colocation, a direct link from a customer is connected to the peering edge of GCP. From this peering zone, the connection is forwarded to a gateway in GCP.

The service for direct connectivity in Alibaba Cloud is offered through Express Connect.

Now, how are these connections managed? Most enterprises will use a connectivity broker or a telecom provider to establish and manage connectivity to clouds. In colocation data centers, all cloud providers have PoP, which is, simply put, the front door allowing entrance into the cloud. Network or telecom providers will also have these PoPs, making it easy to connect to the cloud PoPs. In the case of dedicated connections, this is literally a network cable coming from a telecom or network provider going into the router of the cloud provider. That is what makes this a completely different solution than using VPNs over the public Internet.

How does this work? Telecom and network providers have meet-me rooms or zones where they can connect customers to the peering zone of the preferred cloud provider. As a consequence and a benefit to the customer, the connection will be completely managed by the telecom or network provider. One other major advantage is that enterprises that are multi-cloud can get multiple connections to the respective cloud platforms yet managed by one connectivity provider, including secure access, monitoring, and logging. Companies such as Equinix and Digital Realty have global coverage and offer connection services to all major public clouds. The principle is shown in the following Figure 2.10:

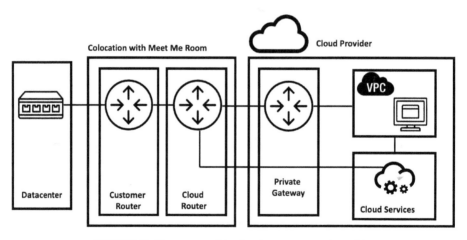

FIGURE 2.10 Direct connectivity via telecom or network provider.

One alternative way of establishing multi-cloud connectivity is by using *network as a service (NaaS)*. A company such as Megaport offers this service. Customers will need a *port* as a stepping stone in a data center of their choice and an account in the Megaport service. Next, the B-port or the destination cloud is defined. Megaport will set up the connection and manage the bandwidth according to the data limits that have been set. Megaport does this for all public cloud providers but also for SaaS services and connecting on-premises data centers. The concept of NaaS is shown in Figure 2.11:

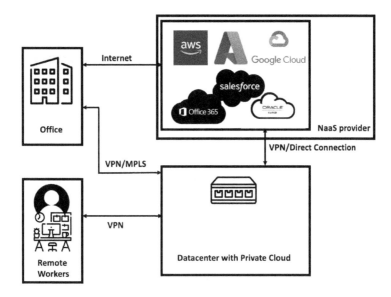

FIGURE 2.11 Concept of network as a service.

Obviously, all of this would not be possible without the possibilities of software-defined networking.

The networks have been virtualized. The next step is virtualizing the resources. The next chapter starts with the storage and explores the storage solutions in clouds and how they can be used in multi-cloud concepts.

CONCLUSION

Moving workloads into the cloud starts with establishing connectivity. This chapter discussed how to set up connectivity to the cloud. Before exploring the various services that clouds offer, the principles of SDN were studied. In the cloud, physical networks will not be managed but networks will be defined as software. This is crucial since public clouds are, by default, multitenant, meaning that customers share services in the cloud. To define a domain in the cloud, an understanding of how to set up a VPC that holds our workloads is needed. To reach and access these VPCs, secure connectivity must be created. This can be done by defining tunnels over the Internet or by setting up direct connections to the clouds that are used. Next was an explanation of how the routing of traffic and protection of workloads can be configured in clouds using gateways, Web application firewalls, and load balancers.

This chapter extensively looked at software defined concepts such as SD-WAN, Edge, and SASE and explained how to extend and manage corporate networks into the cloud. In the final section, the concept of NaaS was discussed, where a NaaS provider takes care of connectivity to various clouds and cloud services.

The next chapter will be about virtualizing and managing storage, exploring the different storage solutions that public cloud providers offer.

KEY POINTS

- Software-defined networking is the cornerstone of networking in clouds; it allows for abstracting the functionality of networking from physical devices.

- All network devices can be virtualized, including switches, routers, firewalls, and load balancers. In the cloud, these devices are offered as services.

- SDN makes it possible to deploy corporate SD-WAN and extend the network to the cloud and the edge of the cloud, close to the user.

- Corporate networks often use MPLS as a private network and are secure. When creating an SD-WAN, security policies must be applied and tools implemented, since security is not natively integrated. This is done through SASE.

- Connections can be established to the cloud with private tunnels over the public Internet (VPN) or by using direct connections that cloud providers offer.

QUESTIONS

1. Corporate networks still often use MPLS. This is considered to be secure. Why?

2. To isolate workloads in Azure, private network segments must be set up. What are these called in Azure?

3. SDN architecture consists of three layers. Name these layers.

4. What is the name of the direct connection service that GCP offers?

Answers appear in the appendix.

VIRTUALIZING AND MANAGING STORAGE

INTRODUCTION

One of the benefits of the cloud is the almost limitless amount of storage that is available to users. However, the cloud is a shared resource model, so an understanding of how storage works in the cloud is needed. How can one ensure the right amount of storage and the right type with the right performance? Cloud architects and admins should know about the different storage types, tiering, and automated scaling of storage. It is covered in this chapter, starting with explaining the virtualization of storage as the basic principle.

STRUCTURE

This chapter discusses the following topics:

- Types of storage virtualization
  - Storage concepts in public clouds
- Managing storage assets in multi-cloud
- Managing storage lifecycles and tiering
- Managing data access

TYPES OF STORAGE VIRTUALIZATION

Before diving into the various types of storage virtualization, the concept of virtualization must be understood. The concept is the same as with networks that were discussed in the previous chapter. The functionality of providing storage capacity is abstracted from the actual storage devices. This can be understood in a very simple way. In the traditional on-premises data center, storage cabinets would need to be attached to servers. If an application on a server needed more storage, the physical storage that was attached to that machine would need to be extended, for instance, by adding discs. With storage virtualization, pools of physical storage devices can be created, acting as if it was one storage device. The software will now allocate storage from that storage pool, using capacity that is available on any of the physical devices that are part of the pool. These physical storage devices are not visible to the user, and the virtual storage appears as one physical machine, drive, or a *logical unit number (LUN)*.

To enable this, a *storage area network (SAN)* must be created, first since the physical storage devices must relate to each other and to the network where the servers are with the hosted applications. A SAN is basically just a network of storage devices, where these devices are separated from the servers in their own dedicated network. This is the main difference with *direct attached storage (DAS)*, where the storage device—typically discs—is directly connected to the server. The problem with DAS is that when the server fails, the storage fails with it, and that might cause data corruption. SAN is much more resilient.

To connect a SAN to servers, the various layers of the SAN technology must be examined. Firstly, there is the host layer in the server that allows the server to connect and communicate with the SAN. In the traditional data center setup, this is typically done through Fiber Channel, a cable that connects the server host to a switch to which the storage devices are connected. This layer with switches, cables, and routers in the SAN is called the fabric layer.

The final layer is the storage layer. To enable traffic to communicate between the devices in the SAN, the *Internet small computer systems interface (iSCSI)* protocol is used. iSCS operates over TCP/IP, linking data storage and providing block-level access. The differences between block and other storage types will be addressed later in this section. Figure 3.1 shows the basic architecture of a SAN:

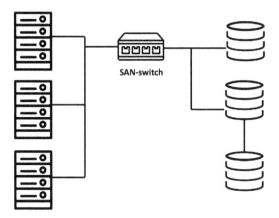

FIGURE 3.1 Basic architecture of a SAN.

A *virtual SAN (vSAN)* does the same thing in principle. However, we need to get back to DAS first. vSAN was invented by VMWare as a solution to aggregate local and DAS and create a single storage cluster that would allow *virtual machines (VMs)* to use one pool of storage devices within the virtualization cluster. In different words, by virtualizing the storage that was attached to the servers, it creates a virtual SAN using that storage, but now as a logical layer instead of physical machines in one network attached to server farms using a fiber channel. Figure 3.2 shows the setup of a vSAN:

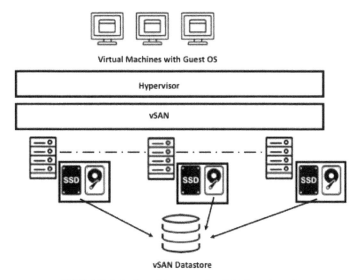

FIGURE 3.2 Basic architecture of a vSAN (host-based).

To connect servers to the vSAN cluster that are outside of the cluster, an iSCSI connection must be set up between these servers and the vSAN. In that way, the vSAN can also be presented to servers that are not part of the cluster, enabling these servers to use the storage in the cluster.

Everything that was discussed so far was related to block storage. Now, the different types of storage should be explored. There are five types of storage virtualization:

- *Host-based*: The most common type of storage virtualization, where the virtualization host presents storage to the guest operating system. A good example is the virtual disks that are attached to a virtual machine. Figure 3.2 shows the host-based principle.
- *Array-based*: With this type of storage virtualization, storage tiering can be created in the hardware that is used to virtualize the storage. For example, solid state disks (SSDs) are used to provide high performance, fast storage, and *hard disk drive (HDDs)* for slower storage.
- *OS-level*: Some operating systems allow implementation of array-based storage as a function of the operating system itself. An example of this is Windows Storage Spaces.
- *File system*: This typically refers to Microsoft's *Distributed File System (DFS)*. The technology divides data into files across various file servers or *server message blocks (SMB)*, but to the user, it appears that the data is still on only one file server.
- *Fiber Channel*: This might be a confusing term since it typically refers to the virtualization of the SAN switches, enabling VMs to connect to a SAN or a storage array.

It all comes down to providing access to data that is still stored on a physical device but using virtualization, and these devices can be used in an optimized way by dynamically allocating storage space to that data. Virtualization software does that by creating maps of paths to where data is stored, typically through metadata. As with any form of virtualization, it abstracts the functionality of storage from physical devices. Administrators will not have to worry about the physical infrastructure anymore, making it easier to execute tasks such as backup and archiving data.

Understanding this principle is essential to grasp the different storage concepts. Next, it is necessary to understand the differences in storage types: file, block, and object.

With file storage, the data is not broken into blocks but written to storage as a complete file in a hierarchical folder structure. These folders can be placed in other folders. By using a directory path, the folder and the specific file are located. File storage is typically used by *network attached storage (NAS)* as centralized, dedicated file storage to multiple clients such as servers or PCs. Applications and users will be able to retrieve documents, images, and other files, based on name and location.

Block storage divides data into equal blocks and then writes it to the storage device. It is a more efficient way of using storage capacity since it optimizes the allocation of the capacity. With block storage, a disk is divided into maximum volumes and then attached to an operating system. The blocks do not contain any metadata, but each has a unique address. This address matches the stored data. The moment the data is accessed, the storage layer checks whether the addresses are correct. Do the addresses match? Then the data will be retrieved and presented. Block storage is the technology that is typically used in the cloud.

The last storage option that we must discuss is object storage. In this case, data is divided into separate units—objects—and spread across storage devices. However, the objects are stored in a single repository. One of the major differences between block and object storage is the fact that object storage does contain metadata. This metadata and the unique identifier of the object allow storage systems to retrieve the data quickly. Object storage is the best solution for storing large amounts of unstructured data because of the search capabilities—using the metadata—and the scaling that object storage provides. This type of storage is designed for storing large amounts of unstructured data, such as images, videos, and audio files. It is highly scalable and can handle a high volume of read and write requests. For that reason, object storage is the most popular form of storage in clouds.

The next section looks at the various storage solutions that public clouds offer.

Storage Concepts in Public Clouds

As may have been understood from the previous section, it very much depends on what is to be done or achieved in terms of using storage in the cloud. Cloud providers offer a variety of solutions, and every one of them serves a specific use case. As an example, *https://azure.microsoft.com/en-us/products/ category/storage/* shows a comprehensive overview of all offerings that Azure provides. For AWS, refer to *https://docs.aws.amazon.com/whitepapers/latest/ aws-overview/storage-services.html*.

AWS and Azure offer a range of storage options to suit different needs, including file storage, object storage, and block storage, the various storage types discussed in the previous section.

One of the main storage options in both AWS and Azure is object storage. In AWS, this type of storage is provided by Amazon S3 (*Simple Storage Service*), while in Azure, it is provided by Azure Blob Storage.

Another option in both AWS and Azure is file storage. This type of storage is used for storing files that can be accessed via the *network file system (NFS)* protocol. It is suitable for storing files that need to be accessed and edited by multiple users, such as documents and spreadsheets. In AWS, this type of storage is provided by Amazon *Elastic File System (EFS)*, while in Azure, it is provided by Azure Files.

In addition to object storage and file storage, both AWS and Azure also offer block storage options. In AWS, this type of storage is provided by Amazon *Elastic Block Store (EBS)*. In Azure, it is provided by Azure Disk Storage.

Both AWS and Azure also offer options for storing data in a database. AWS offers Amazon *Relational Database Service (RDS)* for storing data in a variety of relational database management systems, such as MySQL, PostgreSQL, and Oracle. Azure offers Azure SQL Database for storing data in a SQL-based database, as well as Azure Cosmos DB for storing data in a NoSQL database.

AWS and Azure also offer other types of storage solutions, such as archival storage and in-memory storage. Archival storage is used for storing data that is not accessed frequently and is typically less expensive than other types of storage. In-memory storage is used for storing data in memory for fast access, making it suitable for applications that require low latency.

Next are the storage options in GCP and Alibaba Cloud. GCP offers a range of storage options to suit different needs and use cases. Some of the main storage options provided by GCP are:

- *Cloud storage*: Object storage service designed for storing large amounts of unstructured data, such as images, videos, and audio files. It is highly scalable and can handle a high volume of read and write requests.

- *Cloud filestore*: File storage service that allows us to store and access files using the *network file system (NFS)* protocol. It is suitable for storing files that need to be accessed and edited by multiple users, such as documents and spreadsheets.

- *Cloud Bigtable*: A NoSQL database service that is designed for storing large amounts of structured data. It is suitable for applications that require fast read and write performance, such as real-time analytics and *Internet of things (IoT)* applications.

- *Cloud SQL*: A fully managed SQL database service that is based on the MySQL and PostgreSQL database engines. It is suitable for storing structured data and running SQL queries.
- *Cloud Datastore*: A NoSQL document database service that is designed for storing and querying structured data. It is suitable for applications that require flexible, scalable data storage.

GCP also offers other types of storage solutions, such as Cloud Memorystore for in-memory storage and Cloud Spanner for globally distributed database storage.

Alibaba Cloud offers the following storage options:

- *Object Storage Service (OSS)*: Object storage service designed for storing large amounts of unstructured data, such as images, videos, and audio files. It is highly scalable and can handle a high volume of read and write requests.
- *Elastic File System (EFS)*: File storage service that allows for storing and accessing files using the NFS protocol. It is suitable for storing files that need to be accessed and edited by multiple users, such as documents and spreadsheets.
- *Block Storage Service (BSS)*: Block storage service that is used to store data in fixed-size blocks, like how a hard drive stores data. It is suitable for storing data that needs to be accessed quickly, such as the operating system and application files.
- *ApsaraDB*: A fully managed database service that is based on the MySQL, SQL Server, and PostgreSQL database engines. It is suitable for storing structured data and running SQL queries.
- *Table Store*: A NoSQL database service that is designed for storing and querying structured data. It is suitable for applications that require flexible, scalable data storage.

Alibaba Cloud provides other types of storage solutions, such as MaxCompute for big data processing and Data Lake Analytics for data analytics.

Multi-cloud is being discussed, so a choice may be made to run storage in various cloud platforms. How can these storage assets be managed in the various clouds? That is the topic for the next section.

MANAGING STORAGE ASSETS IN MULTI-CLOUD

Multi-cloud storage is when multiple cloud computing and storage services from different providers are used in a single environment. This may offer many benefits, such as increased flexibility, cost optimization, and improved data protection, but it also introduces new challenges in terms of storage management. This section discusses some best practices for managing storage in a multi-cloud environment.

One of the main considerations when managing storage in a multi-cloud environment is making sure that the data is stored in the most suitable location: the right cloud with the right solution that suits its needs. This may involve placing data in the cloud that is closest to the users who will be accessing it or choosing a cloud provider that offers the best price for a particular type of storage.

Next is to consider the specific requirements of different types of data, such as whether it needs to be stored in a compliant manner or if it requires a certain level of performance. Compliance and performance are crucial requirements in picking the most appropriate type of storage solutions. Only when it has been validated that requirements are met can migrating data to that storage start.

Migration can be a complex process, especially if moving large amounts of data between different cloud providers. The migration process must be carefully planned and the migration tested before moving all the data to ensure that everything goes smoothly. There are several tools and services available that can help with data migration, such as CloudEndure Migration, which allows for migrating data to the cloud with minimal downtime. CloudEndure Migration is an AWS solution—AWS acquired CloudEndure in 2019—that helps in migrating workloads and data to AWS by means of agents that support lift and shift to the cloud. Basically, the solution continuously replicates the data between the source and the target environment, ensuring that there is no downtime and data loss during the migration.

Of course, there are many more solutions that will help in migrating data. Azure Data Box, Google Cloud Transfer Service, and AWS DataSync are good examples:

▪ *Azure Data Box* is a physical device used to securely transfer large amounts of data to and from Azure. Customers can order a Data Box device and then use it to transfer data by loading it with their data and shipping it to an Azure data center, where the data is uploaded to their Azure account. Azure Data Box is useful for transferring large amounts of data more quickly and securely than over the Internet.

▪ *Google Cloud Transfer Service* is a managed service that enables customers to transfer data to and from the Google Cloud Platform. Customers can use Transfer Service to move data from on-premises storage, another cloud provider, or an Internet-connected device to Google Cloud. Transfer Service supports a range of transfer protocols and provides scheduling, notification, and reporting capabilities.

▪ *AWS DataSync*: AWS DataSync is a managed data transfer service that simplifies moving large amounts of data to and from AWS. DataSync can be used to transfer data between on-premises storage, AWS storage services, and other cloud storage services. DataSync uses a high-speed, parallel data transfer mechanism to optimize transfer performance and supports automated scheduling, bandwidth throttling, and checksum verification to ensure data integrity.

The next section discusses one of the main risks in migrating and managing data, which is the loss of data.

Protecting Data from Data Loss

Data loss is likely one of the main concerns in managing storage in the cloud. Once the data is in the cloud, it is important to ensure that it is protected against data loss and unauthorized access. This can be achieved using backup and recovery solutions, such as snapshotting and replication, as well as security measures, such as encryption and access controls. It is also important to consider the risks associated with storing data in a single location and to implement strategies to mitigate these risks, such as storing data in multiple locations or using a cloud provider with a strong track record of data protection.

In a multizone architecture, data is replicated across multiple availability zones within the same region. This ensures that if one availability zone goes down or experiences an outage, data is still available from another availability zone. Multizone architectures provide high availability and can help prevent data loss due to infrastructure failures or disasters within a single region. In a multiregion architecture, data is replicated across multiple regions, which are in different geographic locations. This ensures that if an entire region experiences an outage or disaster, data is still available from another region.

Using both multizone and multiregion architectures together can ensure maximum availability and data durability. Data can be replicated across multiple availability zones within the same region for high availability and then also replicated to multiple regions for disaster recovery.

When talking about data, data migration, and protecting data, the costs that come with managing the required storage must also be discussed. There is one huge misconception about storage costs in the cloud. When entering a console of a cloud provider, storage can be really cheap per gigabyte. However, if storage is not actively managed, the costs can become very high. The storage usage must be regularly monitored and optimized to ensure that costs are not higher than necessary. There are several ways to optimize storage costs, such as by reducing the amount of data stored and by choosing the right type of storage to fulfill requirements. Choosing the right type of storage is related to something called tiering. It is discussed extensively in the next section.

One of the key benefits of a multi-cloud storage strategy is the ability to take advantage of the strengths of different cloud providers; for example, choosing to use one provider for data storage and another for computing resources or choosing to use a combination of different types of storage—such as object storage and block storage—from different providers. Following these best practices can effectively manage storage in a multi-cloud environment and take advantage of the benefits that this approach offers.

Using Third-Party Storage Products

Something not touched upon yet is the use of third-party storage products in the cloud. So far, the native storage offerings in the different clouds have been discussed, but companies will likely still have data in on-premises storage that needs to be connected to the cloud. It might be a good decision to extend the technology that is used on-premises to the cloud. A reason to do so could be commercial benefits for using that same technology in both on-premises and cloud or for compliance reasons.

Products that are of interest here are, for instance, NetApp or file systems built with Lustre. Let us start with NetApp Cloud Volumes ONTAP, a popular solution to manage storage in various environments. ONTAP uses a scale-out architecture, which means that it can scale up or down in capacity and performance as needed by adding or removing storage nodes. The solution supports the most commonly used storage protocols, including NFS, SMB, and iSCSI, and storage use cases such as file, block, and object storage. NetApp is typically associated with so-called filers and physical storage systems, but the Cloud Volumes ONTAP solution can also be used in the cloud. For example,

- *AWS*: Cloud Volumes ONTAP for managing storage on AWS instances, Cloud Sync for syncing data between on-premises storage and AWS, and Cloud Volumes Service for migrating and managing data in the cloud.
- *Azure*: Cloud Volumes ONTAP for managing storage on Azure virtual machines, Azure NetApp Files for high-performance file storage, and Cloud Volumes Service for migrating and managing data in the cloud.
- *GCP*: Cloud Volumes ONTAP for managing storage on GCP instances, Cloud Sync for syncing data between on-premises storage and GCP, and Cloud Volumes Service for migrating and managing data.

A basic architecture for NetApp ONTAP—in this example, AWS has been chosen—is shown in Figure 3.3. NetApp ONTAP in AWS uses FSx, an AWS-managed service that takes care of the file shares in the storage environment:

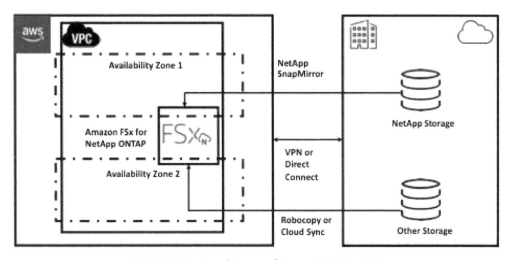

FIGURE 3.3 Basic architecture of NetApp ONTAP in AWS.

As Figure 3.3 shows, NetApp and non-NetApp storage can be attached on-premises or to other clouds to the storage in AWS. NetApp storage is synchronized with Snap Mirror and the other storage with, for example, Robocopy or Cloud Sync. NetApp has its own solution for this, called *NetApp XCP*, for data migration any-to-NetApp or NetApp-to-NetApp.

This is just an example of a third-party product that can be used to connect external storage to the cloud. Other examples include Veeam and Acronis.

The open-source file system Lustre is commonly used for applications that require fast and extremely scalable storage in the cloud, particularly in high-performance environments where data-intensive workloads are common.

In AWS, Lustre can be deployed on EC2 instances, and storage can be provided using Amazon Elastic Block Store (EBS) or S3. Lustre can be used to store and manage data for a wide range of applications, including big data analytics, scientific simulations, and media processing. Think of use cases in financial modeling or in the development of new medicines using genomics.

In Azure, Lustre can be deployed on Azure VMs, and storage can be provided using Azure Premium SSDs or Azure Files. There are many more solutions to provision storage in the cloud. It is not one size fits all, especially when looking for solutions that connect on-premises systems to the cloud. A variety of hybrid cloud storage solutions might be explored, such as AWS Storage Gateway, Azure StorSimple, and Google Anthos:

- *AWS Storage Gateway* is a hybrid cloud storage service that provides a way to connect on-premises applications to AWS cloud storage. It enables on-premises applications to access AWS storage services, such as S3, Glacier, and EBS, through standard storage protocols such as NFS, SMB, and iSCSI. AWS Storage Gateway can be deployed as a virtual appliance or as a hardware appliance.

- *Azure StorSimple* is a hybrid cloud storage solution that helps organizations manage and store data across on-premises and cloud environments. It provides cloud-integrated storage, automated data tiering, and data protection capabilities. StorSimple uses a hybrid storage array that combines solid-state drives, hard disk drives, and cloud storage to provide high-performance and cost-effective storage.

- *Google Anthos* is a hybrid and multi-cloud application platform that enables organizations to build, deploy, and manage applications across on-premises, multi-cloud, and hybrid cloud environments. Anthos allows organizations to modernize existing applications and build new cloud-native applications with Kubernetes, an open-source container orchestration system. Anthos also provides tools for application lifecycle management, service mesh, and policy management across multi-cloud environments.

Once the storage solution has been deployed, it needs to be designed and continuously optimized using tiering and lifecycle management to prevent storage costs from going out of control. This is the topic for the next section.

MANAGING STORAGE LIFECYCLES AND TIERING

The previous section discussed the need to choose the appropriate storage solution to match requirements, optimize the solution, and manage costs. *Storage lifecycle management (SLM)* and tiering can be of great help in this. It involves the management of data storage from the time it is initially created, to the time it is no longer needed, including the transition of data between different storage tiers through lifecycles. First, the principles of tiering need to be understood.

Data storage is typically classified into different tiers based on its accessibility and usage. The most expensive tier is usually the one that provides the highest level of accessibility and performance, such as the cloud provider's native object storage or a cloud-based file system. Examples would be Azure Blob and AWS EFS. The least expensive tier is typically the one that provides the lowest level of accessibility and performance, such as cold storage or archival storage.

A good example of typical archive storage would be AWS Glacier, which is used for low-cost backup and storage of data. But even when using Glacier, there are still options to evaluate. If fast retrieval of archived data is required, S3 Glacier Instant Retrieval should be chosen. If fast retrieval is not needed but the data still needs to be stored for a long time, then S3 Glacier Deep Archive is a better choice. In that case, data retrieval can take up to twelve hours.

There is still more to consider. Storage pricing for Glacier starts at 0.0036 cents per Gb when hosting in U.S.–East. That is the pure cost of the storage. The retrieval costs come on top of that, and that comes in three offerings: expedited, standard, and bulk. Something that is often forgotten is the fact that data transfer is charged as well: data transfer into Glacier is free of charge, and data transfer out of Glacier varies between 0.05 per Gb up to 0.09 per Gb per month. And then it also depends on where the data is transferred to: data transferred to an EC2 instance in the same region, for instance, is free of charge.

The other cloud providers have similar propositions, so it does make sense to have SLM in place. SLM helps organizations to optimize their storage costs by automatically transitioning data from the most expensive tier to the least expensive tier as it ages and becomes less frequently accessed. This process is known as *tiering*. For example, an organization may choose to store its most frequently accessed data in the cloud provider's native object storage and transition the data to cold storage or archival storage as it becomes less frequently accessed. Figure 3.4 shows an example of storage tiering:

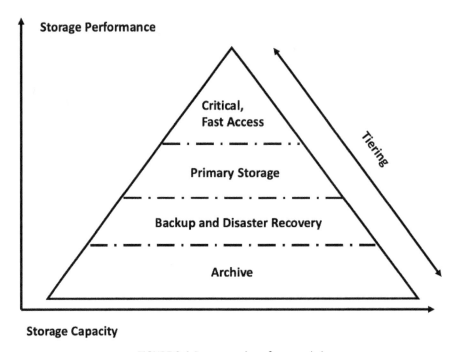

FIGURE 3.4 Representation of storage tiering.

Archive storage will usually have the least performance but will also use the most capacity. Data that requires fast access should be hosted on high-performance storage, but likely only in a limited capacity. Storage will typically be tiered from frequently accessed to archive and not the other way around, but in theory, this is, of course, possible.

In summary, SLM helps organizations to reduce their storage costs by automatically transitioning data to the least expensive tier as it ages. This can be a requirement for organizations that generate a large amount of data and need to store it for an extended period of time. SLM can also be applied to enhance the performance of storage systems through the same principle: by storing frequently accessed data in the most expensive tier and less frequently accessed data in the least expensive tier. This will be the use case for applications that require fast access to data, such as databases and big data analytics platforms.

Lastly, SLM helps organizations to comply with regulatory and legal requirements by automatically transitioning data to the appropriate storage tier based on its retention period. This can be particularly useful and even a hard legal requirement for organizations that are required to store data for a specific period of time, such as financial institutions and healthcare organizations.

There are several factors to consider when implementing SLM in the cloud. First, it is important to define the storage tiers that will be used and the criteria for transitioning data between tiers. This may involve setting up rules based on the age of the data, the frequency of access, or the retention period. Next to be considered are the tools and technologies that will be used to implement SLM. This may involve using the cloud provider's native storage management tools, such as Azure Blob Lifecycle Management and AWS S3 lifecycle, or third-party tools that are specifically designed for SLM, such as Spectra StorCycle.

Be aware that implementing SLM and storage tiering must be tested intensively, especially in terms of the performance of the storage tiers. A lot of this can and should be automated. Tiering, scaling storage, and even performance testing can be automated. Before implementing SLM, the various storage performance metrics must be understood. Understanding these metrics is crucial in determining the appropriate storage tiers and optimizing storage performance, also because cloud providers use these metrics to categorize the different tiers. Examples of these metrics are:

- *IOPS (input/output operations per second)*: This metric measures the number of read and write operations that can be performed per second. IOPS is important for measuring the speed of random-access workloads, such as databases.
- *Throughput*: This metric measures the amount of data that can be transferred per unit of time, usually in MB/s or GB/s. Throughput is important for measuring the speed of sequential access workloads, such as large file transfers.
- *Latency*: This metric measures the time it takes for a storage system to respond to a request, usually in milliseconds. Latency is important for measuring the speed of workloads that require low response times, such as online transaction processing.

- *Queue depth*: This metric measures the number of pending I/O requests in a storage system. Higher queue depths can improve performance for workloads with high concurrency but can also increase latency and reduce throughput.

- *Bandwidth*: This metric measures the amount of data that can be transferred per unit of time, usually in bits per second. Bandwidth is important for measuring the maximum network speed that a storage system can achieve.

- *CPU usage*: This metric measures the percentage of CPU resources used by a storage system. High CPU usage can indicate that the system is processing I/O requests at its maximum capacity.

SLM is the best practice for managing storage tiers and related costs. Consider other cost optimization strategies, too, such as data deduplication, compression, and thin provisioning that can help to manage storage costs in multi-cloud environments.

Automating Tiering

Automating the tiering of storage involves the use of tools and technologies to automatically transition data from the most expensive tier to the least expensive tier as it ages and becomes less frequently accessed. Automating tiering will be discussed for Azure and AWS.

In Azure, the Azure Storage Account can be configured to automatically tier data to the appropriate storage tier based on the age of the data or the frequency of access. This can be done using the Azure Management Portal or the Azure Storage REST API. Azure also provides several tools and technologies for automating the tiering of storage, including Azure Blob Storage Lifecycle Management, Azure Data Lake Storage Gen2, and Azure Archive Blob Storage. This type of action is executed by defining a rule stating that if data is not accessed at least once per month, it can be automatically moved to the archive.

For reference, an example for Azure in PowerShell format is provided as follows:

```
# List the files in the storage account

$files = Get-AzStorageFile -StorageAccountName <storage-account-name>

-ShareName <file-share-name>
```

```
# Filter the list of files based on last access time

$oldFiles = $files | Where-Object { $_.LastModified -lt (Get-Date).
AddMonths(-1) }


# Copy the old files to the archive storage

foreach ($file in $oldFiles) {

  Start-AzStorageFileCopy -SourceUri $file.Uri -DestinationShare
  <archive-file-share-name> -DestinationPath $file.Name



}
```

This is what it will do: the script will list the files in the storage account: The Get-AzStorageFile cmdlet is used to retrieve a list of all the files in that account. The name of the storage account and the file share or directory to be listed will need to be specified.

Next, the list of files is filtered using the Where-Object cmdlet. It filters the list of files based on the last time they were accessed. The Last-Modified property of the file object can be used to determine when the file was last accessed.

Last, the filtered files are moved to archive storage using the `Start-AzStorageFileCopy` cmdlet that copies the filtered files to a separate storage account or file share being used as an archive. Optionally, the original copies of the files can now be deleted. Be aware: the script demonstrates how to list files, filter them based on their last access time, and copy them to archive storage.

In AWS, the Amazon S3 storage service can be configured to automatically tier data to the appropriate storage tier using the S3 Lifecycle policies. This can be done using the AWS Management Console or the AWS SDKs. Like Azure, AWS provides several tools and technologies for automating the tiering of storage, including S3 Intelligent-Tiering, S3 Standard-Infrequent Access, and S3 Glacier.

Automating Scaling of Storage

Automating the scaling of storage involves the use of tools and technologies to automatically increase or decrease the capacity of the storage system based on the demand for storage.

In Azure, the Azure Storage Account can be configured to automatically scale up or down based on the demand for storage using the Azure Management Portal or the Azure Storage REST API. Various tools and technologies are available for automating the scaling of storage, including Azure Storage Scalability and Performance Targets and Azure Storage Autoscale.

Obviously, S3 can be scaled automatically as well through the AWS Management Console or SDKs. Tools and technologies for automating the scaling of storage include S3 Auto Scaling and S3 Transfer Acceleration. S3 does not have a native autoscaling mechanism for storage capacity, as it automatically scales based on the amount of data stored. S3 Transfer Acceleration can be enabled for faster data transfer, but scaling the storage capacity itself is not required.

In the following YAML script, an S3 bucket is defined and scaling policies set up to increase and decrease the number of replicas of the bucket based on the size of the bucket. This could be used as a template in CloudFormation. The script can be used in the scenario where there is an S3 bucket whose replicas are managed by an Auto Scaling Group. In this specific use case, the template is designed to increase or decrease the number of replicas based on the S3 bucket size. In most scenarios, S3 automatically scales to accommodate the amount of data stored without requiring manual intervention or scaling policies.

NOTE *Before getting to the increase and decrease statements, it is necessary to specify the resources and define the roles that these resources have in AWS. This is not included in the example. The script defines a CloudWatch alert that triggers the resizing of storage.*

```
IncreaseReplicaCountPolicy:

  Type: AWS::AutoScaling::ScalingPolicy

  Properties:

    AdjustmentType: ChangeInCapacity

    AutoScalingGroupName: !Ref MyBucket

    Cooldown: 300

    ScalingAdjustment: 1
```

```yaml
DecreaseReplicaCountPolicy:

  Type: AWS::AutoScaling::ScalingPolicy

  Properties:

    AdjustmentType: ChangeInCapacity

    AutoScalingGroupName: !Ref MyBucket

    Cooldown: 300

    ScalingAdjustment: -1

BucketSizeAlarmHigh:

  Type: AWS::CloudWatch::Alarm

  Properties:

    AlarmDescription: "Alarm when bucket size exceeds 10GB"

    MetricName: BucketSize

    Namespace: AWS/S3

    Statistic: Maximum

    Period: 300

    EvaluationPeriods: 1

    Threshold: 10000

    ComparisonOperator: GreaterThanThreshold

    AlarmActions:

      - !Ref IncreaseReplicaCountPolicy

BucketSizeAlarmLow:

  Type: AWS::CloudWatch::Alarm

  Properties:

    AlarmDescription: "Alarm when bucket size falls below 5GB"

    MetricName: BucketSize

    Namespace: AWS/S3

    Statistic: Maximum

    Period: 300
```

Let us review the various parameters in the script in more detail:

- *IncreaseReplicaCountPolicy*: This is a CloudFormation resource of type `AWS::AutoScaling::ScalingPolicy`. It defines a policy to increase the number of replicas in an Auto Scaling Group (referred by !Ref MyBucket) by 1 when triggered.

- *DecreaseReplicaCountPolicy*: Similar to the previous resource, it's also of type `AWS::AutoScaling::ScalingPolicy`. It defines a policy to decrease the number of replicas in the Auto Scaling Group by 1 when triggered.

- *BucketSizeAlarmHigh*: This resource is a CloudWatch alarm that triggers when the bucket size exceeds 10 GB. If this condition is met, the alarm will trigger the `IncreaseReplicaCountPolicy` scaling policy.

- *BucketSizeAlarmLow*: This is another CloudWatch alarm that triggers when the bucket size falls below 5GB. In this case, the alarm doesn't have any associated action, so it won't trigger any scaling policy.

Examples in Azure and AWS have been studied for reference. Obviously, GCP and Alibaba Cloud offer services for autoscaling. GCP offers Cloud Storage Transfer Service and Cloud Storage Nearline for tiering and automated scaling of storage. In Alibaba Cloud, OSS Cold Storage and OSS Archive Storage are used.

By using the tools and technologies provided by the cloud providers, organizations can automate the process of transitioning data between storage tiers and scaling the storage capacity based on the demand, even in real time. This can help organizations to optimize and scale their storage capacity to meet the changing needs of their applications and workloads.

MANAGING DATA ACCESS

Storage is just a technology that enables storing data in a secure way. But not just anyone should be able to access the data. Hence, managing storage is mainly about managing data access. This will be discussed in this final section.

Managing data access in a multi-cloud environment can be a complex task, but it is an essential part of ensuring the security, compliance, and performance of the data. First, policies need to be set that define who, when, and why data may be accessed: it must be specified exactly which users, groups, or applications are authorized to access which data. These policies should be based on the principle of least privilege, which means that users should only have the minimum level of access required to perform their job duties.

To achieve this, the identity and access management (IAM) tools in the clouds need to be used. For access management in data, consider multi-cloud management platforms like Flexera, Scalr, and Morpheus. These platforms offer centralized management of storage, compute, and networking resources across multiple cloud environments and can help simplify the process of managing storage assets in multi-cloud scenarios.

Most enterprises use Active Directory (AD) as a main identity source. Alternatives for access management are Okta, ForgeRock, CyberArk, and Ping. These tools can help to manage and enforce data access policies across multiple cloud platforms. They allow the creation of users, groups, and roles with specific permissions, as well as tracking and monitoring access to data. But this is just a first step. Best practices are as follows:

- *Data encryption*: Encrypting data is an effective way to protect it from unauthorized access, even if it falls into the wrong hands. Many cloud platforms offer encryption services, but third-party tools such as GnuPG or Cloud KMS can also be used to encrypt data before it is uploaded to the cloud. It is good to know that per January of 2023 all data that is entered in S3 buckets is encrypted at 256 bits per default.
- *Apply data access controls*: Access controls such as ACLs and object-level permissions can help in restricting access to specific data sets or objects. For example, ACLs can be used to allow only certain users or groups to read or write to a particular object in an S3 bucket, or object-level permissions can be used to grant or revoke access to specific objects in a Google Cloud Storage bucket.
- *Monitor and audit data access*: Regularly monitoring and auditing data access is essential for detecting and preventing unauthorized access. Many cloud platforms offer tools for monitoring and auditing data access, such as AWS CloudTrail and Azure Activity Logs. Third-party tools such as Splunk or Sumo Logic can also be used to centralize and analyze log data from multiple cloud platforms.

None of this will be effective if the data access policies are not regularly reviewed. Policies and controls must be updated frequently to ensure that they are effective and aligned with the compliance standards and requirements of the organization.

This concludes the chapter about storage. Now there is a good understanding of networks and storage in clouds. Next, machines must run the workloads. Although containers and serverless are gaining popularity, a vast amount of workloads still run on virtual servers in the cloud. Setting up compute infrastructure will be studied in the next chapter.

CONCLUSION

This chapter discussed the various options that cloud providers offer in terms of storage. First, the differences between storage types were discussed. It is important to be able to make a distinction between file, block, and object storage in order to pick the right type of storage in the cloud.

Next, it was explained that managing storage is mainly about optimizing the storage, for instance by using SLM and tiering. Data that is not frequently accessed could be moved to a cheaper type of archive storage, as an example, saving a lot of costs. It was stressed that tiering should be automated as much as possible. The last section studied the best practices of managing data access by implementing data access policies and controls.

Data protection was also discussed. The importance of data redundancy and disaster recovery strategies in multi-cloud storage must be emphasized. This chapter explained concepts of data replication across multiple cloud providers or regions, as well as disaster recovery.

KEY POINTS

- Before defining and designing storage solutions in cloud, the differences in storage types, for instance block, file, or object-based storage, must be understood.
- Cloud providers offer a wide variety of storage solutions. The appropriate solution must be chosen based on the requirements for the environment. Requirements can be set for performance, durability, and compliance.
- It is strongly recommended to apply storage tiering and SLM. Tiering and SLM can reduce storage costs by automatically transitioning data to the least expensive tier as it ages.
- Storage holds data and that data must be protected at all times. Data redundancy and disaster recovery are crucial topics to consider in storage

architecture and management. Monitoring and auditing data access is essential to ensure security and compliance in multi-cloud storage management.

- Cost management is an important aspect of storage management. The price per Gb of storage can be very low, but there might be additional costs for data transfer, for instance.

- Storage is about data. This means that strict principles and policies for accessing data must be considered. IAM is needed to ensure that only authorized users can access data, but there are more controls available. For example, data can and should be encrypted.

QUESTIONS

1. What is the most common way of storage virtualization?

2. Name the three storage types.

3. What is the most used storage solution in Azure?

4. To archive data in AWS, what solution can be used?

Answers appear in the appendix.

## CHAPTER 4

VIRTUALIZING AND MANAGING COMPUTE

INTRODUCTION

Networks and storage have been discussed, but there is one more component that is needed to run workloads in cloud: compute power. This chapter is about the basics of compute, starting with virtual machines which are still often used in clouds, despite the rise of serverless and containers (discussed in later chapters). Public cloud providers offer a wide variety of compute power with different deployment models. It is important to understand how compute in cloud works regarding, for instance, CPU and memory. Next, the various deployment models are discussed, from spot to reserved. This chapter also looks at the on-premises propositions of cloud providers, such as Azure Stack and AWS Outpost.

STRUCTURE

This chapter discusses the following topics:

- Comparing compute models in public clouds
- Key considerations for choosing compute
- Rightsizing compute in deployment and autoscaling
- Exploring on-premises propositions of public cloud
- Deploying and managing compute assets from consoles
- Automating infrastructure management

COMPARING COMPUTE MODELS IN PUBLIC CLOUDS

Previous sections discussed setting up networks and connectivity in the cloud and explored how to store data. But compute power is also needed to run applications that can process this data and present the outcomes to users. Azure, AWS, GCP, and Alibaba Cloud offer a variety of solutions to host applications and services. Applications and services are typically referred to as workloads. Each of the mentioned providers offers different compute models to meet the needs of different types of workloads. Virtual machines, containers, and serverless are all different compute models that can be used to run applications and services in the cloud.

Before comparing, it is good to have an understanding of virtualization of servers, just as was done in the previous chapter about virtualizing storage. The traditional data center had physical servers. Each server would host one application. The server was sized to the expected usage of that application, meaning that it was expected to use a certain amount of processing power and memory in the machine. However, it could happen that the application was not using all the resources that were available in the machine, or that the application was too heavy for the machine, maxing out the CPU and memory and with that causing severe performance issues or even crashes.

Virtualization of servers was invented to make more efficient usage of compute power by dynamically distributing the resources of servers across workloads. Server virtualization allows for running multiple virtual servers on a single physical server. The technology that enables it is the hypervisor, which sits between the physical hardware and the virtual servers. The hypervisor dynamically allocates the physical resources of the server, such as CPU, memory, and storage, to the different virtual servers. It also isolates the virtual servers from each other, so that they cannot interfere with each other's operation.

When a virtual server is created, the hypervisor creates a VM that acts as a software representation of a physical server. The VM includes virtual versions of physical resources, such as a virtual CPU, virtual memory, and virtual storage. The virtual server runs on top of the VM, and it is able to access the virtual resources as if they were real physical resources.

One of the main benefits of server virtualization is that it allows for greater resource utilization. Instead of having a single operating system and application running on a physical server, multiple virtual servers can run on the same physical server, each with their own operating system and applications. This allows for more efficient use of the physical resources, as well as more flexibility in terms of scaling and deploying new servers. With that, it is fair to say that virtualization is the cornerstone of public clouds.

VMs are likely still the most popular compute model. VMs provide on-demand, scalable computing resources. They emulate a physical computer and can run a variety of operating systems and configurations. They are typically used to run traditional, monolithic applications that require a full operating system and a specific set of dependencies. VMs are well-suited for applications that require a high degree of customization and control over the underlying infrastructure.

Containers are becoming increasingly popular since they are lighter than VMs. Containers allow applications to be packaged in a portable and lightweight format. Containers are built on top of the host operating system, and they share the same kernel. This allows them to be lighter and efficient than VMs. Containers are typically used to run microservices-based applications, which are composed of many small, independent services. They are well-suited for applications that require a high degree of scalability and portability. The difference between VMs and containers is shown in Figure 4.1:

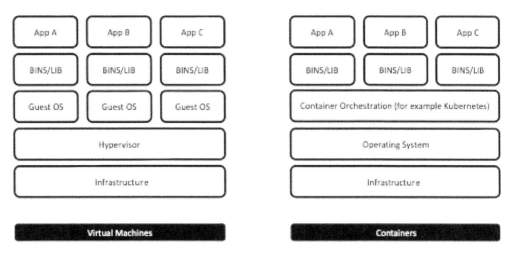

FIGURE 4.1 Difference between VMs and containers.

Serverless is the last compute model that will be discussed. The term serverless might cause confusion since there is still server technology involved.

However, now we can run code without the need to provision or manage servers. In a serverless model, the cloud provider is responsible for managing and scaling the underlying infrastructure, and users only pay for the compute resources used by their code: think of processing power of the CPU and memory. Serverless is typically used to run event-driven and code-based applications, which are composed of small, independent functions. They are well-suited for applications that require a high degree of scalability and cost-efficiency.

Now, the various propositions that Azure, AWS, GCP, and Alibaba Cloud offer will be explored. Azure offers the following services:

- *Virtual machines (VMs)*
- *Azure Container Instances (ACI)* to run Docker containers in serverless mode
- Azure Functions as a serverless compute option

AWS offers several compute models, including:

- *Elastic Compute Cloud (EC2)* to run VMs
- *Elastic Container Service (ECS)* to run and manage Docker containers
- Lambda as a serverless compute option

Google Cloud Platform offers:

- Compute Engine for VMs
- Kubernetes Engine to run containers on Kubernetes clusters
- Cloud Functions as a serverless compute option

And lastly, Alibaba Cloud:

- *Elastic Compute Service (ECS)* for VMs
- Container Service
- Function Compute as a serverless compute option

In summary, Azure, AWS, Google Cloud, and Alibaba Cloud all offer a range of compute deployments to meet the needs of different types of workloads. These include virtual machines, container orchestration, and serverless computing. The choice for a certain option will depend on the specific use case.

KEY CONSIDERATIONS FOR CHOOSING COMPUTE

To cut it short, the key considerations in choosing compute instance are cost, scalability, and performance. Cost will first be addressed, since one of the misperceptions of using public cloud is that it is always cheaper. This is not the case. Cloud will bring a lot of benefits, but only if done right and if all options have been explored in terms of "best fit" to a specific business case.

The pros and cons of the various compute models that were discussed in the previous section will now be explored.

When choosing among virtual machines, containers, or serverless technologies, there are several considerations to take into account. Each option has its own set of pros and cons, and the decision depends on factors such as the specific use case, scalability requirements, resource utilization, development workflow, and operational preferences.

Pros of using virtual machines include:

- *Isolation*: VMs provide strong isolation between applications, allowing different operating systems and software stacks to be run.
- *Compatibility*: VMs can run legacy or specialized software that may not be compatible with other technologies.
- *Flexibility*: VMs offer more configuration options, allowing the fine-tuning of resources such as CPU, memory, and storage.
- *Security*: VMs provide a higher level of security through isolated environments.

Cons of using virtual machines are:

- *Resource overhead*: VMs require a dedicated operating system and consume more resources, leading to higher costs and slower startup times.
- *Scalability*: VMs are slower to scale since they need to be provisioned and booted individually.
- *Management complexity*: VMs require more manual management, including patching, updates, and infrastructure provisioning.

The pros of using containers are:

- *Lightweight*: Containers share the host operating system kernel, resulting in faster startup times, lower resource consumption, and higher density.

- *Scalability*: Containers can be rapidly scaled up or down, allowing for efficient resource utilization and responsiveness to demand.

- *Portability*: Containers can be deployed consistently across different environments, from development to production, reducing compatibility issues.

- *DevOps integration*: Containers integrate well with modern DevOps practices, enabling reproducible builds and streamlined deployment pipelines.

Cons of containers might include:

- *Weaker isolation*: Containers share the host OS, so there is a possibility of security vulnerabilities or conflicts between containerized applications.

- *Limited compatibility*: Containers may not support applications with specific hardware or kernel-level dependencies.

- *Orchestration complexity*: Managing containerized applications at scale requires additional tools (for example, Kubernetes) that add complexity to the infrastructure.

Lastly, using serverless options might have the following pros:

- *No infrastructure management*: Serverless abstracts away the underlying infrastructure, allowing developers to focus solely on writing code.

- *Autoscaling*: Serverless platforms automatically scale resources based on demand, providing high scalability and cost-efficiency.

- *Pay-per-use*: With serverless, only the actual execution time of the code is paid for, which can be cost-effective for sporadic workloads.

- *Easy integration*: Serverless platforms often offer seamless integration with other cloud services and event-driven architectures.

Serverless will also have cons. Although debatable, these might include:

- *Cold start delay*: Serverless functions experience a slight delay during the initial invocation due to container initialization (cold start).

- *Limited execution time*: Serverless platforms impose limits on execution time, which may not be suitable for long-running or resource-intensive tasks.

- *Vendor lock-in*: Adopting serverless can make it challenging to migrate to a different provider or switch to a different architectural approach.

Ultimately, the choice between virtual machines, containers, or serverless depends on the specific requirements, the level of control and isolation needed, scalability demands, resource utilization goals, and the expertise of the development and operations teams. In some cases, a combination of these technologies may be the most suitable solution.

Each public cloud provider offers a variety of pricing options, including on-demand, reserved, and spot instances. On-demand instances are the most flexible option, where only what is used is paid for, without any upfront costs. Reserved instances, on the other hand, require an upfront payment in exchange for a lower hourly rate. This is an important topic: cloud is often chosen by companies since it is mainly *operational expenditure (OPEX)*, meaning that the company only pays for what it is using at that time. With *capital expenditure (CAPEX)*, a company typically has to make upfront investments that it has to depreciate over time, regardless of if the machines that have been invested in are used or not. Now think about reserved instances once more: in that case, an investment is made upfront so that capacity is reserved. Indeed, this is considered CAPEX in the financial world and might lead to debates with controllers in companies.

The last type of instances to mention are spot instances, which are available on AWS and GCP. These allow bidding on unused capacity at a discounted rate but come with the risk of being terminated if the bid is too low. Hence, there is a high risk on the availability of these instances, and they are therefore not recommended to run production workloads.

Another important factor to consider is scalability. All three public cloud providers offer scalable compute options, but each has a slightly different approach. AWS offers the ability to automatically scale instances up or down, based on demand, while Azure offers a similar option called *autoscale*. GCP offers a more manual approach, where instances can be added or removed manually, based on demand. So, there are differences in the approach of scaling among the providers.

The last point to consider is that of performance. Many factors can impact performance in cloud, such as:

- *Resource allocation*: The amount and type of resources allocated to workloads can significantly affect performance. Factors such as CPU, memory, storage, and network bandwidth must be appropriately provisioned to meet the workload's demands.

- *Scalability*: The ability to scale resources up or down based on workload requirements is crucial for achieving optimal performance. Elastic scaling allows us to handle sudden spikes in traffic or adjust resources during periods of low demand.

- *Network latency*: The speed and reliability of network connections between the cloud infrastructure and end-users or other services can impact performance. Higher latency will lead to slower response times and decreased user experience.

- *Geographic location*: The physical location of the cloud infrastructure can affect latency and response times. Choosing data centers that are closer to the target audience or integrating *content delivery networks (CDNs)* can help reduce latency and improve performance.

- *Storage performance*: The type and configuration of storage used can impact the performance of workloads. For example, solid-state drives (SSDs) generally offer faster read/write speeds compared to traditional hard disk drives (HDDs). Refer to *Chapter 3: Visualizing and Managing Storage* to read more about storage options in cloud.

- *Instance types*: Cloud service providers offer different instance types with varying levels of computing power, memory, and networking capabilities. Choosing the right instance type for a workload's requirements is important to ensure optimal performance.

- *Software optimization*: Optimizing software and application code can greatly enhance performance. Techniques such as caching, efficient algorithms, and parallel processing can help minimize resource usage and improve response times.

- *Load balancing*: Distributing incoming traffic across multiple instances or servers can help distribute the workload and prevent any single resource from becoming a performance bottleneck. Load balancers ensure that requests are evenly distributed and help achieve higher availability and scalability.

- *Monitoring and performance analysis*: Regular monitoring of the workload's performance metrics helps to identify bottlenecks, analyze resource utilization, and make informed decisions for optimization. Utilize monitoring tools to track KPIs and identify areas for improvement.

- *Third-party services*: Integrating third-party services, such as databases, content delivery networks, or external APIs, can introduce dependencies and impact performance. Performance characteristics and reliability of these services must be carefully assessed before incorporating them into workloads.

All this needs to be considered in choosing the right compute option for the workloads. Additionally, staying up to date with cloud provider offerings and best practices can help leverage new technologies and optimizations for improved performance.

Different compute models may offer different levels of performance, depending on the type of workload. For example, if *high performance computing (HPC)* is needed for scientific or engineering applications, GCP offers Preemptible VMs, which are a cost-effective option for batch workloads and other fault-tolerant workloads.

The most important thing to consider is the specific needs of our workload. Each public cloud provider offers a variety of options, including VMs, containers, and serverless computing. VMs are the most traditional option and offer the most control over the underlying infrastructure. Containers, on the other hand, offer a more lightweight and portable option, and are well suited for microservices and other cloud-native applications. Serverless computing, available on AWS, Azure, and GCP, allows running code without provisioning or managing servers, and is well suited for event-driven, ephemeral workloads. Different deployment options are discussed extensively in a further section of this chapter.

It is important to remember that the different options must be evaluated and compared to make an informed decision that aligns with the specific needs of the business.

RIGHTSIZING COMPUTE IN DEPLOYMENT AND AUTOSCALING

When it comes to cloud computing, rightsizing compute models can save both time and money. Different topics must be considered when defining the size of the compute power. There is actually a big advantage here, in comparison to physical machines. When equipment had to be ordered in the data center, the architect also had to calculate the required capacity that a server should have. Ordering a bigger server would mean a higher investment. If that machine would sit idle for most of its capacity, it would be a disinvestment. Thus, the role of the architect was to define the right capacity for the workloads of the company.

It works the same in cloud, but the cloud is more flexible and has more options to really tailor the capacity to the requirements. Still, these parameters must be considered:

▪ The type of workload that is running. Different types of workloads have different resource requirements.

▪ The number of instances planned to be run. The more instances there are, the more resources will be needed.

▪ The size of the instances. Larger instances tend to have more resources than smaller instances.

▪ The number of hours that instances are running. The more hours the instances are running, the more resources will need to be taken into account.

To define the capacity of compute models in AWS, the AWS Cost Explorer tool is used, which helps in identifying underutilized instances and resources. Additionally, the AWS Auto Scaling feature can be used to automatically adjust the number of instances based on the workloads. Azure has the Azure Cost Management tool available. The Azure Autoscale feature can also be used to automatically adjust the number of instances. The alternatives to GCP are the Cost Management tool and the Autoscale feature.

Thus, when deploying an instance type, it is important to consider the right size in order to ensure optimal performance and cost efficiency. The size of the compute system refers to the number of resources, such as CPU and memory, which are available in the system.

One of the key considerations when determining the right size of compute in deployment is the workload that the system will be handling. If the workload is expected to be high, then a larger compute system may be necessary to ensure that the system can handle the increased load. On the other hand, if the workload is expected to be low, a smaller compute system may be sufficient. It might be tempting to select a smaller instance for cost reasons. However, selecting an instance type that is too small for the workload can lead to poor performance and decreased user satisfaction. On the other hand, selecting a system that is too large can lead to wasted resources and increased costs. Hence, there is a delicate balance that must be weighed in choosing the right instances or other forms of compute power.

Be aware that this section mainly discusses instances or VMs. In serverless propositions this works differently, since in that case, the automation will ensure that only the required CPU and memory is really allocated to the workload. Having said that, not all workloads—applications—are suitable to run serverless.

The cost of sizing has already been discussed. As the size of the compute system increases, so does the cost. Therefore, it is important to consider the cost-benefit trade-off when selecting the size of the compute system. To minimize costs, it is often best to start with a smaller compute system and then scale up as necessary.

RIGHTSIZING USING AUTOSCALING

Once the right size of compute in deployment has been determined, it is important to be able to change the size as needed, preferably dynamically. One way to do this is by using autoscaling. Autoscaling is the process of automatically adjusting the number of resources in an instance, in response to changes in the workload. This allows the system to automatically scale up or down as necessary, ensuring that the right number of resources are available at all times.

AWS, Azure, GCP, and Alibaba Cloud all offer autoscaling capabilities for their computer systems. AWS offers autoscaling for its EC2 and ECS services, allowing users to automatically scale their compute resources in response to changes in demand. Azure offers autoscaling for its virtual machines, and GCP offers autoscaling for its Compute Engine instances. Alibaba Cloud also offers autoscaling for its ECS instances:

- In AWS, autoscaling can be achieved by using Amazon Auto Scaling, which allows the user to automatically increase or decrease the number of Amazon EC2 instances or Amazon ECS tasks in a group based on CloudWatch Alarms.

- In Azure, Virtual Machine Scale Sets can be used, which enables the user to create and manage a group of identical, load balanced VMs.

- In GCP, autoscaling is done through Autoscaler, a tool that automatically adjusts the number of instances in a managed instance group based on demand.

- In Alibaba Cloud, Auto Scaling is provided to automatically adjust the number of ECS instances based on demand.

By using autoscaling, the size of the compute system can be changed as necessary, ensuring that the right number of resources is always available. AWS, Azure, GCP, and Alibaba Cloud all offer autoscaling capabilities for their compute instances, thus making it easy to implement this feature in deployment. There are a few things to be aware of in terms of using autoscaling. For one, autoscaling can lead to unexpected costs if not configured properly. Automatic scaling can have an impact on performance. This can be mitigated by monitoring the performance of instances and adjusting resources as needed. In other words, monitoring resource utilization is crucial.

One topic that has not yet been addressed is security. But it is crucial in selecting compute options and implementing automation such as autoscaling. It is important to note that while VMs offer stronger isolation compared to containers and serverless, they also come with increased overhead in terms of resource utilization and management complexity. Containers and serverless platforms provide more lightweight and scalable options, but they may require additional security measures and careful configuration to ensure isolation and protect sensitive data.

Security is a critical consideration when choosing compute models in the cloud. The choice between VMs, containers, and serverless can have implications for isolation and data security. The three models are compared as follows:

Virtual machines:

- *Isolation*: VMs provide strong isolation by running applications on separate virtualized operating systems. Each VM operates independently, reducing the risk of one application compromising the security of another.
- *Data security*: VMs allow the implementation of security measures at both the host and guest OS levels. Security patches, firewall rules, and access controls can be applied specifically to each VM. Data within VMs can be encrypted, and VM snapshots can help protect against data loss or corruption.

Containers:

- *Isolation*: Containers share the host operating system's kernel, which means that they have a lower level of isolation compared to VMs. However, containerization technologies employ mechanisms like namespaces and control groups to provide isolation between containers, preventing direct access to other containers' resources.
- *Data security*: Container images should be carefully constructed to include only necessary components, reducing the attack surface. Isolating sensitive data within containers can be achieved using encryption and access control mechanisms. Regular image scanning and updates are crucial to address security vulnerabilities.

Serverless:

- *Isolation*: Serverless functions run in a managed environment provided by the cloud provider. Each function executes in its own isolated container or runtime environment. While serverless platforms handle isolation, the underlying implementation details and level of isolation can vary between providers.

- *Data security*: With serverless, the user relies on the cloud provider's security measures for the underlying infrastructure. Data security within serverless functions involves applying appropriate security controls to the code and using encryption techniques for sensitive data. The responsibility for securing the application and implementing access controls lies with the developer.

Regardless of the chosen compute model, best practices for securing cloud workloads apply, such as regular updates and patches, secure coding practices, least privilege access controls, encryption of data in transit and at rest, and proper monitoring and auditing of the environment. Evaluating the security features, compliance certifications, and documentation provided by the cloud provider is also essential in making an informed decision about the compute model that aligns with the user's security requirements.

Isolation and data security will also greatly drive the choice to keep workloads on premises. That is the topic of the next section, where other infrastructure propositions that cloud providers offer are explored, extending the public cloud to on premises.

EXPLORING ON-PREMISES PROPOSITIONS OF PUBLIC CLOUD

Many organizations must run applications and keep data on premises for various reasons. In a lot of cases, compliancy is an important driver to implement hybrid solutions. Some applications and sensitive data are kept on premises, while organizations can still benefit from the advantages of clouds. The major cloud providers provide solutions for these hybrid setups. This section concentrates on the main offerings: Azure Stack, AWS Outposts, and Google Anthos. Lastly, this section will look at a solution that extends VMWare environments to public clouds.

Azure Stack, AWS Outposts, and Google Anthos are all hybrid cloud solutions that allow organizations to run their applications and services both on premises and in the public cloud. Each of these solutions offers its own set of features and benefits, making them suitable for different use cases.

Azure Stack and Azure Arc

Azure Stack is a hybrid cloud platform from Microsoft that allows organizations to run Azure services on premises. This solution is particularly useful for organizations that have strict data sovereignty and compliance requirements, as it allows them to keep sensitive data within their own facilities while still being able to take advantage of the scalability and flexibility of the Azure public cloud. Azure Stack also provides consistent development and deployment experience, allowing organizations to use the same tools and processes for both on-premises and public cloud deployments.

The two major offerings of Azure Stack are Azure Stack HCI and Stack Hub. Stack HCI is built on top of the *Windows Server Software-Defined (WSSD)* program, which is a partnership between Microsoft and its hardware partners. In essence, it allows the user to run workloads on hardware of partners, such as Dell and HP, and to manage these workloads as if they were hosted in Azure.

Azure Stack Hub, on the other hand, is a hybrid cloud platform that allows organizations to run Azure services on premises. It includes a subset of Azure services, such as virtual machines, storage, and networking, and allows organizations to develop and deploy applications using the same tools and APIs, as they would in the public Azure cloud. The main difference between Azure Stack HCI and Azure Stack Hub is that the former is focused on virtualized workloads, while the latter is focused on providing a hybrid version of Azure services.

One service that needs mentioning here is Azure Arc, which also allows the management of non-Azure workloads from the Azure cloud. The key feature of Azure Arc is its ability to extend Azure management capabilities to resources, regardless of where they are running. This can be in other clouds or on premises, and it includes Windows and Linux servers, Kubernetes clusters, and applications. Arc uses ARM templates to deploy and manage resources, Azure Policy for compliance and governance, and Azure Monitor for monitoring and logging.

AWS Outposts

AWS Outposts is a hybrid cloud solution from AWS, providing an on-premises solution to run workloads, while managing these from the AWS cloud. Like Azure Stack, this solution is particularly useful for organizations that have strict data sovereignty and compliance requirements. AWS Outposts also provides consistent development and deployment experience, allowing organizations to use the same tools and processes for both on-premises and public cloud deployments. One important thing to remember is that Outposts is a fully managed service, providing a solution for computing and storage. Outposts come in preconfigured computer racks, with customizable capacity.

With AWS Outposts, organizations can run a wide range of AWS services on premises, including EC2 and ECS. Additionally, organizations can use the same management and operational tools and services on premises as they do in the cloud, such as AWS Management Console, AWS IAM, and AWS Security Group.

There is a second offering on AWS Outposts that includes the implementation of VMWare. This too is a fully managed service that allows organizations to run VMware Cloud on AWS on premises. In this case, the same VMware control plane and APIs can be used on premises as would be used in the cloud. VMWare will be discussed later in this section.

Google Anthos

The hybrid solution that Google offers is Anthos. Like Azure Stack and AWS Outposts, it allows the running of applications on premises, in the public cloud, or in other clouds such as AWS and Azure. However, Anthos is different than the solutions previously discussed. Of course, it is an on-premises solution, managed by GCP. So, firstly, the environment must be set up in GCP. Next, to use Google Anthos, a Kubernetes cluster must be running on premises. Anthos GKE can be used on premises to set up a cluster or connect an existing cluster to GCP. That is the big difference with the other propositions: Anthos is relying on Kubernetes.

Once the on-premises cluster is connected to GCP, the Kubernetes Engine, Cloud Build, and other GCP services can be used to deploy and manage applications.

Extending VMWare

Other hybrid options are VMWare on public cloud, extending on-premises VMWare environments to respective public clouds. The basic architecture for this is shown in Figure 4.2:

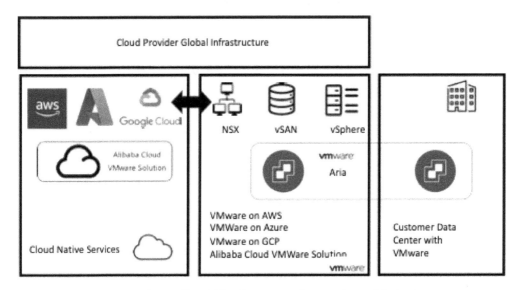

FIGURE 4.2 Extending VMWare from on premises to various public clouds.

The solution uses VMWare Aria, previously known as vRealize, that enables management of resources built with VMWare products across on-premises infrastructures and various public clouds. It is beyond the scope of this book to discuss the different components of Aria. Please refer to *https://www. vmware.com/nl/ products/aria.html* for more information.

This is a popular solution, since many organizations, and especially larger enterprises, have IT environments that are operated with VMWare virtualization products such as vSphere for compute, vSAN for storage, and NSX to virtualize networks. These organizations still want to benefit from the scalability and flexibility in cloud but might not want to change their technology stack completely. Extending VMWare to public clouds can be a good solution, providing a consistent way of managing assets on premises and in the cloud.

DEPLOYING AND MANAGING COMPUTE ASSETS

Deploying compute assets in cloud environments such as Azure, AWS, GCP, and Alibaba can be a daunting task. However, with the right set of best practices in place, it is possible to make the process more efficient and less error prone. The following are some of the best practices:

- First is the most obvious option that cannot be stressed enough: work with a plan. Before deploying any compute assets such as instances, it is essential to have a clear plan in place. This should include details on the type of infrastructure needed, including instances and the number of instances that are required. The plan should also include the configurations that will be used. This plan will serve as a road map for deployment and will help us to stay on track throughout the process.

- Next, the different compute options that are available need to be explored. Each of the cloud providers offers a variety of compute options, including VMs, containers, and serverless. It is important to understand the pros and cons of each option and choose the one that best fits the use case. For example, VMs are great for applications that require a specific operating system or software stack, while containers are more suitable for microservices-based applications. Serverless options are mainly used in event-based functionality.

- In clouds, as much should be automated as possible, which is easier than in the traditional data center. The reason for this is the fact that in cloud, the user is working with code. Basically, everything is code, which makes it easier to blueprint, template, script, and, with that, automate. Automation and configuration management tools such as Terraform, Ansible, and Chef should be used. These tools can help streamline the deployment process and ensure consistency across different environments. These tools can automate the provisioning of compute assets, as well as configure and manage them once they are deployed.

- Lastly, leverage cloud-native services to deploy and manage compute assets. For example, AWS offers ECS for container orchestration, Azure offers *Azure Container Instances (ACI)* for serverless container deployment, GCP provides *Google Kubernetes Engine (GKE)* for container orchestration, and Alibaba Cloud offers *Alibaba Container Service for Kubernetes (ACK)* for container orchestration.

Once the assets have been deployed, they need to be managed. That starts with observability: assets have to be monitored to see how they perform and to identify issues in a timely manner. All providers offer their own monitoring and logging tools: CloudWatch and CloudTrail for AWS, Log Analytics and Azure Monitor for Azure, Google Cloud Monitoring (previously Stackdriver) for GCP, and CloudMonitor for Alibaba Cloud.

Part of monitoring is making sure that the assets are secured. Security is a critical aspect of any deployment, and it is important to have security measures in place to protect compute assets. Each of the cloud providers offers a variety of security options, such as network segmentation, firewalls, and security groups. It is important to understand the security options available and implement them as needed.

Now that the overarching guiding best practices have been examined, a closer look is needed at the various deployment methods that the cloud providers offer. The following are the various methods in AWS:

- *Manual deployment*: This is the simplest method, where instances are manually created and configured using the AWS Management Console or command-line tools. This method is suitable for small-scale deployments or for testing and development environments.
- *Auto Scaling*: This allows for automated increase or decrease of the number of instances. In this case, a group of instances known as an Auto Scaling group is set up, and policies are configured to automatically add or remove instances from the group based on certain conditions.
- *Elastic Beanstalk*: This is a fully managed service that makes it easy to deploy, run, and scale Web applications and services. It handles the provisioning of instances, load balancing, and automatic scaling for the user.
- *EC2 Fleet*: This allows for provisioning a fleet of instances with a mix of instance types, purchase options, and *Amazon Machine Images (AMIs)*.
- *CloudFormation*: This is the infrastructure-as-code service of AWS that enables the user to model infrastructure and provision it in an automated and repeatable way. CloudFormation templates can be used to define the configuration of instances and other AWS resources, and then the CloudFormation service can be used to deploy and manage them.
- *Lambda*: This is a serverless compute service that can be used to run code without provisioning or managing servers. Lambda functions can be run in response to certain events, such as changes to data in an S3 bucket.

- *ECS and EKS*: These are container orchestration services that make it easy to deploy, run, and scale containerized applications.

- *App Runner*: This is a fully managed service that makes it easy to build and deploy containerized applications quickly. It automates the creation, configuration, and scaling of the underlying infrastructure and provides an easy-to-use console to define an application.

- *CodeDeploy*: This is a deployment service that automates the deployment of applications to a variety of compute services, including EC2 instances, Lambda functions, and ECS tasks.

Azure offers the following options:

- *Virtual Machines (VMs)*: This is the most basic method of deploying compute instances in Azure. VMs can be manually created and configured using the Azure Portal, Azure CLI, or Azure PowerShell. This method is suitable for small-scale deployments or for testing and development environments.

- *Autoscaling*: To automatically increase or decrease the number of VMs, Autoscaling can be used by setting up a group of VMs known as an Auto-Scale set. Next, policies are configured to automatically add or remove VMs from the group based on certain conditions.

- *Azure Kubernetes Service (AKS)*: This is a fully managed Kubernetes service in Azure. AKS handles the provisioning and management of the underlying infrastructure for containers that run on Kubernetes.

- *Azure Container Instances (ACI)*: This serverless compute service allows the user to run containers without provisioning or managing servers.

- *Azure App Service*: This is a fully managed *platform-as-a-service (PaaS)* that makes it easy to build and deploy Web, mobile, and API applications. Azure handles the provisioning and management of the underlying infrastructure.

- *Azure Functions*: The serverless compute service that enables the execution of code without provisioning or managing servers. It is the equivalent of Lambda in AWS.

- *Azure DevOps*: This is a special one and can be best described as the Swiss Army knife to build and deploy applications through CI/CD pipelines. Azure DevOps is a set of services that provides a collaborative environment for software development. Azure DevOps can be used to plan, build, test, and deploy code to Azure.

- *Azure Resource Manager (ARM) templates*: These are JSON templates that can be used to define the configuration of Azure resources and deploy them in an automated and repeatable way. ARM templates are used to deploy and manage all types of Azure resources, including VMs, AKS clusters, and other Azure services. ARM is likely the service that administrators will use most of the time in managing and automating resources in Azure. The final section of this chapter will look at an example.

The following are the deployment options for compute in GCP:

- *Manual deployment*: Compute instances can be manually created and configured through the GCP Console or the *command-line interface (CLI)*.
- *Automatic scaling*: By defining autoscaling groups, GCP can automatically create and terminate compute instances.
- *Preemptible instances*: This is a very specific GCP service. The service terminates instances that are not being actively used, to free up resources for other customers. It is somewhat comparable to the technology that Azure and AWS use to free up capacity and offer spot instances.
- *Kubernetes Engine*: GKE is the service to deploy and manage containerized applications using Kubernetes. Automated scaling is done through Cloud Run.
- *Cloud Deployment Manager*: This allows the use of templates in YAML or JSON format to create and manage deployments. It also helps to automate the process of deploying resources, as will be shown in the last section of this chapter with two examples.
- *Cloud Functions*: This is the GCP equivalent of Azure Functions or AWS Lambda. With functions, code can be run without provisioning or managing servers.

All public clouds offer similar methods to deploy compute instances to their respective cloud platforms. To conclude this section, the following are the options that Alibaba Cloud offers:

- *Elastic Compute Service (ECS)*: This is probably the service that is most used to create and manage compute instances in Alibaba Cloud. It can be used to deploy instances with both Windows and Linux operating systems in a wide variety of distributions.

- *Auto scaling*: This service automatically increases or decreases the number of compute instances.

- *Container service*: Deploying and managing containerized applications using Kubernetes is enabled with this service.

- *Serverless computing*: The equivalent for the serverless options that AWS, Azure, and GCP offer, allowing the user to run code without provisioning or managing servers. However, Alibaba Cloud also offers Function Compute that is specifically developed to build and run event-driven applications and services in the cloud.

It is clear that there are a variety of choices in terms of provisioning and managing compute manually or automating this using the advantages of *infrastructure as code (IaC)*. Preferably, the user wants to automate as much as possible in the cloud. The final section of this chapter looks at that and gives some examples on how to automate IaC by using common YAML scripts.

AUTOMATING INFRASTRUCTURE MANAGEMENT

Deploying compute assets in cloud environments such as Azure, AWS, GCP, and Alibaba can be a complex process, but with the right set of best practices in place, it is possible to make the process more efficient and less error prone. By creating a clear plan, understanding the different compute options available, leveraging automation and configuration management tools, utilizing cloud-native services, utilizing monitoring and logging tools, considering security, and testing and iterating, organizations can ensure that their compute assets are deployed successfully and are running smoothly.

However, these assets should not be managed manually, especially not in large environments. Hence, infrastructure management needs to be automated. This is what IaC enables. Most importantly, IaC allows for the use of version control systems such as Git, allowing for easy tracking of changes and rollbacks. However, there are more benefits from working with IaC. Templates and modules are reusable, reducing the amount of code that needs to be written. Obviously, it enables the automation of the infrastructure provisioning process, reducing the risk of human error, and increasing the speed of deployment.

In DevOps especially, the concept of IaC is very relevant. IaC empowers DevOps teams to treat infrastructure as code, bringing automation, consistency, scalability, traceability, and collaboration to the infrastructure provisioning and management processes. It aligns with the core principles of DevOps, enabling faster and more reliable software delivery and promoting efficient collaboration between development and operations teams:

- IaC allows infrastructure provisioning and configuration to be treated as code. By using declarative or imperative scripts, infrastructure can be automatically provisioned, configured, and managed, reducing manual effort and human error. This automation enables faster and more reliable deployments.

- With IaC, infrastructure configurations are defined in a code repository, ensuring consistent and repeatable deployments across various environments, such as development, testing, staging, and production. It eliminates the inconsistencies that arise from manual configurations, reducing the risk of deployment issues and increasing reliability.

- IaC allows for easy scaling of infrastructure resources by defining desired configurations and specifying the desired number of instances, load balancers, storage, and other resources. This scalability ensures that the infrastructure can handle varying workloads efficiently, improving performance and responsiveness.

- IaC treats infrastructure configurations as code, enabling the use of version control systems like Git. This brings traceability to infrastructure changes, allowing teams to track and review modifications, roll back changes if needed, and collaborate effectively. Version control also helps in auditing and compliance by providing a clear history of infrastructure changes.

- IaC encourages collaboration between developers, operations teams, and other stakeholders by providing a common, version-controlled codebase for infrastructure configurations. Infrastructure changes become more transparent, and teams can work together to improve processes, review code, and share knowledge. It also ensures that infrastructure can be easily reproduced across different environments or by different teams.

- IaC integrates seamlessly with CI/CD pipelines, enabling the automation of infrastructure deployments along with application deployments. Infrastructure changes can be automatically tested, validated, and deployed in a controlled manner, reducing manual intervention, and accelerating the delivery of software updates.

- IaC allows for automated testing of infrastructure configurations. Tests can be written as code to validate that the infrastructure is provisioned and configured correctly. These tests can check for security compliance, performance, availability, and other criteria, ensuring that the infrastructure meets desired standards.

- IaC promotes agility by enabling infrastructure changes to be implemented quickly and reliably. Infrastructure can be easily modified or replaced as needed, providing flexibility to adapt to changing business requirements and technology advancements.

If all the assets are as code, then scripts can manage the code. Assume a user wants to regularly deploy new instances of exactly the same type, with the same policies and configured in a consistent way. Scripting tools such as PowerShell, Bicep, or AWS CloudFormation templates can be used to do so.

Automating deployment of instances in Azure could be done through scripting an ARM template. In that case, the variables must first be defined: VM name, VM size, admin username, admin password, storage account name, storage account type, image, and location. The script can then be put together in YAML, and it would be something like this:

```yaml
# Resources
- name: myVM
  type: Microsoft.Compute/virtualMachines
  apiVersion: 2018-04-01
  location: "[parameters("location")]"
  properties:
    hardwareProfile:
      vmSize: "[parameters("vmSize")]"
    storageProfile:
      imageReference:
        publisher: "[parameters('imagePublisher')]"
        offer: "[parameters('imageOffer')]"
        sku: "[parameters('imageSku')]"
        version: latest
      osDisk:
        name: myOsDisk
```

```
        caching: ReadWrite
        createOption: FromImage
        diskSizeGB: 30
        vhd:
          uri: "[concat('http://',parameters('storageAccountName'),'.
          blob.core.windows.net/vhds/',parameters('vmName'),'-osdisk.
          vhd')]"
    osProfile:
      adminUsername: "[parameters('adminUsername')]"
      adminPassword: "[parameters('adminPassword')]"
      computerName: "[parameters('vmName')]"
    networkProfile:
      networkInterfaces:
        - name: myNic
          properties:
            primary: true
            ipConfigurations:
              - name: myIpConfig
                properties:
                  privateIPAllocationMethod: Dynamic
                  subnet:
                    id: "[variables('subnetId')]"


- name: myStorageAccount
  type: Microsoft.Storage/storageAccounts
  apiVersion: 2019-04-01
  location: "[parameters('location')]"
  properties:
    accountType: "[parameters('storageAccountType')]"
```

```
- name: myNic
  type: Microsoft.Network/networkInterfaces
  apiVersion: 2018-04-01
  location: "[parameters('location')]"
  properties:
    ipConfigurations:
      - name: myIpConfig
        properties:
          privateIPAllocationMethod: Dynamic
          subnet:
            id: "[variables('subnetId')]"
```

In AWS, CloudFormation templates would be used for this. In the following example, a t2.micro EC2 instance is deployed, again using YAML:

```
---
AWSTemplateFormatVersion: '2010-09-09'
Resources:
  MyEC2Instance:
    Type: 'AWS::EC2::Instance'
    Properties:
      InstanceType: t2.micro
      ImageId: ami-0ff8a91507f77f867
      KeyName: MyKeyPair
      SecurityGroupIds:
        - sg-01234567890abcdef0
      SubnetId: subnet-01234567890abcdef0
```

This example creates a single EC2 instance of type t2.micro using an AMI with ID ami-0ff8a91507f77f867, using the key pair MyKeyPair for SSH access, within the specified security group and subnet. Obviously, the properties can be replaced with other values, but it should be clear that the main principle is the same as in Azure: variables are defined that can be inserted into a template that can be reused. It is the basic first step to automation using IaC.

In GCP, YAML can also be used to create templates. Like in Azure and AWS, some parameters need to be specified to the instance, such as name, type, and location. The template can then be deployed from the gcloud CLI, which is the easiest way to work with GCP. In the example, a VM has been defined with the name my-instance. The only thing needed to do next is triggering the command through gcloud:

```
gcloud deployment-manager deployments create my-instance --config my-instance.yaml
```

Updating the deployment is also very easy:

```
gcloud deployment-manager deployments update my-instance --config my-instance.yaml
```

The past three chapters discussed virtualization of networks, storage, and compute as foundation to understand how public clouds work. However, this book is about multi-cloud. How can environments in different clouds communicate with each other? That requires interoperability. It is the topic for the next chapter.

CONCLUSION

This chapter explained the various compute models that can be deployed in clouds, from virtual machines to serverless options. It explored the many offerings that Azure, AWS, GCP, and Alibaba Cloud provide to run workloads from their platforms. It is not only about the public cloud. Azure, AWS, and GCP have solutions for on premises too: physical machines that can be managed from the respective clouds to create a hybrid platform. It was shown that in some cases, organizations need to have compute and data on premises, for instance, because of latency or compliance reasons. Next, the deployment and management of compute assets were discussed, starting with manual deployments and expanding to fully automated deployments including autoscaling.

The chapter also discussed the concept of IaC and the benefits of having everything as code. IaC plays a vital role in DevOps by bringing automation, consistency, scalability, and traceability to the infrastructure provisioning and management processes. The final section provided examples to automate with IaC, using YAML.

KEY POINTS

- Before deploying compute assets in cloud, the use case must be considered. Some applications might need virtual machines, but in more cloud-native environments, containers or even serverless options can be used.

- Organizations might have a need to keep environments on premises. There are solutions that cater to hybrid setups. These solutions include offerings such as Azure Stack, AWS Outposts, Google Anthos, and VMWare, extended into public clouds using VMWare Aria.

- The main concept of compute in cloud is built on the principles of IaC, making it easy to configure templates and blueprints and with that, create repeatable, scalable solutions to provision infrastructure in cloud.

- Infrastructure is also about cost management. It means that the user has to carefully consider the required capacity and rightsize the assets in cloud. Autoscaling and automation can be of great help in rightsizing environments.

QUESTIONS

1. What is needed to enable virtualization of servers?

2. Rate True or false: rightsizing is important in terms of cost control.

3. What is the name of the on-premises proposition of AWS?

4. Name the three main compute models in cloud.

Answers appear in the appendix.

5

CREATING INTEROPERABILITY

INTRODUCTION

One of the biggest challenges in multi-cloud is interoperability. Systems must be able to communicate with each other between public clouds, between clouds, and on-premises stacks. Interoperability must be defined on various levels, and this chapter will explain how to ensure interoperability between environments. The chapter will show why this is so important, as well as how to use solutions such as containers and service mesh to create interoperability.

STRUCTURE

This chapter discusses the following topics:

- Defining interoperability
- Requirements for interoperability
- Explaining the difference between portability and interoperability
- Solutions to create interoperability in public and hybrid clouds
- Working with Open Compute Project

DEFINING INTEROPERABILITY

Ask any company why interoperability in the cloud is important, and the most likely answer is probably to avoid vendor lock-in. That is the rationale behind the decision to adopt a multi-cloud strategy and not to have all workloads in one cloud. Multi-cloud is a strategy that promises to have the best of various worlds, with opportunities to reduce costs while improving flexibility and scalability.

The simple definition of interoperability is the ability of different systems, applications, or components to communicate and exchange data with each other in a seamless manner. In the context of multi-cloud, interoperability refers to the ability of different cloud platforms to work together seamlessly and exchange data, services, and applications. With the increasing popularity of multi-cloud, it is becoming more critical for organizations to ensure that cloud platforms are indeed interoperable. However, the use of multiple cloud platforms also presents new challenges, particularly in terms of interoperability.

Some of these challenges are discussed as follows:

- Although this might seem contradictory in itself, one of the biggest challenges with multi-cloud is the risk of vendor lock-in. One might wonder how that is possible. Each cloud provider may use different technologies, tools, and services, which can make it difficult for organizations to transfer their data and applications from one cloud to another. That is why technologies are needed to achieve interoperability and the ability to move data and applications between environments, thus helping to avoid vendor lock-in without encountering technical or compatibility issues.

- Data gravity is often forgotten about when discussing interoperability and portability, but it can be a real issue. Data gravity refers to when data attracts more data and applications to it as it grows in size and value. If data can be easily transferred from one location to another without any loss of quality or function, then we use the term data portability. The problem is that data gravity can make it difficult for organizations to move their data to other platforms or services, as the data becomes more difficult to extract and transfer as its size and complexity increase. Data portability can help organizations overcome the challenges posed by data gravity.

- Interoperability helps reduce costs. In multi-cloud concepts, the user can take advantage of the best features and pricing offered by different cloud providers. For example, one cloud provider can be used for storage and another for computing, taking advantage of the lower prices and better performance offered by the different clouds. However, this will impose a real risk. Managing these various solutions might become a challenge: it means that skills must be developed in each of the solutions that are used. It is essential to include this in the entire business case. The costs for upskilling and the need to have staff trained in multiple solutions might outweigh the reduction of the actual cloud spent. Introducing, adopting, and managing the cloud means more than just technology.

- The possibility of switching between various clouds will make the environment flexible and scalable. For example, if one cloud suffers from an outage, it can fail over to another provider, even without interrupting services. Business continuity and disaster recovery are one of the most common use cases for adopting multi-cloud or hybrid cloud with on-premises systems and a public cloud. However, this also has consequences for the management of these environments. They might become very complex in implementation and management. For one, both environments need to be kept in sync, depending on the requirements defined for *Recovery Time Objective (RTO)* and *Recovery Point Objective (RPO)*.

One use case was mentioned, business continuity, as well as disaster recovery. Other use cases are cloud bursts from the data center to the cloud to increase capacity fast or move applications and data closer to the user to overcome latency issues. The latter use case is often used in content delivery. Not every cloud provider has the same global presence, making it necessary to work with various providers to enable the delivery of services to users in a specific area. This can also be for compliance reasons, for instance, delivery of services in the China region using a native Chinese provider such as Alibaba Cloud or Tencent, where AWS might be used in other parts of the world. It should be clear that interoperability is crucial in multi-cloud for multiple reasons.

There are several approaches to choose to achieve interoperability in multi-cloud, including the following:

- Standardization is the first option to consider. Standards and protocols should be adopted that are supported by multiple cloud platforms. Examples are the OpenStack open-source cloud platform or the *Cloud Data Management Interface (CDMI)* standard. The Open Compute Project is another example that will be studied in detail in the final section of this chapter.

- Use of *application programming interfaces (APIs)*. APIs allow different cloud platforms to communicate and exchange data and services by providing a standardized interface for accessing data and applications.

- Implement a hybrid cloud as a combination of public and private cloud services. By using a hybrid cloud, organizations can take advantage of the best features of both public and private clouds and move data and applications between them as needed. The previous chapter discussed the on-premises offerings of public clouds, such as Azure Stack and AWS Outposts, that enable the creation of a hybrid environment. A widely adopted solution is VMware, which can be used on-premises and in various clouds, enabling shifting workloads between the different platforms.

- Cloud brokers can help by providing tools and services to manage and integrate cloud deployments, including data migration, security, and monitoring. The setup of a cloud broker is demonstrated in Figure 5.1:

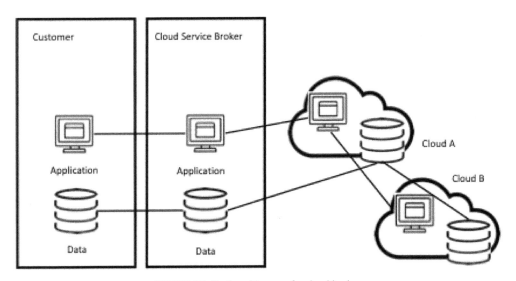

FIGURE 5.1 Basic architecture for cloud broker.

- The same applies to cloud gateways that provide a unified access point for cloud services, enabling access and management of multiple cloud platforms from a single interface. Examples of such gateways are the *Internet Business Exchange (IBX)* of Equinix or the services that Megaport provides.

When discussing cloud brokers and gateways, the benefits and limitations of these solutions should be elaborated. Generally spoken, brokers have the following benefits:

- A cloud broker provides flexibility by offering multiple cloud service options from different providers. It allows users to select the most suitable cloud services based on their specific requirements, such as cost, performance, and geographic location.
- Cloud brokers can analyze the pricing models and offerings of different cloud providers to help users optimize their costs. They can identify cost-effective options and provide recommendations to minimize expenses.
- A cloud broker simplifies the management of cloud services by providing a single interface or platform to manage multiple cloud environments. It eliminates the need to interact with different cloud providers individually.
- Cloud brokers can enforce security and compliance policies across multiple cloud platforms. They provide centralized control and visibility, making it easier to implement security measures and ensure compliance with industry regulations.

Some limitations would be the dependency on the cloud broker, possible vendor lock-in, and even potential latency. Since a cloud broker act as an intermediary between the user and the cloud providers, there may be additional network latency introduced in the data transmission process. The benefits of a gateway would be somewhat comparable to the usage of a broker:

- A cloud gateway provides a secure and simplified connection between an organization's on-premises infrastructure and cloud services. It allows seamless integration and data transfer between the two environments.
- Cloud gateways typically offer robust security features, such as encryption, authentication, and access control. They help protect data during transit and ensure secure communication between on-premises systems and cloud services.
- Cloud gateways can optimize network performance by caching data, reducing latency, and optimizing bandwidth usage. They can accelerate data transfer and improve application performance.
- Cloud gateways often support protocol translation, allowing different systems or applications with incompatible protocols to communicate and exchange data effectively.

Like brokers, gateways have downsides that must be considered carefully in the architecture:

- A cloud gateway may have limitations in terms of the cloud services it can connect to. Some gateways are designed to work with specific cloud providers or have compatibility constraints, restricting the choice of available services.

- Organizations need to deploy and manage the cloud gateway infrastructure, which may require additional resources, expertise, and maintenance.

- While cloud gateways aim to improve network performance, there can be cases where the additional overhead introduced by the gateway negatively impacts network latency or bandwidth utilization.

- If a cloud gateway becomes unavailable or experiences a failure, it can disrupt the connectivity between on-premises systems and cloud services, leading to downtime or service interruptions.

Interoperability is perceived as a must-do in multi-cloud architecture. However, it requires a well-thought-out architecture that takes all aspects into account, including skills that are needed to manage the solutions. Interoperability, as such, can be a requirement for adopting the cloud:

- It must be possible to adapt the cloud service to requirements that are specific to a particular business. Think of specific business rules and associated values. This needs to be considered with every service of the provider because many cloud provider processes can and will be set up quite standardly.

- Organizations do not want to be too dependent on a specific supplier. Changes in a specific service should not have a direct impact on the user organization and the application landscape. This means that a supplier should not simply remove functionality and allow customers of a specific service to migrate to a new version of this service at their own speed. Interfaces should be backward compatible because they are intertwined with the application landscape of the organization that uses the service. Suppliers should also notify their customers of significant changes in a timely manner.

- Sourcing choices are not forever, meaning that organizations must be able to easily choose other products. They must therefore require suppliers to have access to the data managed by the service so that it can be migrated to a new product. Legal agreements are also necessary, for example, to cover the risk if the supplier goes bankrupt. Think of exit strategies and associated exit plans. Consider, for example, an escrow agreement that ensures that customers have access to the (intellectual) property if a supplier goes bankrupt. Having said that, it is very unlikely for the larger providers discussed in this book to go bankrupt, but services might be stopped, which effectively leads to the same situations.

The next section discusses the definition of requirements in more detail.

REQUIREMENTS FOR INTEROPERABILITY

It was learned in the previous section that interoperability is critical for multi-cloud computing to be successful. By using standardized interfaces, data portability, security, and flexibility, it can be ensured that the multi-cloud environments are able to meet the specific needs discussed previously. This section explores the requirements for achieving interoperability in multi-cloud concepts, and also looks at some use cases for both on premises to cloud and between various public clouds.

Requirements that must be considered for achieving interoperability in multi-cloud would include:

- *Standardized interfaces*: To achieve interoperability, the various cloud platforms must have standardized interfaces that allow for seamless communication between them. This includes APIs, protocols, and data formats that are common across all platforms.
- *Security*: This is very obvious but still very important to mention. Interoperability must not compromise security. Cloud platforms must implement robust security measures to ensure that data is protected as it is transferred between platforms. Having said that, cloud platforms such as Azure, AWS, GCP, and Alibaba Cloud are probably the best-protected platforms in the world. They have no other option than to implement maximum security for the thousands of customers that they host in their clouds. However, these clouds offer customers an extensive toolbox with security controls. It is always up to the customer to apply these controls.
- *Flexibility*: Interoperability must be flexible enough to accommodate different use cases and requirements. This includes the ability to easily add or remove cloud platforms from a multi-cloud environment, as well as the ability to scale resources as needed.

▦ *Data portability*: As discussed, with data gravity being something that must be avoided, data must be able to move easily between different cloud platforms. Data portability is likely the most important requirement. This requires that the data be stored in a format that is compatible across platforms, such as Open Data Formats.

Data portability has become increasingly important. Organizations may want to migrate their data from one cloud provider to another due to factors such as cost, performance, or service offerings. Data portability allows for a seamless transfer of data, minimizing disruption and enabling a smooth transition. However, there are many more use cases, for example, when software has to be upgraded. When organizations upgrade their software systems or switch to different applications, they often need to transfer their existing data to the new system. Data portability ensures that important data is preserved and can be effectively migrated to the new platform. Other examples include:

▦ *Data backup and disaster recovery*: Having data portability enables organizations to create backup copies of their data and store it in different locations or systems. In the event of a data loss or disaster, data portability allows for the recovery of critical data from backups, ensuring business continuity.

▦ *Cross-platform collaboration*: Data portability facilitates collaboration between different platforms or applications. It allows users to share and transfer data seamlessly between systems, enabling teams to work together, integrate workflows, and leverage data from various sources.

▦ *Personal data management*: Individuals may want to have control over their personal data and be able to move it between different online services or social media platforms. Data portability empowers individuals to manage their data, switch platforms, or delete their data from a particular service.

▦ *Compliance with data regulations*: Data portability is often a requirement under data protection regulations, such as the *General Data Protection Regulation (GDPR)*. It ensures that individuals have the right to receive their personal data in a structured, commonly used, and machine-readable format, allowing them to transfer it to another organization if desired.

These are just a few examples of how data portability can be utilized in various scenarios. The ability to transfer data seamlessly between systems and platforms enhances flexibility, data control, and interoperability in digital environments.

By following these practices, the user can create interoperability from on premises to the cloud and between various clouds. Both use cases might be equally important for enterprises. Think of migrations of workloads: many organizations are looking to move some or all of their on-premises workloads to the cloud. Interoperability is essential for this migration, as it allows for the seamless transfer of data and workloads between the on-premises environment and the cloud.

In multi-cloud, different public cloud platforms are used for different purposes, for example, AWS for computing and storage and GCP for big data and analytics. Interoperability between these platforms is essential to ensure that data can be easily transferred between them.

One aspect of interoperability that must be addressed is unified monitoring. Interoperability implies that there will be multiple platforms where applications are hosted and data is stored. With that, the need for unified monitoring rises. Unified monitoring provides a single, centralized view of the performance and health of resources across multi-cloud environments. This allows admins to monitor and manage all of the cloud resources, regardless of the underlying cloud infrastructure or platform.

Without unified monitoring, different tools and interfaces may need to be used to monitor each cloud environment, making it difficult to get a comprehensive view of cloud resources and quickly identify and resolve any issues. Unified monitoring can also help to optimize our cloud usage and spending.

One might wonder why all of this is important. It can be illustrated with an example in a specific industry: healthcare. Healthcare has been chosen since interoperability in this industry can literally be lifesaving, as discussed:

- In healthcare, patient data needs to be accessible to multiple stakeholders, including physicians, hospitals, and insurance companies. Interoperability ensures that this data can be easily shared and accessed regardless of where it is stored.

- By having interoperable systems, healthcare providers can access and share relevant patient data in real time, leading to improved patient outcomes. This is especially important in emergency situations where quick access to patient data can mean the difference between life and death.

- Healthcare organizations are subject to strict regulations regarding patient data privacy and security. Interoperability ensures that these regulations are adhered to as data is shared between different systems.

    ■   Interoperable systems can help healthcare organizations reduce costs by avoiding the need for redundant data storage and management systems.

Of course, this is just one example, but it hopefully makes clear why we should architect for interoperability. The next section studies how interoperable systems can be managed with the use of containers and microservices. First, it is necessary to understand the difference between interoperability and portability.

EXPLAINING THE DIFFERENCE BETWEEN PORTABILITY AND INTEROPERABILITY

Data portability was already mentioned a few times in the previous sections. The terms portability and interoperability tend to get mixed up. They are certainly related but are also quite different things, and it is important to understand the differences. The term interoperability defines the capability of easily moving workloads and data from one cloud provider to another or between private and public clouds. This also implies the portability of applications and especially data. So, the question is: how are interoperability and portability different, and how are they related?

Interoperability describes the capability of systems, applications, or platforms to work together and exchange data without changing the data or the application. Interoperable systems can communicate with each other and exchange information in a way that is seamless and transparent to the user.

Portability, on the other hand, refers to the ability of software or applications to run on different platforms or environments without any modifications or changes to the code. This means that applications can be easily moved from one platform to another, preserving their functionality and performance. Portability is important because it allows organizations to take advantage of new platforms and technologies as they emerge without having to worry about the compatibility of their existing applications.

It is important for organizations that are moving environments to the cloud as part of the digital transformation because portability helps in avoiding vendor lock-in since, in theory, organizations can easily switch to a different platform if needed without having to rewrite their applications from scratch. This is *in theory*, because in practice, this might be sometimes difficult, especially when native cloud solutions from a specific provider have been used.

Interoperability and portability both contribute to the overall flexibility and accessibility of data and applications. Interoperability helps ensure that different systems can communicate and exchange data, while portability ensures that applications can run on different platforms without altering the code.

In the context of cloud computing, interoperability and portability are especially important. By ensuring that different cloud platforms and services are interoperable and that applications are portable, organizations can ensure that their cloud deployments are flexible and scalable and that they can easily adapt to changing business needs. This is the true goal of going multi-cloud.

SOLUTIONS TO CREATE INTEROPERABILITY IN PUBLIC AND HYBRID CLOUDS

Why do companies hesitate to move their IT systems into the cloud? There are a couple of reasons for that, and all will be recognized. It can be because of compliance with local laws and regulations or because of technical constraints. But most companies hesitate because of the lack of cloud interoperability and the fear of *lock-in*.

Achieving interoperability in systems, and particularly cloud, starts with architecting for interoperability. But first, the areas where we need this interoperability need to be identified:

- *Data portability*: Enabling data to be freely moved between platforms.
- *Application portability*: Enabling the use of application components such as PaaS on various platforms.
- *Platform portability*: This is mainly about the processing layer on top of the infrastructure. For example, can operating system images be moved between platforms?
- *Application interoperability*: Enabling application or application components to communicate with each other, even when these are on different platforms.

That is the *what* of interoperability. Now, *how* needs to be defined, since that will form the solution to create interoperability. Let us explore the *how*:

- *Adopt open standards*: Utilize widely adopted standards, such as HTTP, JSON, XML, and so on, to ensure that different systems can communicate with each other.

▩ *Use APIs*: Design and implement APIs that allow different systems to communicate with each other. This needs more explanation, since APIs are often seen as a sort of magic wand. First, it is necessary to understand the multiple forms of APIs and API architecture types.

● *REpresentational State Transfer (REST)*: This is the most used API type on the Web. It can use JSON, XML, HTML, or plain text. REST APIs are very lightweight and flexible.

● *GraphQL*: This is a query language for APIs and uses a schema to describe data. GraphQL is typically used in applications that require low bandwidth to fetch specific data in a single endpoint.

● *Simple Object Access Protocol (SOAP)*: This is used in secured environments. It is protocol independent, but it uses a strictly defined messaging framework.

● *Remote Procedure Call (RCP)*: This is used for distributed systems as an action-based protocol, utilizing only HTTP GET and POST commands.

● *Apache Kafka*: This one is becoming more and more popular. It is used for event streaming and can process, publish, and store data as it occurs. It captures and delivers data in real time. Kafka utilizes TCP.

▩ *Implement security*: Security is intrinsic. Secure communication between systems must be established by using secure protocols such as HTTPS and by properly authenticating and authorizing access to APIs. Remember data gravity. When moving applications or application components between platforms, data is likely moving with it. For a lot of companies, data is absolutely crucial and, therefore, must be extremely well-protected.

▩ *Consider containerization*: Containerize applications to ensure that they can run in any environment, making them more portable and interoperable. This will be discussed in more detail in this section.

▩ *Utilize service brokers*: Use service brokers that allow different cloud platforms to communicate with each other, such as the Azure Service Broker for AWS or the Google Cloud Interconnect for GCP.

Before continuing, the use of the services should not be oversimplified. APIs, for instance, can be very tricky. There are some challenges to be addressed in implementing and managing APIs across multiple cloud platforms:

▩ *API compatibility*: Different cloud platforms may have their own proprietary APIs, which can vary in terms of functionality, structure, and syntax. Ensuring compatibility between APIs from different providers can be complex and require additional development efforts to translate or adapt API calls.

- *Feature parity*: Cloud platforms may offer different sets of features and services. When using APIs across platforms, it can be challenging to find equivalent functionality or services in each platform. This can lead to limitations or gaps in the capabilities available through the APIs.

- *Authentication and authorization*: Each cloud platform typically has its own authentication and authorization mechanisms. Managing user credentials and access control across different platforms can be cumbersome, requiring additional effort to handle authentication and authorization logic consistently.

- *Error handling and logging*: Error handling and logging mechanisms can differ among cloud platforms. Consistently handling errors and logging information across different platforms and API responses may require additional code or integration logic to ensure uniformity.

- *Performance and latency*: APIs rely on network connectivity, and utilizing APIs across different cloud platforms introduces potential latency due to varying network infrastructure and data transmission protocols. Optimizing performance and minimizing latency in API interactions across platforms can be challenging.

- *Documentation and support*: The quality and comprehensiveness of API documentation may vary across different cloud platforms. Inconsistent or inadequate documentation can make it more difficult to understand and effectively use APIs, leading to longer development cycles and increased troubleshooting efforts.

- *Versioning and compatibility*: Cloud platforms often release new versions of their APIs, introducing changes and deprecating older versions. Ensuring compatibility and managing version dependencies across multiple platforms can be demanding, requiring ongoing monitoring and maintenance.

- *Governance and compliance*: When using APIs across different cloud platforms, it can be more complex to maintain governance and compliance standards consistently. Managing data privacy, security, and compliance measures across multiple platforms may require additional controls and monitoring.

Addressing these challenges requires careful planning, architectural considerations, and robust integration strategies. API management tools and practices can also help mitigate some of the complexities and provide a unified approach to using APIs across different cloud platforms.

Cloud providers offer various services. For each of the clouds, the solutions that ensure interoperability must be considered. The following are some concrete examples in the various clouds, starting with Azure:

- *Azure Active Directory* can be used for authentication and authorization across different systems and cloud platforms.
- *Azure API Management* can be used to create, publish, and manage APIs to ensure secure and scalable communication between different systems.

Some examples in AWS are:

- *AWS Direct Connect* can be used to establish a dedicated network connection between AWS and on-premises systems.
- *AWS App Mesh* can be used to manage intercommunication between microservices, ensuring that they can communicate with each other securely and efficiently. Service mesh will be discussed in more detail later in this section.

Alibaba Cloud includes the following:

- *Alibaba Cloud OpenAPI* is a collection of APIs that allow developers to interact with Alibaba Cloud services programmatically. Think of creating and managing virtual machines and integrating Alibaba Cloud services with other cloud platforms and applications.
- *Alibaba Cloud Interconnect* is a service that enables organizations to connect their on-premises data centers to Alibaba Cloud, creating a hybrid cloud environment.

Finally, here are some examples in GCP:

- *GCP Cloud Interconnect* can be used to connect GCP to other cloud platforms or on-premises systems.
- *GCP endpoints* can be used to manage APIs and ensure secure communication between different systems.

Interoperability is needed for network levels, data, and applications. Systems must be able to connect to each other in the first place, and then it must be ensured that data can be exchanged in readable and usable formats. Following that, applications must be able to process that data and present outcomes to users. Containers are a great technology to achieve this, but microservices and service mesh will also be explored, including how they can help in achieving interoperability.

It was already mentioned that containers should be considered, since they can help in achieving interoperability by enabling applications to run in any environment without dependencies on the underlying infrastructure. This abstraction from the infrastructure makes containers portable, meaning that they can run on any operating system and in any cloud environment. To deploy and manage containers, an orchestration layer is needed to operate these containers. Kubernetes has become the industry standard for container deployment and management. There are definitively more technologies available, but in this book, we will use Kubernetes.

First, Kubernetes must be defined. Simply put, it is an open-source orchestration system to deploy and operate containers. It features automated deployment, scaling, and management of containerized applications. How does that help in achieving interoperability? By using Kubernetes, organizations can run the same containerized application on different platforms, ensuring that the application can run on any infrastructure. That is the theory. Indeed, Kubernetes can be deployed on multiple cloud platforms such as AWS, GCP, and Azure. However, it does require specific Kubernetes runtime environments in these clouds. It will require *Azure Kubernetes Services (AKS)* in Azure, *Elastic Kubernetes Services (EKS)* in AWS, and *Google Kubernetes Engine (GKE)* in GCP. However, the good news is that the deployment principles are the same, as shown in Figure 5.2:

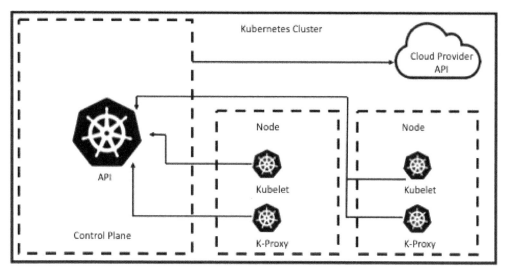

FIGURE 5.2 Basic architecture for Kubernetes.

As shown in the figure, to operate Kubernetes in a cloud, the specific cloud API that connects the control plane with the cloud services must be configured. If that has been done, then the clusters can be managed from cloud services, such as AKS, EKS, and GKE. The control plane holds the scheduler for scaling the cluster nodes and the controller manager. The Kubelet is the node agent that connects to the control plane; the Kube-proxy or k-proxy takes care of the traffic to the node.

The user might want to deploy and run containers on premises, too, and even in edge or Internet of things (IoT) deployments, to enable applications to connect from edge devices to the clouds. For that, there is a lightweight version of Kubernetes called K3S. This was designed to run containers on edge and IoT devices, enabling applications to run on any environment, regardless of the underlying infrastructure, making it easier to ensure interoperability across different environments.

Thus, by using containers and orchestration engines such as Kubernetes and K3S, it can be ensured that applications can run on any platform, making these applications more portable and interoperable. Figure 5.3 shows the principal architecture for K3S. It resembles Kubernetes architecture. The main difference is that the control node runs a different server with the agent nodes, the Kubelets in the Kubernetes architecture, on separate devices:

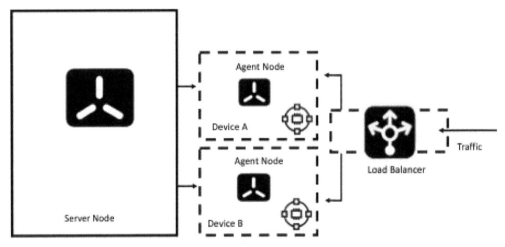

FIGURE 5.3 Basic architecture for K3S.

The agent nodes can run on devices with minimal resources. Containers can help in achieving portability and interoperability. Containers are also used to deploy services independently from each other in a microservices architecture.

To recap once more what interoperability means: it is the ability of different systems, applications, or components to work together seamlessly. In the context of microservices, interoperability refers to the ability of individual services to communicate and exchange data with each other effectively. This can be a significant challenge in a microservices architecture, particularly as the number of services and their complexity increase. A basic architecture for microservices is shown in Figure 5.4:

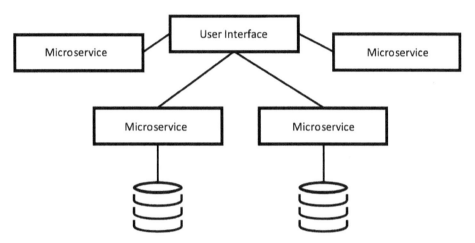

FIGURE 5.4 High-level architecture for microservices.

Thus, interoperability does come with challenges to overcome, especially when implementing a microservices architecture and working with containers. The advantage of microservices is that the services can be used for multiple applications. When an upgrade is needed, it is not necessary to bring down the entire application but only the services that are concerned with the upgrade, thus making development and operations more agile and flexible. The major challenge in microservices architecture, however, is to establish and manage the communication between the services. With the decentralization of functionality into individual services, communication between services becomes more complex and difficult to manage. This can result in issues such as increased latency and decreased reliability.

Microservices will use data, and it might be the case that services use their own data stores. That might become a challenge in making sure that data is consistent across the various services, meaning that if data in a specific service is changed, these changes are reflected in all other associated services. Keep in mind that microservices, per default, operate independently from each other.

Lastly, the configuration of the services needs to be managed. As every service is an independent function, it will require its own configuration. In complex environments where the number of services is vast, updates and changes of services can become challenging. It calls for some form of centralized management to keep the overview. That is where service mesh comes in as a solution.

Service mesh is a solution to these challenges of interoperability in microservices. It is, however, not easy to explain how service mesh works. In essence, it is a configurable infrastructure layer for microservices that enables the communication between the services by a common set of rules and functions that are used to manage the services and help to keep data consistent when it is transferred between the services. These common sets of rules and functions are *attached* to the service or app using sidecars. A typical service mesh architecture using sidecars can look like Figure 5.5:

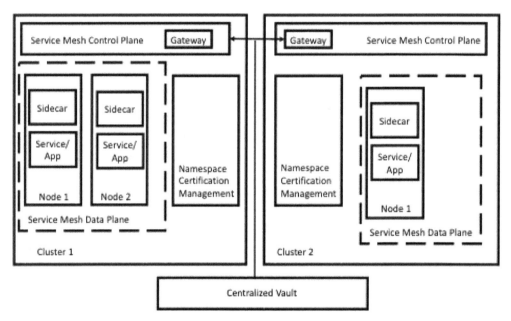

FIGURE 5.5 High-level architecture for service mesh using sidecars.

To summarize it shortly: service mesh helps reduce the complexity of managing the communication between services, and it improves the reliability of the overall system. It provides a centralized configuration mechanism that makes it easier to manage the configuration of services, particularly as the number of services grows. Services will be configured consistently while the risk of configuration errors is reduced.

Service mesh also provides improved visibility between services by providing detailed metrics and logging information about the communication between services. This information can be used to identify and resolve issues, improve performance, and make informed decisions about the architecture and configuration of the system. A service mesh can be perceived as a platform that integrates security services into the microservices architecture. Security policies are stored in so-called sidecars that can be connected to the various services, ensuring that each service is compliant with that specific policy.

Service mesh is a dedicated infrastructure layer that handles service-to-service communication in a microservices architecture. It provides a set of capabilities to manage and control the interactions between services. It takes care of the following functionality:

- *Service discovery*: Service mesh typically employs a service registry to handle service discovery. The registry maintains a centralized catalog of available services and their network locations. When a service needs to communicate with another service, it queries the service registry to obtain the necessary network endpoint information.
- *Load balancing*: Service mesh incorporates load balancing techniques to evenly distribute incoming requests across multiple instances of a service. It ensures optimal utilization of resources and prevents individual services from being overwhelmed. Load balancing algorithms can be configured within the service mesh to suit specific requirements, such as round-robin, least connections, or weighted load balancing.
- *Failure recovery*: Service mesh helps manage failure recovery by implementing various mechanisms such as retries, timeouts, and circuit breakers. If a service encounters an error or becomes unavailable, the service mesh can automatically retry the request, apply timeouts to avoid waiting indefinitely, or open a circuit breaker to stop sending requests to a failing service temporarily.
- *Metrics*: Service mesh collects metrics related to network traffic, latency, error rates, and other relevant data points. It gathers these metrics from the communication flow between services. These metrics provide insights into the health and performance of services and can be used for monitoring, troubleshooting, and performance optimization purposes.
- *Monitoring*: Service mesh offers built-in monitoring capabilities to track and visualize the behavior of services within the mesh. It provides observability into communication patterns, latency, error rates, and other metrics. Monitoring tools and dashboards within the service mesh help operators and developers gain real-time visibility into the system, detect issues, and troubleshoot performance bottlenecks.

By abstracting these functionalities into the service mesh layer, developers can focus on building services without worrying about the intricacies of network communication, load balancing, or failure handling. Service mesh simplifies and standardizes these essential capabilities, making it easier to manage and scale microservices architectures effectively.

Obviously, technology is needed to take care of all of this, preferably solutions that are agnostic to the different cloud platforms. Service mesh platforms such as Istio, Linkerd, or Consul often provide features and integrations to handle the discussed functionalities. They incorporate sidecar proxies (such as Envoy) alongside each service instance, enabling fine-grained control and management of service-to-service communication.

Some of the popular service mesh solutions that are available for different clouds include the following:

- *Istio* is probably the most used solution for service mesh. It is an open-source solution that is supported by many cloud providers, including GCP, AWS, and Azure. It is also compatible with Alibaba Cloud Service Mesh.
- *Linkerd* is also open-source and supported by many cloud providers. Linkerd provides a lightweight and efficient service mesh solution that is easy to deploy and manage.

Next to these two popular cloud-independent solutions, the cloud providers offer service mesh solutions themselves as follows:

- *AWS App Mesh* is a service mesh solution by AWS and, as such, is integrated with the AWS ecosystem. It provides a native service mesh solution for microservices that are deployed in AWS.
- *Google Cloud Traffic Director* is the GCP service mesh solution. Google Cloud Traffic Director provides a fully managed service mesh solution for microservices deployed in GCP.
- *Microsoft Azure Service Fabric Mesh* is the fully managed service mesh solution for microservices that are deployed in Azure.
- Lastly, *Alibaba Cloud Service Mesh* is a fully managed service for microservices in Alibaba Cloud.

To realize interoperability, it is important that cloud providers support open standards. The *Open Compute Project (OCP)* is such a standard. OCP will be discussed in the closing section of this chapter.

WORKING WITH OPEN COMPUTE PROJECT

Interoperability is realized when technology providers agree on open standards. An example from the past is a home video. In the 1980s, there were three technologies introduced for home video: Video 2000, Betamax, and VHS. A Video 2000 tape could not be used in a VHS machine or vice versa. The consumer had to choose one system but was then constrained to the use of specific tapes for that system. The entertainment industry did learn from this: when the CD player was released, the manufacturers agreed upon one format. Be aware that in the gaming industry, there are still different consoles that are not truly interoperable.

The key message is this: interoperability issues can be avoided if vendors support open standard initiatives. The OCP is such a standard. Better yet, it is a community of hardware and software developers dedicated to sharing designs for efficient data centers and cloud computing infrastructure. OCP was founded by Facebook in 2011 but has grown to include several big tech firms, including Microsoft, Intel, and Google.

In the multi-cloud world, the importance of the OCP has only increased. Interoperability and portability between different cloud providers is a major challenge for many organizations. The OCP helps to address these challenges by providing a set of standards and guidelines for data centers and cloud infrastructure, which can be used by any organization, regardless of which cloud provider they use. This helps to ensure that data centers and clouds can communicate with each other, share data, and work together, even if they are built on different hardware or software platforms.

OCP integrates with leading cloud providers, including AWS, Azure, and GCP. For example, AWS has adopted OCP hardware and standards for its data centers, and GCP has integrated OCP into its cloud infrastructure. Azure has also been a strong supporter of the OCP and is using its standards to help build their own data centers and cloud infrastructure.

It helps customers of these providers to easily move workloads between different clouds without having to worry about compatibility issues, avoiding vendor lock-in. The underlying hardware and software infrastructure is consistent, regardless of the cloud provider. This reduces the risk of technical issues and improves the overall stability of the infrastructure.

There is criticism, of course. OCP and using infrastructure standards are only a part of the interoperability solution. Standards, guidelines, and guardrails for exchanging data and coding applications are equally important.

Talking about data: the next chapter is about managing data in multi-cloud.

CONCLUSION

Companies try to avoid vendor lock-in, and that is the main reason behind implementing a multi-cloud architecture. Multi-cloud, however, comes with challenges. Interoperability and portability are the two biggest challenges. How can one make sure that applications and data can be freely moved from one platform to another, and how can communication between systems that are on different platforms be established? This chapter explained the differences between portability and interoperability. Next, various methods to create interoperability were discussed.

This chapter looked at containers, microservices, and service mesh that will enhance the level of interoperability, but it was also noticed that these cloud-native architectures can become complex, especially when our environments grow. Nonetheless, in multi-cloud, it is essential to have a good understanding of these emerging technologies. In the final section, the Open Compute Project was studied as a concept that aims at full interoperability between systems on premises and in the cloud.

KEY POINTS

- Interoperability and portability are related, but they are different things. Interoperability is about the capability to communicate between applications and exchange data, even when these are in different systems on different platforms. Portability refers to the capability to freely move applications and data from one platform to another.

- Both interoperability and portability are essential in multi-cloud architecture.

- Cloud-native technologies such as containers and microservices can improve both portability and interoperability. These architectures can become complex when environments grow with a lot of containers or microservices that must be managed. Centralized orchestration and management plans such as Kubernetes for container management and service mesh concepts for microservices can lift the heavy weight for administrators.

QUESTIONS

1. What has become the industry standard for container management?

2. What is used when attaching configuration policies from a centralized vault to microservices and apps?

3. What is K3S?

4. If an application or data attracts (more) data, how is this described?

Answers appear in the appendix.

MANAGING DATA IN MULTI-CLOUD

INTRODUCTION

With multi-cloud, data can be everywhere in theory. It is one of the major challenges in multi-cloud: where is the data, where should it be, who may access it, who can access it, and how to ensure that data is available at the right time and the right place? Hence, a clear data strategy is needed on migration, where data is stored and who and what may access data, what the usage of data is, and how to prevent events such as data leaks and loss. Migrating and managing data in multi-cloud is all about data governance. This chapter will cover the most important aspects of data management in the cloud.

STRUCTURE

This chapter discusses the following topics:

- Defining a data strategy
- Planning data migration
- Managing data governance
- Improving data quality
- Securing data

DEFINING A DATA STRATEGY

In today's digital era, data is increasingly becoming the true new gold for organizations. Almost every company will make an enormous effort to collect the right data, analyze it, and on the basis of the outcomes make decisions for the future of the business. Organizations that effectively harness their data and turn it into actionable insights will make significant gains in terms of efficiency, productivity, and profitability.

However, with the explosion of data comes the need for advanced tools, infrastructure, and expertise to manage it effectively. This is where cloud computing comes in. Cloud computing has revolutionized the way businesses handle their data, providing them with an agile and scalable infrastructure that can store, process, and analyze vast amounts of data quickly and efficiently. However, it does not happen overnight. Companies will need to develop a data strategy.

This section discusses the required activities to define such a strategy. In terms of cloud computing, the focus will be on the three major providers: AWS, Azure, and GCP. What follows is a step-by-step explanation. There are seven critical steps in defining a data strategy:

1. *Define the business objectives*: The first step in developing a data strategy for cloud computing is to define business objectives. What are the key business problems the company is trying to solve with data? There will be various use cases. The company might be looking to gain a competitive advantage through data insights or have a need to optimize business processes and reduce costs. Once there is a clear understanding of the business objectives, the type of data to be collected and analyzed to achieve those objectives can be determined. Typically, this is done on the enterprise level of the company. The enterprise architect will closely work together with the business to determine the strategy. Based on the strategy, the next step can occur.

2. *Determine the data requirements*: This step is about the type of data that must be collected and analyzed. This also determines what sources will be used. What are the requirements regarding data quality and security measures? This is also a good time to identify any data governance and compliance requirements that must be adhered to. The following section will extensively discuss data governance.

3. *Develop the data architecture*: The next step is to develop the data architecture. This includes designing the data models, data pipelines, and data workflows. It must be determined how data flows through the architecture, how it is transformed and analyzed, and how it is stored and secured. This architecture was developed by the enterprise architect and the data architect. Make no mistake here: this is on the data layer that doesn't necessarily already involve technology. The technology will follow the data models.

4. *Choose a cloud and a cloud provider*: After defining the data architecture, one can further drill down to the technology layer. The first thing to do on this layer is choose the right cloud and the associated cloud provider. Each cloud provider has its own strengths and weaknesses, so it is important to choose the one that best meets the specific needs. Azure is known for its integration with Microsoft products, AWS has a vast array of services, and GCP is known for its cutting-edge technology and innovation. Consultancy firms typically use battle cards to map the requirements of the enterprise to the capabilities of a specific cloud, including the type of technology that can be used to meet the requirements. Figure 6.1 shows an example of such a battle card:

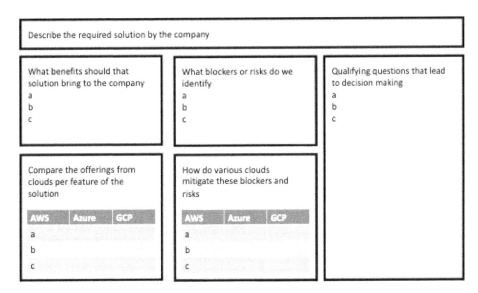

FIGURE 6.1 Battle card for cloud comparison.

5. *The cloud infrastructure architecture*: Once the cloud and cloud provider have been selected, the cloud infrastructure requirements must be architected. What type of storage and computing resources are needed? What level of availability and redundancy does the company require? Cloud providers will help in providing best practices and blueprints for the so-called landing zones. That is the reason why Azure, AWS, GCP, and Alibaba Cloud have developed cloud adoption and well-architected frameworks that contain guidelines for setting up cloud infrastructure that must support specific use cases. It is strongly recommended to validate the architecture for a landing zone with specialists from the cloud provider.

6. *Choose the data services*: The next step is to choose the data services, for example, databases, warehousing, data lakes, and analytics services. However, one should also think of disaster recovery and backup strategy. With critical data, a strategy might be developed where data is backed up to a different platform, to ensure that data can always be retrieved. In designing such a strategy, it is also elementary to think about how to keep data in sync. Each cloud provider offers a range of services, as already seen in the chapter about storage, which is closely related to data services. If a highly scalable and flexible database is needed, one might choose AWS's Aurora or GCP's Bigtable. For a powerful data analytics platform, the user may want to choose Azure's Synapse Analytics or GCP's BigQuery.

7. *Implement security measures*: The final but crucial step is securing the data. Security measures must be included to protect the data from unauthorized access, breaches, and other security threats. This includes implementing access controls, encryption, and monitoring tools to detect and respond to security incidents.

Developing a data strategy for cloud computing can be a complex exercise. Topics such as data integrity and separation of concerns between the technology and data layer should also be considered carefully. The following explains what that means.

Data integrity refers to the accuracy, consistency, and reliability of data throughout its lifecycle. It ensures that data remains intact and consistent without any unauthorized modifications or corruption. Maintaining data integrity is crucial for any data architecture because it guarantees the quality and trustworthiness of the information being stored and processed. Data integrity is crucial, or better said: reliable and accurate data is essential for making informed decisions. If data integrity is compromised, it can lead to incorrect analysis and flawed decision-making, which can have significant consequences for businesses. Data integrity builds trust and credibility among users and stakeholders. When data is consistent and accurate, it increases confidence in the systems and processes relying on that data, fostering trust in the organization.

Next, data integrity is also important for compliance. Many industries have strict compliance requirements, such as healthcare (HIPAA) or finance (Sarbanes-Oxley Act). Data integrity plays a vital role in meeting these regulations, ensuring data privacy, and maintaining audit trails.

When talking about data integrity, normalization must also be addressed. This is a technique used in database design to eliminate redundancy and improve data consistency. It involves organizing data into multiple related tables, each containing atomic and nonredundant information. Normalization helps eliminate data anomalies and redundancies by structuring data in a way that prevents duplicate or conflicting information. This ensures that changes made to data are propagated consistently throughout the system.

By reducing redundancy, normalization optimizes storage space and improves query performance. It allows for more efficient data retrieval and minimizes the risk of data inconsistencies or conflicts.

It was discussed that a separate data layer and a technology layer are distinguished in data architecture. It is important to have a good understanding of this separation of concerns. The data and technology layer are two very distinct artifacts, as discussed:

- The data layer focuses on the organization, storage, and management of data. It includes activities such as data modeling, data integration, data quality assurance, and data governance. The data layer ensures that data is structured, standardized, and stored in a consistent manner, enabling efficient access and retrieval.

- The technology layer encompasses the systems, tools, and infrastructure that facilitate data processing, analysis, and delivery. It includes hardware, software, networks, and platforms used to handle data. The technology layer enables data transformation, data analytics, and the presentation of data to end-users.

By separating data concerns from technology concerns, changes can be made in one layer without necessarily impacting the other. This modularity allows for flexibility and adaptability, making it easier to upgrade or replace technology components without affecting the underlying data structure.

Separating concerns allows individuals or teams to specialize in specific areas. Data professionals can focus on designing efficient data models, ensuring data quality, and establishing data governance practices. Technology professionals can specialize in selecting and implementing appropriate tools and technologies for data processing and analysis. This also ensures scalability and performance optimization: the technology layer can be designed to scale horizontally or vertically to handle increasing data volumes and user demands without affecting the underlying data architecture.

There are many best practices that can help organizations achieve success. Here are a few:

- *Involve all business stakeholders*: The success of any data strategy depends on its alignment with business goals and objectives. A strategy must be focused on solving the key business problems and delivering the expected outcomes. For that, the input of all business stakeholders is needed.

- *Start small and iterate*: Define a specific use case, pilot it, and next, refine it. If a use case is successful, the strategy can be expanded. It is important to define the strategy and the solution with scalability as a requirement.

- *Design for scalability*: Cloud provides organizations with an agile and scalable infrastructure that can grow and adapt to changing business needs.

- *Focus on data governance and compliance*: Data governance and compliance are critical aspects of any data strategy, and it is important to establish robust policies and controls to ensure data quality, security, and compliance with regulations such as *General Data Protection Regulation in the European Union (GDPR)* and more specific regulations such as the *Californian Consumer Privacy Act (CCPA)* that were established in 2020. Both acts force companies to show exactly what data they collect, and how they store and protect it.

- *Implement data security*: Unauthorized access, breaches, and other security threats must be detected on time and preferably avoided. If breaches materialize, plans must be in place for mitigating actions. This includes implementing access controls, encryption, and monitoring tools to detect and respond to security incidents. When discussing data security, security by design should be emphasized as the best practice. By integrating security into the data architecture from the outset, potential vulnerabilities and risks can be identified and addressed early on. This proactive approach minimizes the likelihood of security breaches, data leaks, and unauthorized access to sensitive information. Security by design ensures that appropriate measures are in place to protect the confidentiality, integrity, and availability of data. It involves implementing encryption, access controls, and authentication mechanisms to safeguard sensitive data against unauthorized access or modifications.

The next sections will discuss these phases in more detail.

PLANNING DATA MIGRATION

Planning a data migration in a multi-cloud environment requires careful consideration of several factors to ensure a smooth and successful migration. This section discusses the best practices for performing data migration, targeting data storage in AWS, Azure, GCP, and Alibaba Cloud. Besides these best practices, some pitfalls to avoid will be explained.

First and rather obviously, clear migration goals must be defined. This includes the data to be migrated, the timelines, and the expected outcome. Understanding the goals can help to identify the right approach, cloud provider, and tools for the migration.

Selecting the right cloud provider is not an easy task and should be very carefully considered. Each cloud provider has its own set of capabilities and features, which can impact the migration approach and timeline. For instance, AWS provides an extensive suite of migration tools, including AWS Database Migration Service, AWS Snowball, and AWS Transfer for SFTP. Similarly, Azure offers several migration tools, such as Azure Migrate, Azure Site Recovery, and Azure Database Migration Service.

Choosing the migration feature depends on a lot of aspects, for instance, the quantity of the data, but also how critical the data is. Data security will be discussed in a later section, but first the quantity will be discussed. The size of data files and the total amount of data that must be migrated will set the migration strategy. This can be online using an Internet connection, but in a number of cases, this will simply take too long. A common strategy is to freeze the data source and then copy the data to a device that can contain bulk data.

AWS Snowball is such a device. The data is copied to the Snowball device, which is then transferred to an AWS data center. The concept is shown in Figure 6.2:

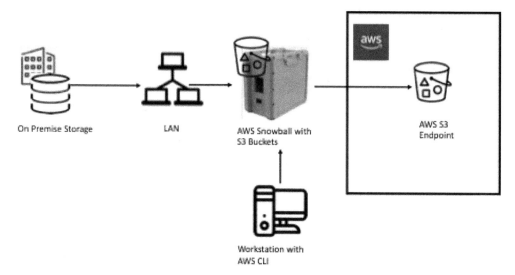

On Premise Storage   LAN   AWS Snowball with S3 Buckets   AWS S3 Endpoint

Workstation with AWS CLI

FIGURE 6.2 The AWS Snowball concept.

The data is now loaded to the AWS storage of choice, typically S3. As soon as the data is inside the AWS cloud, the data can be synced with the original data source up until the point where both the datastores contain the exact same data. From that point onward, the original data source may be decommissioned since the data is now in the AWS cloud. Other clouds do offer similar strategies.

Of course, AWS is not the only provider that offers these services. Azure offers Azure Data Box, and GCP uses Google's Transfer Appliance. Both offer physical data transfer solutions that help overcome challenges associated with moving large datasets to the respective cloud platforms. The Azure Data Box comes in various formats, such as:

- *Azure Data Box Disk*: A portable SSD storage device available with capacities of 8 TB or 16 TB. It is suitable for transferring smaller amounts of data (up to 40 TB) and is typically used for offline data transfer.

- *Azure Data Box*: A ruggedized, tamper-resistant storage appliance with storage capacities of up to 100 TB or 560 TB. It is used for transferring larger volumes of data (from a few terabytes to multiple petabytes). Customers can connect the device to their network, copy the data onto it, and then ship it to Microsoft Azure for ingestion into Azure Blob Storage.

■ *Azure Data Box Heavy*: A larger, rack-mountable variant of Azure Data Box with a capacity of 1 PB. It is suitable for massive data transfers and is typically used for offline data migration at scale.

Google's Transfer Appliance comes in two models: the Online model, with a capacity of 100 TB, and the Rack model, with a capacity of 480 TB. These devices allow for efficient and secure data migration in scenarios where transferring over the Internet is not practical or feasible.

Before selecting the cloud and the migration tools, an analysis must be conducted of the data and the associated applications. A thorough analysis of the data and applications is absolutely required to determine the complexity, dependencies, and security requirements. This analysis will help to identify potential migration challenges and develop a migration plan accordingly.

Of course, data security must be taken into consideration from the start. Adequate security measures must be in place to protect the data during migration. For instance, the data must be encrypted in transit and at rest to prevent unauthorized access. AWS offers several security services, such as AWS *Identity and Access Management (IAM)* and AWS *Key Management Service (KMS)*, to secure data during migration. As in *Chapter 3: Virtualizing and Managing Storage*, when the various storage concepts were discussed, all cloud providers encrypt data by default upon entry into the cloud. This is typically about data at rest. But since data is being moved, attention must be focused on securing data in transit. The following technologies ensure secure data in transit:

■ *Transport Layer Security (TLS) encryption*: TLS is a protocol that encrypts data sent over the Internet to ensure that it remains confidential and secure. It is important to ensure that TLS encryption is enabled for all data transfers between on-premises and cloud environments or between different cloud environments. All major public cloud providers, AWS, Azure, GCP, and Alibaba Cloud, support TLS encryption for data in transit.

■ *Virtual Private Network (VPN)*: VPNs provide a secure, encrypted tunnel for data to travel between on-premises and cloud environments. VPNs can help to protect data in transit by ensuring that it is not intercepted by unauthorized parties.

- *Direct connections*: In data transfer scenarios, direct connections might be a good option. AWS Direct Connect or Azure ExpressRoute can provide more secure and reliable connectivity for data migration.

- *Secure File Transfer Protocol (SFTP)*: SFTP is a secure protocol for transferring files over the Internet. It uses encryption to protect data in transit, making it an ideal choice for migrating large amounts of data between on-premises and cloud environments. All cloud providers support SFTP for data transfers.

- *Multifactor authentication (MFA)*: MFA adds an additional layer of security to data transfers by requiring users to provide more than one form of authentication to access cloud resources. This can help to prevent unauthorized access to data in transit.

A final step in planning the data migration includes test and validation. The migration plan must be tested and validated before the actual migration. Tests will help spot potential issues and address them before the migration. It is crucial to design and execute comprehensive test cases that cover a wide range of data scenarios, including different data types, formats, and use cases relevant to the specific migration. Automated testing frameworks and tools can help streamline the testing process and ensure consistent and repeatable results. Tests must aim to validate the integrity, accuracy, and completeness of the data. Tests must include the following:

- Data consistency and integrity:
  - *Perform data integrity checks*: Compare the source data with the migrated data in order to ensure that it remains consistent and accurate.
  - *Verify data relationships*: Validate the relationships between different data elements, such as foreign key constraints or referential integrity.
  - *Check data types and formats*: Ensure that the data types and formats are correctly preserved during the migration process.

- Data completeness:
  - *Conduct record counts*: Compare the total number of records in the source data with the migrated data to ensure all records have been successfully transferred.

- *Validate data subsets*: Verify the presence of specific data subsets or categories to ensure that critical data has not been omitted during the migration.

- *Data quality and validation*:
  - *Perform data quality checks*: Evaluate the quality of the migrated data by comparing it against predefined quality standards and business rules.
  - *Validate data transformations*: If any data transformations or conversions were performed during the migration, validate that the transformations were accurately applied and did not introduce any errors.

- Performance and scalability testing:
  - *Assess data retrieval and processing performance*: Test the performance of data retrieval and processing operations to ensure that the migrated data can be accessed efficiently in the cloud environment.
  - *Evaluate scalability*: Verify that the cloud infrastructure can handle the increased workload and data volume, particularly if the migration involves significant data growth.

- Integration and interoperability:
  - *Test data integration*: If the migrated data needs to integrate with other systems or applications, validate the integration points and ensure data flows seamlessly between different components.
  - *Validate data access controls*: Test the access controls and permissions to ensure that only authorized users can access and modify the migrated data.

- Error handling and exception scenarios:
  - *Conduct error and exception testing*: Test various error and exception scenarios to ensure that the system handles them appropriately and provides meaningful error messages or notifications.

- Backup and recovery testing:
  - *Test data recovery procedures*: Validate backup and recovery mechanisms to ensure that in the event of data loss or corruption, data can be restored successfully from the backup.

All these steps are crucial in defining a data migration strategy. Skipping steps may lead to severe risks of data breaches. As an example, failure to consider dependencies can lead to data loss, data corruption, or application downtime. Therefore, it is crucial to analyze dependencies between data and applications and prioritize the order of migration accordingly.

Poor planning will definitively lead to delays, cost overruns, and failed migrations. A data migration plan must address all aspects of the migration, including timelines, budgets, and resource allocation. This includes the setup of the data governance, a topic that will be discussed in detail in the next section. Inaccurate data governance policies can lead to data breaches, compliance violations, and, again, loss of data. Data governance should include governance policies and tools in place to ensure data security, privacy, and compliance.

The importance of testing has already been stressed. With proper testing, the capabilities and features of the designated cloud can be validated. This is a vital step in the data migration plan and the execution of that plan: the capabilities and features of the cloud provider must be understood and the right migration tools and approaches selected accordingly. Lack of testing can lead to migration failures, data loss, and downtime.

It is strongly advised to have data governance in place before starting to execute the data migration. It is the topic of the following section, which concerns best practices for managing data governance.

MANAGING DATA GOVERNANCE

Implementing and managing data governance in multi-cloud concepts is essential to ensure that data is managed efficiently, effectively, and securely. Data governance involves a set of policies, procedures, and processes for managing data throughout its lifecycle. In a multi-cloud environment, where data is stored in multiple cloud environments, data governance becomes even more complex. Implementing proper data governance is a complex task in multi-cloud environments. This section explores some guidelines for implementing data governance, but first addresses the concept of data governance in more detail.

Data governance involves the process of managing the availability, usability, integrity, and security of data used by an organization. It includes the creation of policies, procedures, and standards for managing data throughout its entire lifecycle, from creation to disposal. The primary goal is to ensure that data is managed in a way that meets business needs and regulatory requirements while also mitigating risks associated with data misuse, loss, or theft.

Data governance demands collaboration among different departments and stakeholders within an organization, including IT, legal, compliance, risk management, and business units. A data governance framework must be drafted to define the roles and responsibilities, policies, and procedures. Lastly, the technological solutions that will support the secure management of data must be defined and decided upon. The framework will contain principles on various aspects of data:

- Data quality
- Data security
- Data privacy
- Data lifecycle management
- Data ownership
- Data architecture

Implementing a robust data governance framework will ensure that data is accurate, secure, and compliant with legal and regulatory requirements. But what steps should be taken to compose this framework?

As a first step, data governance policies must be defined that align with the goals, compliance requirements, and regulatory standards of the organization. This includes policies for data classification, data privacy, security, and retention. It must be specified how critical data is; who is allowed to read, use, or even change data; and how long the organization needs to keep the data, either directly available or in the archive. Who is responsible for managing these policies? The policies themselves are defined on an enterprise level, but owners need to make sure that policies are followed in specific data domains. In the industry, these owners are referred to as *data stewards*. They are responsible for managing specific data domains or datasets. Data stewards are responsible for ensuring that data is accurate, complete, and available when needed.

Having stewards on specific data domains does not mean that data management should be distributed. It is recommended to have data management centralized. This will ensure that data is managed consistently across all cloud environments. This includes establishing a centralized data governance team responsible for managing data policies, processes, and procedures. Policies include adherence to data quality standards and ensuring that data is accurate, complete, and consistent across all cloud environments. Of course, this must be monitored. Just monitoring the infrastructure is not sufficient; the data usage must also be monitored to identify potential data breaches. This can be done by defining monitoring metrics such as usage patterns and data access protocols. Any deviation or abnormal usage will be flagged by the monitoring.

Before monitoring can begin, it is necessary to know what is being monitored and what is being monitored against. Hence, data security principles must be specified. How can data be protected from unauthorized access, modification, and deletion? This will lead to designing solutions for encryption, access controls, and data backup and recovery procedures.

All of this is about policies and technology, but do not forget that people are needed to operate it all: the data administrators. Train data administrators to ensure that they have the necessary skills and knowledge to manage data in a multi-cloud environment. The role of the data administrator is critical in implementing and managing data governance in multi-cloud concepts. The administrator will have to have knowledge about the various components of the cloud technologies that are used. The data administrator is responsible for managing data across all cloud environments, ensuring that data is accurate, complete, and secure and that data is being used appropriately.

Everything discussed previously starts with the data administrator. He will define data quality standards and be responsible for setting up monitoring of data quality metrics. He is also responsible for defining data governance policies and procedures that align with organizational goals, compliance requirements, and regulatory standards. But even more important: he will need to work closely with the data owners, the data stewards. These data stewards must be trained so that they have the necessary skills and knowledge to manage data in a multi-cloud environment.

To put it in simple words: the data administrator plays a critical role in implementing and managing data governance in a multi-cloud environment. However, it starts with having the right data in an organization. That data must have a specified quality to ensure that it is useful to the organization. The next section discusses data quality and how that quality can be improved using cloud technology.

IMPROVING DATA QUALITY

The governance of data management and the role of the data administrator have been discussed. However, data has a purpose. Typically, organizations use data to make informed decisions, gain insights, and improve business processes. This can only be achieved if data meets quality requirements. However, maintaining data quality can be challenging when dealing with large volumes of data that are stored across different platforms and systems.

High-quality data is essential for accurate and informed decision-making. Business leaders rely on data to analyze trends, identify opportunities, mitigate risks, and make strategic decisions. If the data is of poor quality, decision-makers may draw incorrect conclusions, leading to flawed strategies and inefficient resource allocation. As an example, a retail company analyzes sales data to identify customer preferences and optimize inventory management. If the data contains errors, such as duplicate records or incorrect product codes, the analysis may lead to inaccurate insights, resulting in inadequate stock levels or wrong product promotions.

However, data quality also involves compliance and regulations. Compliance with data protection and privacy regulations is crucial for businesses across various industries. Think of the healthcare provider maintaining patient records. Inaccurate or incomplete patient data can lead to medical errors, compromised patient safety, and violations of privacy regulations, impacting the organization's compliance and reputation.

Lastly, organizations increasingly rely on data-driven insights and innovation to gain a competitive edge. High-quality data serves as a foundation for advanced analytics, machine learning, and artificial intelligence applications, enabling businesses to uncover valuable insights and drive innovation.

First, the parameters that set out the quality of data will be explored. Data quality refers to the degree to which data meets the needs and requirements of its intended use. In other words, data quality is a measure of how well data satisfies its intended purpose. There are various dimensions that define data quality, including:

- *Accuracy*: Data must be free from errors, omissions, or inconsistencies. Accurate data is essential for making informed decisions and avoiding costly mistakes.

- *Completeness*: Data must contain all the necessary information for its intended use. Incomplete data can lead to incorrect conclusions and inaccurate insights.

- *Consistency*: Data must be uniform and consistent across different systems, platforms, and time periods. Inconsistent data can lead to confusion and errors in decision-making.

- *Timeliness*: Data must be up-to-date and relevant to its intended use. Timely data is essential for making informed decisions and taking timely action.

- *Relevance*: Data must be useful for its intended purpose. Relevant data is essential for making informed decisions and gaining valuable insights.

- *Validity*: Data must conform to the rules and requirements of its intended use. Valid data is essential for ensuring the accuracy and reliability of insights and decisions.

Improving data quality is important for almost every organization. A lot of companies today operate data driven or might even use *artificial intelligence (AI)*. To get the best decisions out of data-driven concepts and AI and continuously improve these decisions, data is needed from which these concepts can be trained. A good and actual example of how this principle works is ChatGPT. Basically, ChatGPT formulates answers with the data that is available to ChatGPT. It cannot work with data it does not have, and part of the answer might be missed. ChatGPT can be told that it is missing data and provide that data, and it will then incorporate that data the next time. ChatGPT is a wonderful example of how AI works with data and how it trains itself with that data.

Cloud providers offer various tools and technologies that can help organizations improve their data quality by ensuring that data is accurate, consistent, and complete. The following are some of these tools in the different clouds.

Data Quality in AWS

AWS offers a suite for designing and managing data quality, as shown in Figure 6.3.

It shows the data quality cycle:

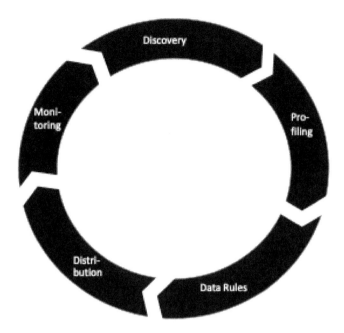

FIGURE 6.3 The AWS data lifecycle.

To work according to this quality cycle, AWS offers a variety of tools, including:

- *AWS Glue DataBrew*: This is a data preparation tool that can help improve the quality of the data. It automatically identifies and fixes errors, such as missing values or inconsistent data types, in large volumes of data.

- *Amazon SageMaker Data Wrangler*: Like Glue DataBrew, this is a tool for data preparation that cleans and transforms data. It automatically identifies and removes duplicates, outliers, and other data errors.

- *Amazon Redshift*: This is probably already a well-known tool. It is a cloud-based data warehouse that automatically analyzes data for errors and inconsistencies and provides recommendations for improving data quality.

- *Amazon QuickSight*: This is a business intelligence tool that can help to visualize and analyze data. Like Redshift, it provides recommendations for improving data quality.

There is a very good blog post about data quality in AWS. It can be found at *https://aws.amazon.com/blogs/industries/how-to-architect-data-quality-on-the-aws-cloud/*. That post also discusses tools like Athena that help in analyzing data in S3 using standard SQL queries.

Data Quality in Azure

Azure provides tools and services under the umbrella of Azure *Data Quality Services (DQS)*. The process within DQS works with two main stages, build and use. In the build, the data is explored and policies are matched against that data. In use, the data is corrected, standardized, and cleaned, and then deduplicated. After cleansing and deduplication, the data flows back into the build for exploration and matching. This way, data quality is continuously improved. It is shown in Figure 6.4:

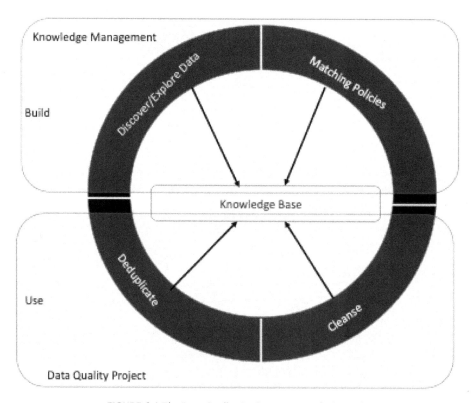

FIGURE 6.4 The Data Quality Services concept of Microsoft.

Azure offers a variety of tools:

- *Azure Data Factory*: This is a cloud-based data integration service that automatically identifies missing values or inconsistent data types in large volumes of data. Data Factory is used to train data models by cleansing and deduplication of data.
- *Azure Data Lake Storage and Synapse Analytics*: With these tools, data can be analyzed for errors and inconsistencies and provide recommendations for improving data quality.
- *Azure Databricks*: This is a very popular tool to clean and transform data. It can automatically identify and remove duplicates, outliers, and other data errors.

However, DQS offers an integrated toolset with Data Quality Server and Data Quality Client. These are implemented within SQL Server, and that sets it apart from the other tools that have been mentioned. DQS is designed for SQL Server to provide tools to clean and analyze data in SQL Server by using a knowledge base. More information can be found at *https://learn.microsoft.com/en-us/sql/data-quality-services/introduction-to-data-quality-services?view=sql-server-ver16*.

Data Quality in GCP

When searching for data quality programs in GCP, there is a solution called Dataplex. The principle is similar to the one discussed under Azure, with a phase where the data is explored and one in which the data is cleaned and prepared. With Auto data quality, GCP offers a tool that provides insights about the data. It automates and simplifies quality definition with recommendations and workflows. In the next stage, the Dataplex data quality task will be used to enable the management of rules to which data is analyzed, cleaned, and deduplicated.

Next to Dataplex, GCP offers more tools to improve data quality:

- *Cloud Dataflow*: This tool automatically identifies errors, such as missing values or inconsistent data types.
- *Cloud Dataprep*: As the name suggests, it helps in data preparation with cleansing and transformation. It also identifies and removes duplicates.

- *BigQuery*: This tool was discussed in the chapter about storage. BigQuery is GCP's data warehouse that also automatically analyzes data for errors and inconsistencies.

- *Cloud data loss prevention*: This is a GCP service that can help organizations protect their sensitive data. It automatically identifies and classifies sensitive data and provides recommendations. Of course, AWS and Azure offer tools for *Data Loss Prevention (DLP)* as well. In Azure, Azure Information Protection can be used. AWS does not offer a native solution for DLP, but with Macie and GuardDuty for S3, there is a solution for *Data Loss Detection (DLD)*. There are third-party solutions that can be used in AWS, such as stackArmor.

Data Quality in Alibaba Cloud

Alibaba Cloud offers an integrated suite for managing data quality: DataWorks. Like tools discussed in the other clouds, DataWorks helps in automatically identifying errors, such as missing values in large volumes of data. In DataWorks, the rules are specified by which data is analyzed and processed, including scheduling tasks.

DataWorks allows for integrating data from various sources, including structured and unstructured data, and supports batch and real-time data processing. Next, it provides data quality checks, profiling, and cleansing to ensure the accuracy and consistency of data. It can use *machine learning (ML)* algorithms to get better insights from data.

Of course, this overview of tools in various clouds is not complete. Azure, AWS, GCP, and Alibaba Cloud continuously improve their services to gain more and better insights from data, including the integration of AI and ML.

SECURING DATA

In a multi-cloud environment, securing data can be a complex task. As discussed in a previous section about governance, data administrators are responsible for managing data access, ensuring data integrity, and monitoring data usage. They must implement a data security plan that holds policies and procedures to safeguard sensitive data from unauthorized access, data breaches, and other security threats. To ensure data security in multi-cloud, data administrators must follow several guardrails when setting up data security policies. These guardrails are as follows.

Securing data, first of all, means it is necessary to understand what sort of data to protect and to what extent. Not all data is equally critical. Protecting all data at the highest level would be a very costly endeavor and, above all, very hard to manage. Hence, securing data starts with proper classification. That is the first task of the data administrator: it must classify data based on its sensitivity level and define access controls accordingly. Sensitive data, such as financial and personal data, must be encrypted and given restricted access to prevent unauthorized access.

Encryption must be implemented for all data in transit and at rest to prevent data breaches. Data administrators should use strong encryption algorithms and encryption keys to secure data. All cloud providers encrypt data, but there are differences in how this is done.

Amazon S3, EBS, and Glacier use *server-side encryption (SSE)* with the choice to use keys provided by AWS (SSE-S3 or SSE-KMS) or customer-managed keys (SSE-C). Amazon S3 also supports *client-side encryption (CSE)*, where users can encrypt their data before uploading it to S3. Data in transit is encrypted using SSL/TLS.

Azure and GCP have a similar offering. Azure supports SSE with customer-managed keys (SSE-CMK) or Microsoft-managed keys (SSE). Azure Disk Storage and Azure File Storage also support the encryption of data at rest using SSE. Azure also provides options for encrypting data in transit using SSL/TLS.

GCP provides multiple encryption options for data at rest and in transit. Google Cloud Storage supports SSE with customer-managed keys (SSE-C) or Google-managed keys (SSE-S3 or SSE-KMS). Google Compute Engine and Google Kubernetes Engine support the encryption of data at rest using *customer-managed keys (CMEK)*. GCP also provides options for encrypting data in transit using SSL/TLS.

Object Storage Service (OSS) in Alibaba Cloud supports SSE with customer-managed keys (SSE-CMK) or Alibaba Cloud-managed keys (SSE-KMS). As with all other clouds, SSL/TLS is used to encrypt data in transit.

Another important aspect of securing data involves *identity and access management (IAM)*. IAM policies must be implemented to ensure that only authorized users have access to data. Multifactor authentication must be used for accessing sensitive data to provide an additional layer of security.

If proper rules and guardrails are implemented, these must also be audited on a regular basis. Regular security audits must be conducted to detect and prevent security breaches. Data administrators play an important role in implementing automated security monitoring tools and performing periodic security audits to identify vulnerabilities and ensure compliance with data security policies.

Lastly, for critical data, disaster recovery and business continuity planning should be considered. This means that a disaster recovery plan must be in place to ensure business continuity in the event of a security breach or a disaster.

Moving infrastructure and data to the cloud has been discussed, but will that bring the real benefits of using cloud technology? The answer is likely to be no. Environments should be transformed and cloud-native services used to achieve the agility and scalability that businesses are looking for. The next chapter is all about working with cloud-native concepts.

CONCLUSION

This chapter discussed one of the biggest challenges in multi-cloud: managing and securing data. It explained how to define a data and data migration strategy to set guidelines and guardrails on where data must be stored, who is allowed to access it, and how to ensure that the data is available at the right time and in the right place. The quality attributes of data were discussed and how to use cloud technologies to improve data quality through automatic cleansing and deduplicating.

The final sections looked intensively at securing data. Securing data in a multi-cloud environment requires a comprehensive data security policy and procedures. Data administrators must classify data based on its sensitivity, implement strong encryption, define access controls, perform regular security audits, and have a disaster recovery plan in place to ensure data security. By following these guardrails, organizations can ensure that their data is safe and secure in a multi-cloud environment.

KEY POINTS

- Cloud provides an agile and scalable infrastructure in which vast amounts of data can be stored, processed, and analyzed quickly and efficiently. But a data strategy must be defined to make sure that data is stored in a secure way and that it is accessible and available when required.

- Data governance and compliance are critical aspects of any data strategy, and it is important to establish robust policies and controls to ensure data quality, security, and compliance with laws and industry regulations.

- Unauthorized access, breaches, and other security threats must be detected on time and preferably avoided. If breaches materialize, plans must be in place for mitigating actions. This includes implementing access controls, encryption, and monitoring tools to detect and respond to security incidents. This is all part of the data security plan.

QUESTIONS

1. Name three data quality attributes.

2. If large volumes need to be migrated in bulk to AWS, a specific service can be used. What is the name of that service?

3. What are the tasks of a data steward?

Answers appear in the appendix.

7

BUILD AND OPERATE CLOUD NATIVE

INTRODUCTION

Although lift and shift are still a popular way to get started in the cloud, the real transformation starts with building and operating cloud native—making use of native services that the major providers offer. Cloud-native development offers solutions to create scalable applications using, for instance, microservices, container, and serverless concepts, and deploying declarative code. The following chapters will dive deeper into this, but this chapter is the introduction to cloud native.

STRUCTURE

In this chapter, we will discuss the following topics:

- Understanding cloud-native concepts
- Organizing cloud-native with DevOps
- Explaining microservices
- Management of releases in cloud-native

UNDERSTANDING CLOUD-NATIVE CONCEPTS

Cloud-native is a software development approach that leverages cloud infrastructure to build and deploy applications that are scalable, reliable, and flexible. Cloud-native applications are designed to take full advantage of cloud-native services, such as containerization, microservices architecture, and serverless computing. These concepts will be addressed in more detail in this and the following chapters, but here is a short description of these concepts:

- *Containerization*: Containers are a lightweight way of packaging an application and all of its dependencies into a single unit that can be easily moved between different environments. *Chapter 8: Building Agnostic with Containers* is all about containers.

- *Serverless*: To avoid misunderstanding, with serverless, there are still servers involved. The difference is that with serverless, the cloud provider manages and allocates computing resources such as server hardware, networks, and storage automatically, without requiring the user to manage any infrastructure. Users only provide the code for their application or service, which is executed by the cloud provider in a container or runtime environment. *Chapter 9: Building and Managing Serverless* is all about serverless.

- *Microservices*: Microservices are a software architecture pattern in which an application is broken down into smaller, independent services that communicate with each other over a network. In a multi-cloud environment, these microservices can be deployed and operated across different cloud providers. This chapter will talk mainly about microservices.

Cloud-native concepts can be used to improve cloud infrastructure in several ways. First, they allow developers to build and deploy applications faster and more efficiently, which can reduce operational costs and increase agility. Second, cloud-native services provide a more reliable and scalable infrastructure that can handle high volumes of traffic and support the rapid growth of applications. Finally, cloud-native services allow for more granular control over resources, which can improve security and reduce waste.

The following is a look at the various propositions that cloud providers offer in terms of cloud-native concepts (all providers offer concepts for containerization, serverless, and automation):

- AWS offers a wide range of cloud-native services. For containerization and container orchestration, this includes Amazon Elastic Container Service (ECS) and Amazon Elastic Kubernetes Service (EKS). The serverless computing proposition of AWS is AWS Lambda. Amazon RDS is used for managed databases. A serverless option for container orchestration is Fargate. AWS also offers a variety of tools and services for monitoring and managing cloud infrastructure, such as Amazon CloudWatch and AWS CloudFormation.

- Microsoft Azure provides a similar set of cloud-native services, including Azure Kubernetes Service (AKS), Azure Functions for serverless computing, and Azure Cosmos DB for managed databases. Azure also offers a range of tools for managing and monitoring cloud infrastructure, such as Azure Monitor.

- Kubernetes was originally invented by GCP, so it is no surprise that it offers several cloud-native services. For container orchestration, the Google Kubernetes Engine (GKE) is used. Cloud Functions is the option for serverless computing, and Cloud Spanner is for managed databases. GCP also offers a range of tools for managing and monitoring cloud infrastructure, such as Google Cloud Operations, formerly known as Stackdriver, and Google Cloud Deployment Manager.

- Alibaba Cloud provides *Elastic Container Instance (ECI)* and *Kubernetes Container Service (ACK)* for container orchestration. For serverless computing, we can use Function Compute. ApsaraDB is the solution for managed databases. Tools for managing and monitoring cloud infrastructure are CloudMonitor and *Resource Orchestration Service (ROS)*.

There is one thing to be aware of while using these solutions and offerings: operating cloud native is quite different than the more traditional workload concepts such as virtual machines. This will be discussed next.

Cloud-native applications are typically designed using containerization technologies such as Docker, which allows for a more lightweight and portable deployment process. This contrasts with traditional VM deployments, which require the entire operating system to be installed and configured on each virtual machine instance. The fact that these concepts are more lightweight makes them very suitable for microservices architecture, allowing for greater flexibility and scalability. In contrast, traditional monolithic applications are designed as a single, large application, which is more difficult to modify and scale. Microservices will be talked about extensively in the following sections of this chapter.

Next, cloud-native applications can take advantage of serverless computing, which allows for automatic scaling and pay-per-use pricing. This eliminates the need for manual scaling and reduces operational costs. They are commonly used in a DevOps approach for development and deployment, which emphasizes collaboration between developers and operations teams to ensure continuous integration and delivery. This approach allows for faster iteration and deployment cycles and can reduce the time to market for new features.

Organizations that have adopted DevOps will be able to build and deploy applications more quickly and efficiently, with greater reliability and scalability. That introduces the domain of DevOps, which is the central topic of the next section.

ORGANIZING CLOUD-NATIVE WITH DEVOPS

Cloud-native applications are designed to be modular, decoupled, and horizontally scalable, allowing them to run on multiple cloud environments. To achieve that, a set of principles and practices is needed that utilizes the benefits of the cloud infrastructure and services in order to build and deploy these applications. DevOps is a set of practices that emphasizes collaboration and communication between development and operations teams, with the goal of delivering software more rapidly and reliably. Combining cloud-native concepts with DevOps will help in the development processes while reducing deployment times and improving the scalability and reliability of applications that are *born in the cloud*.

Applications that are born in the cloud typically consist of microservices, which are small, independent components that work together to provide the application's functionality. Each microservice can be developed, deployed, and scaled independently of the others, which allows teams to work more efficiently and with greater agility.

DevOps is one word: it brings development and IT operations together and enables the automation of many aspects of the software development process, including testing, deployment, and monitoring. Using DevOps practices, the company can rapidly iterate on and deploy microservices.

DevOps capabilities for the development and deployment of applications, among others, include:

- *Containerization*: The use of containers to develop and deploy an application.

- *Cloud-based development*: Building the application in the cloud using native cloud technologies and tools.
- *API Management (APIM)*: Cloud services will be connected with each other using APIs. This requires API Management (APIM) with the use of tools and services to create, publish, monitor, and secure APIs, as well as to manage their lifecycle.
- *Apps and database migration*: Applications can be built in the cloud, but in a lot of cases, existing applications and databases will need to be migrated to the cloud, transforming them with cloud-native services.
- *Full stack and grand stack*: Full stack refers to an application that typically uses multiple technologies to build the various layers of the application, such as using a front-end framework such as React or Angular for the user interface, a back-end framework like Node.js or Ruby on Rails for the server-side logic, and a database technology like MySQL or MongoDB for data storage. Grand Stack is a different approach; in this case, an application is built using a combination of four technologies: GraphQL for the API layer, React for the user interface, Apollo for the data layer, and Neo4j for the database layer. The term *GRAND* stands for GraphQL, React, Apollo, and Neo4j Database.
- *DevSecOps*: Security is intrinsic; it needs to be a bolt in the entire development and deployment process. In DevSecOps, security is included in every step of development and operations, including *Static Application Security Testing (SAST)* and *Dynamic Application Security Testing (DAST)* as gateways in the development and deployment pipelines.
- *Document As Code*: Documentation is treated as code and is managed using the same version control systems and tools used for software development. This means that documentation is written using markup languages such as Markdown, AsciiDoc, or reStructuredText, and stored as plain text files in a repository such as Git.
- *PaaS deployment*: Using PaaS technologies from cloud providers to build and deploy applications. Think of database services such as Azure SQL and RDS in AWS.
- *Event-driven architecture*: In an event-driven architecture, an application performs an action as a reaction to events triggered by changes in the system or through external inputs. Application components are designed to be loosely coupled and communicate through asynchronous messaging. This means that components can publish events when they perform a task or have new information, and other components can subscribe to those events and take actions based on them.

- *SaaS integration*: Integrating third-party SaaS services into the development and deployment of applications. It includes the connection of different SaaS applications and services through APIs, webhooks, or other integration methods, to enable data sharing, automation, and collaboration across different systems.

One remark has to be made concerning DevSecOps. Of course, DevSecOps goes deeper than implementing SAST and DAST. Incorporating key risk strategies to manage and mitigate security risks effectively, it's a holistic approach to software development that integrates security practices into the entire software development lifecycle (SDLC). This approach aims to ensure that security measures are considered and implemented throughout the development process rather than being added as an afterthought. It involves a collaborative effort between development teams, security teams, and operations teams. Teams work together to integrate security practices into the development process seamlessly.

Key risk strategies to address in DevSecOps are:

- *Secure coding practices*: Developers are trained in secure coding techniques to prevent common vulnerabilities, such as input validation errors, buffer overflows, and injection attacks.

- *Continuous security testing*: Automated security testing tools are used throughout the development process to identify vulnerabilities and weaknesses in the code. This includes SAST, DAST, and penetration testing.

- *Secure configuration management*: Secure configuration practices are implemented for all software components, including servers, databases, and network devices. This involves applying secure settings, removing unnecessary features, and regularly updating and patching software.

- *Access control and privilege management*: Proper access controls are enforced to ensure that only authorized individuals have the necessary permissions to access and modify the software and its underlying infrastructure. Privilege escalation is carefully managed to prevent unauthorized access.

- *Incident response and recovery*: A well-defined incident response plan is established to handle security incidents effectively. This includes processes for identifying, containing, eradicating, and recovering from security breaches. Regular drills and exercises help validate the effectiveness of the plan.

To enable these capabilities, a supporting platform is needed. For that reason, DevOps is now often rebranded as platform services. Capabilities of the platform include:

- *Open platform*: AWS, Azure, GCP, VMWare, OpenStack, Alibaba Cloud, and Tencent, among others, all allow for connecting third-party services to enable DevOps capabilities.
- *Kubernetes capabilities across clouds*: Think of Azure Kubernetes Services (AKS), Elastic Kubernetes Services in AWS (EKS), Pivotal Kubernetes Services, or Tanzu of VMWare and OpenShift.
- *Infrastructure automation*: Think of ARM and BICEP in Azure, CloudFormation in AWS, Ansible, and Terraform.
- *The cultural shift to DevOps*: The organization must be ready to adopt the DevOps practices, for instance, by assembling teams with the right skills.
- *Platform and apps monitoring*: Open-Source monitoring or cloud-based solutions can be chosen.
- *Service mesh deployment*: The platform must enable service mesh as a layer of infrastructure for managing and controlling communication between microservices. This service mesh layer takes care of service-to-service communication, allowing developers to focus on application development rather than infrastructure concerns.

Additionally, DevOps enables teams to implement *continuous integration* and *continuous delivery (CI/CD)* pipelines, which automate the process of testing, building, and deploying applications. This reduces the time it takes to deliver new features and bug fixes, allowing teams to respond to customer needs more quickly. Before exploring cloud-native further, it's good to have a common understanding of CI/CD.

Continuous Integration focuses on merging code changes from multiple developers into a shared repository regularly. The main goal is to detect and resolve integration issues early and frequently. In a CI workflow, developers frequently commit their code changes to a version control system, triggering an automated build process. The CI server compiles the code, runs unit tests, and performs static code analysis. If any issues are identified, developers are notified immediately, allowing them to fix the problems quickly. CI ensures that code changes are continuously integrated and tested, reducing the risk of integration conflicts, and improving code quality.

Continuous Delivery extends the CI process by automating the deployment of applications to various environments, such as development, staging, and production. The CD pipeline allows for the rapid and reliable release of software by automating the steps needed to deliver the application to end users. The CD pipeline includes activities such as packaging the application, configuring the deployment environment, running additional tests (for example, integration tests and acceptance tests), and deploying the application to the target environment. CD ensures that the application is in a deployable state at any given time, making it easier to release new features, bug fixes, and updates to users.

The pipeline comprises the following essential steps:

- *Code integration*: Developers commit their code changes to the version control system.
- *Build and test*: The CI server automatically builds the code, runs tests (unit tests, integration tests, etc.), and performs code analysis.
- *Artifact generation*: If the code passes the tests, the CI server generates an artifact (for example, a compiled application, a Docker image) that represents a deployable version of the software.
- *Deployment*: The CD pipeline takes the artifact and deploys it to the desired environment, such as staging or production. This involves configuring the deployment environment, ensuring dependencies are met, and deploying the artifact.
- *Testing in the deployment environment*: Additional tests, such as integration tests or acceptance tests, are performed in the deployment environment to verify the behavior and functionality of the application in a realistic setup.
- *Approval and release*: Once the application passes all tests and meets the desired quality criteria, it can be approved for release. Release management processes, such as versioning, change management, and user notifications, are typically included in this stage.

By implementing a CI/CD pipeline, development teams can automate and accelerate the software delivery process while maintaining a high level of quality and reducing the risk of errors.

A simple representation of a pipeline is presented in Figure 7.1:

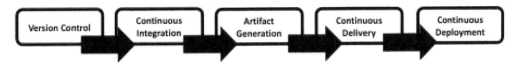

FIGURE 7.1 Simple representation of CI/CD pipeline.

Let us go over the different steps in more detail:

- *Version control*: Developers work on their code changes and commit them to a shared version control system, such as Git.
- Continuous Integration (CI) includes:
  - *Code build*: Whenever code changes are committed, a CI server (for example, Jenkins, CircleCI) automatically triggers a build process.
  - *Compilation*: The CI server compiles the code, ensuring it can be executed.
  - *Automated tests*: Unit tests, integration tests, and other automated tests are executed to verify the code's functionality and quality.
  - *Code analysis*: Static code analysis tools check the code for coding standards, security vulnerabilities, and other potential issues.
- Artifact generation includes:
  - *Packaging*: If the code passes all tests and analysis, the CI server creates an artifact, such as a compiled application or a Docker image.
  - *Versioning*: The artifact is typically tagged with a unique version number or identifier.
- Continuous Delivery (CD) includes:
  - *Deployment*: The artifact is deployed to a staging environment, which closely resembles the production environment.
  - *Additional testing*: Integration tests, acceptance tests, and other tests are performed in the staging environment to validate the application's behavior and compatibility.
  - *User Acceptance Testing (UAT)*: If applicable, stakeholders or users can test the application in the staging environment to provide feedback.
  - *Approval and release*: Once the application passes all tests and receives approval, it can be released to the production environment.

■ Continuous Deployment includes:

• *Fully automated release*: In some cases, organizations may choose to automate the release process directly from the staging environment to the production environment without manual approval.

Note that the CI/CD pipeline can vary depending on the specific tools and practices used by different organizations. The representation provided here gives a general idea of the flow and stages involved in a typical CI/CD pipeline. Figure 7.3 provides a more detailed example of a CI/CD pipeline.

How can working with cloud-native services and implementing the DevOps practice begin? The DevOps approach is depicted in Figure 7.2:

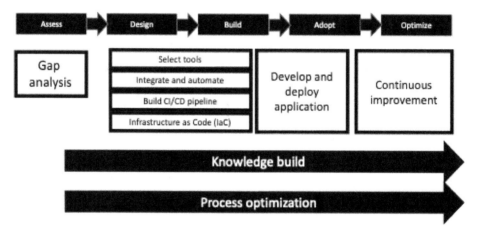

FIGURE 7.2 The DevOps approach.

The first step in building cloud-native concepts using DevOps is to adopt a container-based architecture. Containers can be deployed and scaled quickly, and they help to isolate applications from one another. DevOps teams can use tools such as Docker to build, package, and deploy containers, while Kubernetes can be used to manage container orchestration and scaling. Kubernetes provides a unified API for managing different types of workloads, including stateless and stateful applications, batch jobs, and machine-learning workflows.

Using Kubernetes, DevOps teams can deploy applications to the cloud using a variety of different deployment strategies, including:

■ *Rolling updates*: With rolling updates, systems get updated in a gradual, controlled manner by updating a small batch of nodes or servers at a time rather than all at once. Once a batch has been updated and verified to be working correctly, the next batch is updated, and so on, until the entire system has been updated. Rolling updates are often used in conjunction with other deployment strategies, such as canary releases or blue/green deployments, to ensure that the update process is reliable and safe and does not cause any downtime or disruption to users.

▣ *Blue/green deployments*: In blue/green deployment, there are two identical environments, one representing the current production environment (blue) and the other representing the new environment with the new feature enabled (green). This is a popular methodology to release new software or features. This will be discussed in more detail in the final section of this chapter.

▣ *Canary releases*: New features or software releases are tested with a small subset of users, the so-called canary group, before the feature or release is rolled out to the entire population.

These are just examples of strategies that allow for rapid deployment of new features and updates while minimizing downtime and reducing the risk of application failures.

Implementing DevOps for cloud-native architecture requires a number of key practices, including:

▣ *Automation*: As many aspects of the development and deployment process must be automated as possible. This includes testing, building, and deploying applications. Automation reduces the risk of human error and speeds up the deployment process.

▣ *Containerization*: Containers are used to package and deploy applications.

▣ *Orchestration*: If apps are built using containers, then an orchestration tool is needed to manage our containers. Kubernetes has developed to become the industry standard for automating the deployment, scaling, and management of containers.

▣ *CI/CD*: For effective and efficient DevOps, a continuous integration and continuous delivery (CI/CD) pipeline must be implemented to automate the process of testing, building, and deploying applications. This ensures that applications are thoroughly tested and that new features and bug fixes can be quickly deployed. The concept of CI/CD and a very simple representation of a pipeline were already examined, but a more detailed example is provided in Figure 7.3:

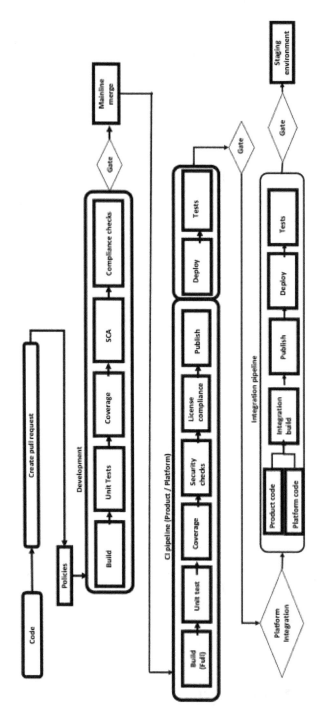

FIGURE 7.3 Example of CI/CD pipeline.

One topic deserves special attention, and that is observability. Proper monitoring is needed that provides a view of the entire stack, from the infrastructure to the application and the containers that are used to deliver the application. Once applications have been deployed to the cloud using cloud-native concepts and DevOps practices, it is important to ensure that they are running smoothly and efficiently. This requires a range of monitoring and observability tools to help DevOps teams track performance metrics, detect, and diagnose issues, and optimize application performance.

One important tool for monitoring cloud-native applications is Prometheus, which is an open-source monitoring system that collects metrics from targets by scraping metrics from HTTP endpoints on those targets. It stores the collected data in a time-series database and provides a powerful query language for analyzing and visualizing the data. Prometheus can be used to monitor a wide range of metrics, including CPU and memory usage, network traffic, and application-specific metrics such as request latency and error rates.

Another important tool for observability is tracing. Tracing as a methodology allows the visualization of the flow of requests through complex distributed systems and identify performance bottlenecks or other issues. One popular tracing tool for cloud-native applications is Jaeger. Jaeger provides a distributed tracing system with an easy-to-use user interface.

Microservices have already been discussed, but it is time to do a proper deep dive into this concept. It is the main topic for the next sections, since building and operating microservices is something completely different from managing traditional applications.

EXPLAINING MICROSERVICES

The previous sections concluded that containers and serverless are typically part of a microservices architecture. *Chapter 5: Creating Interoperability* introduced microservices in *Figure 5.4*. This section will explain how to rearchitect our applications to microservices and how to operate them.

When starting work with microservices, the following architectural artifacts must be considered:

- *Legacy migration*: Unless every application is being built from scratch, legacy, existing applications, and even infrastructure will certainly have to be dealt with. In a lot of cases, these will be monolithic. Some of this legacy might be suitable to rearchitect as microservices, but in that case, the business case must be proof that such a migration is providing benefits to an organization.

▪ *Application modernization*: Application modernization refers to updating, refactoring, or replacing existing applications with newer technologies, architectures, and development methodologies. The goal is to enhance the functionality, performance, and scalability of legacy applications while also reducing their maintenance costs and improving their overall user experience.

▪ *API development and integration*: Microservices are loosely coupled and communicate with each other through APIs. They might and likely will also use PaaS and SaaS services from the cloud provider or third-party vendors. API development and integration are, therefore, crucial elements in developing and deploying microservices.

When operating microservices in a multi-cloud environment, it is important to consider several factors, such as security, network connectivity, and data synchronization. One approach to operating microservices is to use a service mesh such as Istio or Linkerd. *Chapter 5: Creating Interoperability* shows the concept of service mesh in Figure 5.5.

Service mesh provides a dedicated infrastructure layer for managing service-to-service communication, load balancing, and other networking features that are essential to microservices. This can help simplify the complexity of operating microservices in a multi-cloud environment.

Another approach is to use a multi-cloud management platform like Cloudify or Terraform. These platforms enable the deployment and management of microservices across different cloud providers, as well as automate tasks such as scaling, monitoring, and failover.

At the beginning of this section, legacy migration and application modernization were mentioned. Transforming a monolithic application to a microservices architecture in the cloud involves breaking down the application into smaller, independent services that can be deployed and operated separately. This is not an easy process, and a lot of aspects must be considered. It can be broken down into six basic, overarching steps:

1. The first step is to identify the different components of the monolithic application. This can be done by analyzing the application code, database schema, and other relevant documentation.

2. Once the components have been identified, the next step is to group them into logical services. Each service should have a clear and well-defined purpose that can be easily understood and managed.

3. Now that the services have been identified, the next step is taken defining the interfaces between them. These interfaces should be standardized to ensure interoperability and consistency across the different services.

4. The following step is very likely containerization. This involves packaging each service into a container that can be easily deployed and managed using container orchestration tools like Kubernetes.

5. Containers can begin to be deployed to the designated cloud. This can be done using cloud-native tools such as AWS Elastic Beanstalk, Azure Kubernetes Service, or Google Kubernetes Engine.

6. The final step is to manage the new environment with microservices. This involves monitoring the services for performance and availability, as well as automating tasks such as scaling and failover.

Transforming a monolithic application to a microservices architecture in the cloud is a complex process that requires careful planning and execution. It is also important to ensure that the new architecture is properly secured and that data is properly managed across the different services. The final section of this chapter is all about managing microservices.

MANAGING RELEASES IN MICROSERVICES

Microservices are, in essence, distributed systems. The great benefit of this is that specific services are updated without having to touch the entire system. But it also comes with challenges. As soon as an update to service is performed in that system, it must be confirmed that the system as a whole will still be functioning as designed. This is where release management plays a crucial role: it is likely the most important task in managing microservices architectures and systems.

Release management involves managing the deployment and release of individual services as part of a larger system. In order to manage releases effectively, it is important to have a process in place that includes feature management and feature toggling. With feature management, which features are available to users is controlled based on their roles, preferences, or other criteria. This can be done using feature flags, which are toggles that can be used to turn features on or off without the need for a full release.

Using feature toggling, features can be turned on or off based on specific criteria, such as user preferences, geographic location, or other factors. This can be used to gradually roll out new features or to test them in a controlled environment before releasing them to a wider audience. Obviously, tools are needed to execute feature management and toggling. Some of the most popular and multi-cloud-ready tools are LaunchDarkly, CloudBees Rollout, Split. io, and the open-source platform Unleash.

All of these tools provide capabilities in feature flag management that enable management of features across different environments, including the gradual rollout and testing in controlled environments. Most tools are able to perform A/B testing, in which two versions of a Web page, mobile app, or other digital asset are compared to determine which one performs better.

In an A/B test, two different versions of the asset are created and randomly shown to users, with each user seeing only one version. The performance of each version is measured based on a specific goal, such as conversion rate, click-through rate, or user engagement. The version that performs better is then identified and used as the final version.

But how should feature management be implemented? First, the feature requirements must be designed: this includes identifying the target audience for the feature, as well as any business rules or other criteria that should be used to determine when the feature should be enabled. Then the feature flags can be designed that will be used to enable or disable the feature. This may lead to the need to create new code or modify existing code to support the feature flagging functionality.

Now the feature flags can be implemented in the microservices landscape. It starts with updating the code to check for the presence of the feature flag and enabling or disabling the feature accordingly. As already mentioned in the introduction of some tools, testing is of the essence. It is necessary to ensure that the new features are working as expected. The best practice is to run A/B tests or other types of tests to evaluate the impact of the feature on user behavior and system performance.

As with anything in IT, monitoring must be considered. Monitoring of features includes metrics of usage and other performance indicators to ensure that the feature is meeting its objectives, as well as adjusting the feature flags as needed to optimize performance and user satisfaction. This is not a one-time exercise but ongoing. Environments will be constantly updated with new features; that is what CI/CD pipelines are for. Development teams will be continuously looking for ways to enhance applications. To control this continuous development, a specific release methodology called blue/green deployment can be used.

Blue/green deployment provides a way to release new features in a controlled and low-risk manner. Blue/green deployment involves deploying two identical environments, one representing the current production environment (blue) and the other representing the new environment with the new feature enabled (green). Figure 7.4 shows the concept of blue/green deployment:

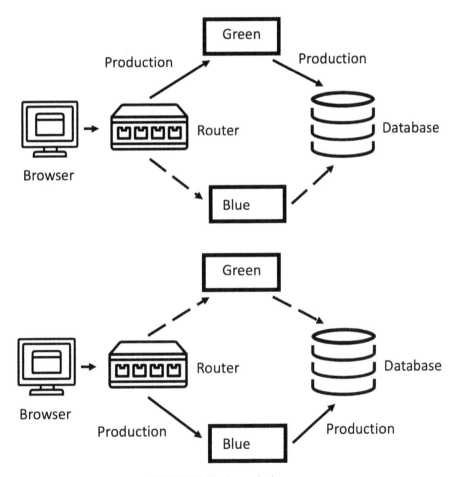

FIGURE 7.4 Blue/green deployment.

Once the green environment is fully deployed and tested, traffic is routed to the green environment while the blue environment is left idle. This allows for easy rollback in case of any issues with the new feature. Once the new feature is fully tested and stable, the blue environment can be decommissioned, and the green environment becomes the new production environment.

In the context of feature management, blue/green deployment can be used to release new features gradually to a subset of users or to test them in a controlled environment before releasing them to a wider audience. By using blue/green deployment in conjunction with feature flags, teams can gradually roll out new features to a subset of users while minimizing the impact of any issues that may arise.

Now having a good understanding of working with cloud-native concepts, containerization and serverless can be discussed in more detail using examples in AWS, Azure, GCP, and Alibaba Cloud. The next chapter will start with containers.

CONCLUSION

This chapter explored the use of cloud-native concepts such as containers and serverless. These concepts offer solutions to create scalable and flexible applications in a microservices architecture, a software architecture pattern in which an application is broken down into smaller, independent services that communicate with each other over a network. With the use of microservices, applications become more scalable and resilient, since the impact of a single service failure can be reduced so that it does not affect the entire system.

Building and managing microservices and cloud-native environments can become complex. The use of CI/CD pipelines in a DevOps setting was extensively explored, building and deploying applications with container platforms and serverless options such as LaMDA in AWS and Azure Functions. Microservices using containers and serverless options are decoupled, making the deployment faster and easier to release new services quickly with minimal disruption to the existing application. For this, methodologies and technologies for feature management and feature toggling must be considered. The last section discussed the use of the blue/green deployment methodology to safely test and manage releases.

KEY POINTS

- Cloud-native concepts are containers, container platforms and orchestration, serverless, and microservices. All major clouds support these concepts. Most clouds have adopted Kubernetes as the industry standard for container orchestration.

- Organizing teams in a DevOps setting is the best practice for the development and deployment of applications with cloud-native offerings. For effective and efficient DevOps, a *continuous integration* and *continuous delivery (CI/CD)* pipeline must be implemented to automate the process of testing, building, and deploying applications. This ensures that applications are thoroughly tested and that new features and bug fixes can be quickly deployed.

- Transforming legacy applications to microservices to run them in the cloud can become very complex. One of the key topics to remember in architecting, building, and managing microservices architectures is APIM, API Management. Since microservices are loosely coupled services, they communicate with each other through APIs, including PaaS and SaaS services from the cloud provider or third-party vendors. API development and integration are, therefore, crucial elements in developing and deploying microservices.

QUESTIONS

1. What does Grand Stack stand for?

2. What is a release called where only a small group of users get the newest version of the software before it is rolled out to the entire population of users?

3. What is the purpose of a CI/CD pipeline?

Answers appear in the appendix.

8

BUILDING AGNOSTIC WITH CONTAINERS

INTRODUCTION

Container technology has become increasingly popular in software development and deployment on cloud infrastructure. It allows for very agile development and controlled distribution in various clouds, promising a form of agnostic cloud deployment. This chapter looks at the concepts of containers, developing and provisioning, and management of container environments in multi-cloud settings.

STRUCTURE

This chapter discusses the following topics:

- Understanding container technology
- Developing and provisioning containers using industry standards
- Exploring container management using a single pane of glass view
- Deep dive into container monitoring and log management

UNDERSTANDING CONTAINER TECHNOLOGY

Container technology has rapidly gained popularity over the past decade to package and deploy applications in a portable and efficient manner. But what are containers? Containers provide an isolated runtime environment for applications, allowing them to run consistently across different computing environments. This consistency is a key benefit of container technology, making it an essential tool for modern software development and deployment.

At its core, a container is a lightweight and portable package that includes all the necessary components to run a specific application. One remark must be made here: Containers are designed to be lightweight, meaning they consume fewer resources than traditional virtual machines. However, it's still important to allocate resources carefully to ensure that containers have enough CPU, memory, and disk space to run efficiently. Failure to allocate resources correctly can lead to performance issues or even container crashes.

The portable package includes the application code, dependencies, libraries, and configurations. Containers also come with an isolated runtime environment that allows them to run consistently across different computing environments, such as different operating systems, cloud providers, or local machines. Figure 8.1 shows the basic architecture of a container and all the components needed to manage containers:

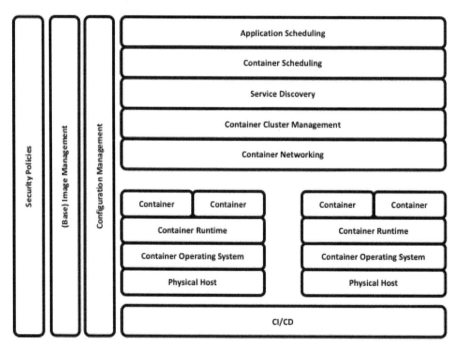

FIGURE 8.1 Basic architecture of container management.

As can be seen from the figure, architecting container technology requires a different approach than traditional application deployment. Containers have unique properties that require careful consideration during the application design and deployment process. The following are some key considerations for architecting for container technology:

- *Microservices architecture*: Containers are an essential tool for implementing microservices architecture. Microservices are a way to break down large monolithic applications into smaller, independent services that can be developed, deployed, and scaled independently. Containers provide a lightweight and portable runtime environment for each microservice, allowing them to run independently of each other. *Chapter 7: Build and Operate Cloud Native* extensively discussed microservices architecture.

- *Resource allocation*: Containers are designed to be lightweight, meaning they consume fewer resources than traditional virtual machines. However, it is still important to allocate resources carefully to ensure that containers have enough CPU, memory, and disk space to run efficiently. Failure to allocate resources correctly can lead to performance issues or even container crashes.

- *Security*: Containers provide an isolated runtime environment for applications, but this isolation is not enough to secure container ecosystems themselves. It is essential to take measures to secure containers, such as using secure container images, applying security patches, and limiting container privileges. Failure to secure containers can lead to security breaches or data loss.

The following are the best practices to deploy and run containers. First, an orchestration platform is needed, such as Kubernetes or Docker Swarm. These platforms provide a way to manage and scale containers across different computing environments. Indeed, Kubernetes and Docker Swarm are cloud platform agnostic, meaning they can operate on different computing platforms such as VMWare, Azure, AWS, GCP, and Alibaba Cloud.

Orchestration platforms automate many of the tasks required to manage containers, such as scheduling, scaling, and load balancing. Using a container orchestration platform simplifies the management of containers and ensures that they run consistently across different environments.

Next, it is recommended to use standardized container images to ensure that containers are consistent. This will also help in managing containers.

Standardized images are created from a base image that includes a minimal operating system and the necessary libraries and dependencies. This base image can then be customized with the application code and configurations. Using standardized images ensures that containers are consistent across different environments, making it easier to manage and scale them. An example of a coded base image for a container is provided in the section under *Guided Plan to Develop and Deploy Containers.*

Containers are designed to be lightweight, but they can still consume resources if not optimized correctly. It is important to optimize container size by removing unnecessary files and dependencies. This optimization reduces container size and improves performance, making it easier to manage and scale containers.

Pitfalls and Risks of Container Technology

There are benefits of using containers, but there are pitfalls too. It might seem contradictory, but vendor lock-in is one of the pitfalls. Container technology is not immune to vendor lock-in. Many container orchestration systems and cloud providers offer their own container solutions, which can make it difficult to switch to a different solution. It is important to consider the long-term implications of choosing a specific container solution and plan accordingly.

Security has already been mentioned, and there are certainly security risks to containers. Containers are vulnerable to security risks such as unauthorized access, malware, and data loss. It is important to take measures to secure containers, such as using secure container images, applying security patches, and limiting container privileges.

Complexity and cost are also key here. Especially when containers are used with microservices, containers can become really hard to manage. For some companies, it's the reason to leave the microservices architecture and return to a more traditional architecture for applications. An example of that and cause for a real debate is the way AWS rearchitected the service for video monitoring at Prime. The service monitors thousands of video streams that Prime delivers to customers. Originally this task was done by a set of distributed components orchestrated by AWS Step Functions, a serverless orchestration service. But the responsible team found out that a monolithic approach to this task did a better job (*https://thenewstack.io/ return-of-the-monolith-amazon-dumps-microservices-for-video-monitoring/*).

Container Services from Major Cloud Providers

Major cloud providers such as Azure, AWS, GCP, and Alibaba Cloud offer containerization services to their customers, allowing them to easily deploy and manage containerized applications. The following response describes the best setup for a containerized application using examples from these cloud providers:

- Azure offers several containerization services, including Azure Kubernetes Service (AKS), Azure Container Instances (ACI), and Azure Container Registry (ACR). The best setup for a containerized application on Azure depends on the specific use case and requirements.
  - For example, if the application requires a high level of scalability and reliability, AKS is a good choice. AKS provides a managed Kubernetes environment that allows customers to deploy and manage containerized applications at scale. AKS also integrates with other Azure services, such as Azure Active Directory and Azure Monitor, to provide a complete containerization solution.
  - If the application requires a more lightweight containerization solution, ACI is a good choice. ACI provides a serverless environment for running containers, allowing customers to easily deploy and scale containerized applications without worrying about infrastructure management. ACI also integrates with other Azure services, such as Azure Virtual Networks and Azure Blob Storage, to provide a complete containerization solution.
- AWS offers Amazon Elastic Container Service (ECS), Amazon Elastic Kubernetes Service (EKS), and Amazon Elastic Container Registry (ECR).
  - For an application that requires a high level of scalability and reliability, EKS is a good choice. EKS is a managed Kubernetes environment that integrates with other AWS services, such as AWS Identity and Access Management and AWS CloudTrail.
  - ECS is a more lightweight containerization solution. ECS also integrates with other AWS services, such as Amazon Virtual Private Cloud and Amazon S3.
- The container solutions of GCP include Google Kubernetes Engine (GKE), Google Cloud Run, and Google Container Registry. If the application requires a high level of scalability and reliability, GKE is the right

solution. GKE integrates with other GCP services, such as Google Cloud IAM and Google Cloud Logging, to provide a complete solution.

- For a lightweight solution, Cloud Run is a good choice. Cloud Run is a serverless environment for running containers and integrates with other GCP services, such as Google Cloud SQL and Google Cloud Storage, making deployment and managing containers easy.

- The final example is Alibaba Cloud. It offers Container Service for Kubernetes (ACK), Elastic Container Instance (ECI), and Container Registry. ACK would be the best fit for applications that require a high level of scalability and reliability, where ECI is the lightweight variant. As with the other clouds, both services integrate with all other services of Alibaba Cloud.

DEVELOPING AND PROVISIONING CONTAINERS USING INDUSTRY STANDARDS

A promise was made in the previous section: containers can run anywhere and on any platform. They are cloud platform agnostic, although it was also mentioned that there's still a risk of vendor lock-in when a specific deployment platform is used for containers. To ensure the interoperability and portability of containerized applications across different cloud platforms, the container technology industry has developed several standards. These standards cover various aspects of container technology, including container formats, container orchestration, and container registry. These are discussed in this section.

To begin with the format that containers have, a good example of such a format is the *Open Container Initiative (OCI)*, which is an open-source project that defines standards for container formats and runtime. OCI specifications ensure that container images are portable across different container runtimes and platforms. The OCI format specifies how to package and distribute container images and how to run them on different platforms. OCI sets definitions for:

- *Image specification*: This concerns the format and layout of a container image. A container image is a lightweight, standalone, and executable package that contains everything needed to run an application, including the application code, runtime, libraries, and dependencies. The OCI

Image Specification provides a standard way of packaging and distributing container images, which can be used across different container runtimes.

▨ *Runtime specification*: This defines the format and behavior of a container runtime. A container runtime is responsible for starting and managing a container instance, including creating and isolating namespaces, managing cgroups, and interacting with the host system. The OCI Runtime Specification provides a standard way of interacting with a container runtime, which allows containers to be portable across different container engines and platforms.

An example of a Dockerfile that contains the specifications according to OCI is as follows:

```
# Use a base image that supports the OCI image format
FROM scratch


# Set the image label according to OCI specification
LABEL org.opencontainers.image.title="My App" \

      org.opencontainers.image.description="This is my app" \

      org.opencontainers.image.authors="Jeroen Mulder <Jeroen.
      Mulder@ example.com>" \

      org.opencontainers.image.created="2023-03-31T14:00:00Z" \

      org.opencontainers.image.version="1.0"



# Add the application binary to the container image
ADD myapp /usr/bin/myapp



# Set the default command for the container
CMD ["/usr/bin/myapp"]

```

The example starts with a scratch base image, which is an empty image that provides no file system or runtime environment. Next, various image labels are set using the LABEL instruction, following the OCI image specification.

Then the application binary is added to the container image using the ADD instruction. Finally, the default command must be specified to run when the container is started using the CMD instruction.

Container orchestration is also needed. Kubernetes is the most popular container orchestration platform, which has become an industry standard for containerized application deployment and management. Kubernetes provides a rich set of features for scaling, scheduling, and managing containerized applications across different cloud platforms.

Lastly, a mechanism is needed to register the containers, where containers can be centrally stored and container images distributed. Docker Hub is the most widely used container registry, but there are other popular alternatives, such as *Google Container Registry (GCR)*, Amazon ECR, and ACR. These registries allow seamless integration with container orchestration platforms like Kubernetes.

In all of this, security plays a big role too. The *Center for Internet Security (CIS)* provides a benchmark for secure container deployment, which is widely adopted in the industry. The benchmark provides best practices and guidelines for securing container images, orchestrators, and hosts. Think of the following:

- *Use trusted base images*: Always use images from trusted sources and verify the integrity of the image by verifying its checksum or digital signature.

- *Use the latest version of container images*: Keep container images up to date to ensure that security patches are applied and vulnerabilities are addressed.

- *Limit container privileges*: Containers should run with the least number of privileges necessary to perform their intended function. For example, avoid running containers as root.

- *Use image scanning tools*: Use tools such as vulnerability scanners or static code analysis tools to scan container images for known vulnerabilities.

- *Apply security patches*: Regularly update container images with the latest security patches to address known vulnerabilities.

- *Implement network segmentation*: Use network segmentation to isolate container traffic and prevent attackers from moving laterally within your infrastructure.

- *Use secure configurations*: Follow secure configuration practices, such as disabling unnecessary services, restricting access to sensitive resources, and enforcing secure communication protocols.

- *Monitor container activity*: Monitor container activity for suspicious or malicious behavior, such as attempts to access sensitive resources or unusual network traffic.

- *Implement access controls*: Use access controls to limit the permissions of containerized applications and ensure that users and applications only have access to the resources they need to perform their tasks.

All these industry standards will help to ensure that containerized applications are portable and can be easily deployed across different cloud platforms, making container technology an attractive option for modern application development and deployment. But how will a containerized application be developed and deployed to the cloud? The next section goes through the essential steps.

Guided Plan to Develop and Deploy Containers

To start working with containers, it's recommended to follow this this ten-step approach:

- *Step 1*: Choose a cloud provider. Select a cloud provider that supports container services. Popular options include Amazon Web Services (AWS), Microsoft Azure, and Google Cloud Platform (GCP). Evaluate their offerings, pricing, and features to find the best fit for the requirements.

- *Step 2*: Set up an account. Create an account with the chosen cloud provider. This typically involves providing contact and billing information.

- *Step 3*: Become familiar with container concepts. Get acquainted with container technology and its key concepts, such as container images, containers, and container orchestration. Understand the benefits of containers, such as portability, scalability, and isolation.

- *Step 4*: Select a container orchestration platform. Choose a container orchestration platform that will manage the containers. The most popular options are Kubernetes and Docker Swarm. Kubernetes has become the de facto standard and offers a rich ecosystem and community support.

- *Step 5*: Set up a container registry. A container registry is a repository for storing and managing container images. Most cloud providers offer their own container registries, such as AWS ECR, ACR, and GCP Container Registry. Create a registry to store container images.

- *Step 6*: Build container images. Create Dockerfiles or build configuration files that define the steps to build container images. These files specify the base image, dependencies, and commands required to run the application within a container.

- *Step 7*: Containerize the application. Use tools like Docker to build container images from the application code. This involves packaging the application, its dependencies, and any required configuration into a container image.

- *Step 8*: Push container images to the registry. Push the container images that have been built to the container registry set up earlier. This step makes the images available for deployment and sharing with the team.

- *Step 9*: Create a cluster. Set up a cluster within the chosen container orchestration platform. This involves provisioning virtual machines or worker nodes that will run the containers. The orchestration platform will manage the scheduling, scaling, and monitoring of containers across the cluster.

- *Step 10*: Deploy containers. Use the orchestration platform's CLI or GUI to deploy the containers to the cluster. Define the desired number of instances, resource requirements, networking, and any other necessary configurations.

Obviously, from this point onward, the health and performance of the containers should be monitored using the tools provided by the cloud provider or third-party monitoring solutions. And automatic scaling rules must be set up to scale the container instances based on resource utilization or incoming traffic.

Still, the very first step is to choose a container platform that best suits the company's needs. There are many options available, including Docker, Kubernetes, and Amazon ECS, as discussed in the first section of this chapter. Evaluate each platform's features and pricing and choose the one that best fits the requirements. That can be quite straightforward: if the environment runs completely in Azure and there are no plans to deploy in other clouds, then Azure seems to be a logical place to start hosting the containers. It really depends on the cloud strategy of an organization.

Next, the application can be developed using the preferred programming language and framework. It is necessary to design the application with containers in mind, ensuring that it is modular and can run in a containerized environment. This is really the job of an application or software architect.

Once the application has been designed and coded, the container images can be developed. Docker, for instance, can be used with a Docker image. A Docker image is a self-contained package that includes the application and all its dependencies. A Dockerfile is used to define the image and its contents. An example of a Dockerfile is given as follows.

It starts with a base image that includes the Python 3.9 runtime and dependencies for the application. The working directory is then set to /app and the contents of the current directory are copied into the container. Any required dependencies are installed using pip and the default command is set to run our app.py script using the Python interpreter:

```
# Use a base image that includes the runtime and dependencies
for your application


FROM python:3.9-alpine

# Set the working directory to /app

WORKDIR /app


# Copy the current directory contents into the container at /app

COPY . /app


# Install any required dependencies

RUN pip install --no-cache-dir -r requirements.txt


# Set the default command to run when the container starts

CMD [ "python", "./app.py" ]
```

This image can be built using the docker build command:

```
docker build -t hello-world .
```

Once the build is completed, the container can be run:

```
docker run -p 5000:5000 hello-world
```

This will start the container and map port `5000` in the container to port `5000` on the host. The `Hello, world!` application can then be accessed by navigating to `http:// localhost:5000` in a Web browser.

Of course, this is a very simple example and probably does not require a lot of testing, but testing the image is a necessity. After creating the Docker image, test it to ensure that it runs as expected. Use a local Docker environment to test the image and make any necessary changes. When changes are made to the application, the Docker image must be updated and redeployed to the container platform. Rolling updates is a methodology to minimize downtime and ensure that the application is always available. Having a central place where images are stored and distributed—the container registry—is essential to stay in control of image consistency.

The application can be deployed to the designated cloud provider using the chosen container platform. Follow the documentation provided by the cloud provider to set up a cluster or a single instance for the application. The reason to set up a cluster is because it is necessary for containers to be able to scale in case the application is used more. As the application grows, it may need to be scaled horizontally by adding more instances, adding more instances automatically or manually.

Now that everything is set up, the behavior of our containers must be monitored to make sure that everything keeps running as designed and secure. The final section of this chapter discusses monitoring and logging in much more detail.

Developing and deploying a containerized application to the cloud involves choosing a container platform, developing the application, creating a Docker image, testing the image, choosing a cloud provider, setting up a container registry, deploying the application, and next scaling, monitoring, and updating the application. Once the containers have been developed and deployed, the container platform and the applications that are hosted on the platform must be managed. That is the topic of the next section.

EXPLORING CONTAINER MANAGEMENT USING A SINGLE PANE OF GLASS VIEW

The deployment of containers has been discussed, but how are these container platforms and the containers that hold the applications managed, especially in multi-cloud settings? The containers must be secure, scalable, and highly available. This section will discuss how container management is done and the tools available in Azure, AWS, GCP, and Alibaba Cloud. Best practices, pitfalls, and security management in container environments will also be discussed.

Managing containers involves various tasks such as creating, deploying, scaling, and monitoring them. Container orchestration tools help to automate these tasks, making it easy to manage containers at scale. Some of the popular container orchestration tools include Kubernetes, Docker Swarm, and Apache Mesos:

- Kubernetes is the most popular container orchestration tool, and it is available in all major cloud providers. Kubernetes automates container deployment, scaling, and management. It provides a platform to deploy and manage containers in a distributed environment. Kubernetes is highly customizable and provides various deployment options, such as rolling updates, blue-green deployments, and canary deployments.
- Docker Swarm is a native clustering and scheduling tool for Docker containers. It is integrated with the Docker engine, making it easy to use for Docker users. Docker Swarm provides automatic load balancing and scaling, making it easy to manage containers at scale.
- Apache Mesos is another popular container orchestration tool. It provides a platform to manage containers across multiple clusters. Apache Mesos provides resource isolation and sharing, making it easy to run different workloads on the same cluster.

To manage containers across multiple clouds, a multi-cloud container management platform can be used. These platforms provide a unified view of container management across different clouds. A multi-cloud container management platform allows management of containers from a single interface, regardless of the cloud provider. An example is Kubernetes Federation. Kubernetes Federation enables the management of multiple Kubernetes clusters across different cloud providers. Federation provides a single pane of glass view for container management across different clouds.

Another solution is to use a container management platform such as Rancher. Rancher is a container management platform that provides a unified view of container management across multiple clouds. Rancher allows the management of Kubernetes clusters across different clouds, including Azure, AWS, GCP, and Alibaba Cloud. Moreover, with Rancher, containers can be managed from a single interface. Next, it offers features such as automated scaling, load balancing, and monitoring, making it easy to manage containers at scale.

One final tool to discuss is Tanzu Mission Control by VMWare. This is a centralized management platform offered by VMware that enables organizations to manage and deploy Kubernetes clusters across multiple cloud environments, just like Rancher does. It provides a single control plane for managing Kubernetes clusters running on different cloud providers, including AWS, Microsoft Azure, and GCP. Tanzu Mission Control also enables organizations to manage the entire container lifecycle, including building, deploying, and scaling containerized applications.

In terms of best practices, the use of container orchestration and registry for images were already discussed in the first section. But there is more that can be done to ensure that container environments are managed in a proper way. Best practices include:

- *Use resource limits*: When running containers, it is important to set resource limits such as CPU and memory usage to prevent containers from consuming too many resources and affecting other applications running on the same host.

- *Monitor container performance*: Monitoring container performance is critical to ensuring that they are running efficiently and reliably. Key metrics such as CPU usage, memory usage, and network performance should be monitored to identify any performance issues and address them proactively.

- *Use configuration management tools*: Configuration management tools such as Ansible and Puppet make it easier to manage and deploy containerized applications. These tools automate the process of configuring and deploying containers, making it easier to manage containers at scale.

▪ *Use version control*: Version control is critical to managing container images and configurations. Version control tools such as Git should be used to track changes to container images and configurations and roll back to previous versions if necessary.

Managing Security in Container Platforms

There is one topic that must be discussed in more detail, and that is managing the security of container environments. Security starts with using a minimal and trusted base image for the containers, such as those provided by the cloud provider or a reputable source. This reduces the attack surface and ensures that the container does not include any unnecessary software or libraries that can introduce vulnerabilities. This also implies that the containers must be kept up to date, making sure that updates are regularly applied to the containers with the latest patches and security fixes to mitigate known vulnerabilities. This includes not only the application code but also the underlying operating system and any dependencies.

Deploying a base image for a container is one, but the containers also need to be configured. This means it is necessary to ensure that containers are secure by default. For example, avoid running containers as root, disable unnecessary services and ports, and enforce strong authentication and access control. Secure networking practices such as encrypting communication between containers must be implemented, using firewalls to restrict access to sensitive ports, and using network policies to control traffic flow.

An important task is to monitor the container platform and the containers running on that platform to discover any suspicious activity, such as unauthorized access or attempts to exploit vulnerabilities. Tools such as logging and auditing can be used to track container activity and investigate any security incidents. The final section discusses this in more detail, since this is of great importance.

Other best practices to secure containers are:

▪ Use container isolation techniques such as namespaces and cgroups to limit the resources and permissions available to each container. This can help prevent containers from interfering with each other or accessing sensitive data or resources.

▩ Use container image scanning tools to detect any vulnerabilities or security risks in container images before they are deployed. This can help prevent the deployment of vulnerable containers that can be exploited by attackers.

▩ Use access control and authentication mechanisms such as *role-based access control (RBAC)* and *multifactor authentication (MFA)* to control access to container environments and containers. This can help prevent unauthorized access and reduce the risk of data breaches.

Overall, managing security in container environments and containers in the cloud requires a comprehensive and proactive approach that includes implementing best practices for configuration, monitoring, and access control. This all fits into the concept of DevSecOps, as represented in Figure 8.2:

FIGURE 8.2 The DevSecOps approach.

DevSecOps is an approach to software development that integrates security into the entire software development lifecycle, from design to deployment and beyond. It emphasizes collaboration among development, operations, and security teams to ensure that security is a shared responsibility and is addressed at every stage of the development process.

Techniques that should be included in DevSecOps are *Software Component Analysis (SCA)*, *Static Application Security Testing (SAST)*, *Interactive Application Security Testing (IAST)*, *Dynamic Application Security Testing (DAST)*, and penetration (Pen) testing:

- SCA is a process that involves analyzing the software components used in an application to identify any potential security vulnerabilities or compliance issues. Obviously, this includes container development. SCA tools scan the software codebase and generate a list of components, including open-source libraries, third-party components, and custom code, along with their versions and dependencies. The SCA tool compares this list against a database of known vulnerabilities and checks for any licensing or compliance issues. The results of the analysis are typically presented in a report that includes a summary of the findings, along with recommendations for remediation.

- SAST is a process that analyzes the source code of an application to identify security vulnerabilities and coding errors before the code is compiled or deployed. SAST tools use a set of rules and heuristics to scan the codebase and identify potential security issues such as SQL injection, *cross-site scripting (XSS)*, and buffer overflows. SAST is relevant when using containers, as it helps identify security vulnerabilities and misconfigurations that could be exploited by attackers, such as image tampering, resource abuse, and container escape attacks. SAST can be integrated into the container image build process to ensure that any potential security vulnerabilities or coding errors are identified before the image is deployed.

- DAST is the process of testing an application from the outside to identify vulnerabilities that may be exploitable by an attacker. DAST tools simulate attacks against the running application to identify potential security weaknesses such as input validation issues, authentication and authorization problems, and misconfigured security settings. It can help identify security vulnerabilities in the containerized application at runtime. Since containers are often used to deploy microservices-based architectures, it can be challenging to ensure that all the microservices are secure and that there are no vulnerabilities in the communication between them. DAST tools can help identify these vulnerabilities by testing the application from the outside.

- IAST focuses on identifying vulnerabilities in applications during runtime. IAST involves instrumenting the application code or runtime environment to gather security-related data while the application is executing within a container. This data includes information about code execution, data flow, inputs, and outputs.

▪ Pen testing can be performed in container environments in the cloud to identify potential security weaknesses in the containerized applications and their underlying infrastructure. In these tests, attacks are simulated on the containerized applications and infrastructure to identify any potential security weaknesses using tools such as Metasploit or Nmap.

One topic that also must be discussed here is the *Software Bill of Materials (SBOM)*. Containers make it easy to deploy and scale applications across different environments. However, this also introduces new security challenges, particularly around supply chain security. An SBOM is a detailed inventory of all the components used in a software application, including its dependencies and their versions. It helps organizations understand the security risks associated with the software they are using, as well as identify vulnerabilities and potential points of attack in the software supply chain.

For container users, having an SBOM can provide visibility into the components used in the container image, including the operating system, libraries, and other software packages. This information can be used to identify and remediate any vulnerabilities or compliance issues associated with these components.

In terms of who benefits from an SBOM when using containers, it would be the organization deploying the containers, as well as any downstream consumers of the container image. This includes developers, operations teams, security teams, and compliance teams that need to ensure the security and compliance of the software they are using. Additionally, SBOMs are becoming increasingly important in regulatory compliance, particularly in industries such as healthcare and finance. As such, collecting and maintaining the SBOM has become a mandatory artifact in DevSecOps.

Managing security in container environments and containers in the cloud fits in well with the DevSecOps approach because it emphasizes a proactive, collaborative, and automated approach to security. By incorporating security best practices into the container development process, teams can ensure that security is not an afterthought but is instead built into the entire process. This includes implementing security testing and scanning as part of the CI/CD pipeline, using automation to enforce security policies, and collaborating between teams to identify and address security risks.

In the DevSecOps approach, security is not a separate function that is added at the end of the development process but is instead integrated into every aspect of the process. This ensures that security risks are identified and addressed early in the development cycle, reducing the risk of vulnerabilities and security incidents. By managing security in container environments and containers in the cloud as part of the DevSecOps approach, teams can build more secure and resilient applications that are better able to withstand cyberattacks and protect user data.

DEEP DIVE INTO CONTAINER MONITORING AND LOG MANAGEMENT

With so many moving parts, it is important to have a robust monitoring strategy in place to ensure that everything is running smoothly. This section is all about monitoring and log management. The following are best practices for implementing the monitoring of containers in cloud environments.

When discussing monitoring, it is necessary to start debating what will be monitored in the first place. Sometimes a simple "heartbeat" is a certain workload, alive or not, can be sufficient, but in most cases, it is necessary to know much more. For instance, how the workload is performing. That is a matter of choosing the right metrics. Metrics such as CPU usage, memory usage, and network traffic are all important, but other metrics like container restarts, container uptime, and resource limits should also be considered. These metrics can help to identify potential issues before they become serious problems.

Setting metrics for container monitoring involves identifying the Key Performance Indicators (KPIs) that are relevant to the application and its infrastructure. The metrics that are chosen will depend on specific use cases and what container monitoring is meant to achieve. Steps to consider in defining metrics are:

- *Identifying application requirements*: This includes identifying the resources that the application needs to run, such as CPU, memory, disk space, and network bandwidth.
- *Defining key performance indicators*: KPIs should be relevant to the overall performance and health of the application. Examples of KPIs include CPU usage, memory usage, network traffic, and disk I/O.

The following Python script uses the Docker SDK for Python to get the container stats and then defines functions to extract the CPU usage, memory usage, and network I/O metrics from the stats. The script then enters an infinite loop to continuously print out these metrics every second for the specified container ID. This script can be customized to monitor other metrics as needed; it is just an example:

```python
import docker
import time


client = docker.from_env()


def get_container_stats(container_id):
    container = client.containers.get(container_id)
    stats = container.stats(stream=False)

    return stats


def get_cpu_usage(stats):
    cpu_stats = stats['cpu_stats']
    precpu_stats = stats['precpu_stats']

    cpu_delta = cpu_stats['cpu_usage']['total_usage'] - precpu_
    stats['cpu_usage']['total_usage']

    system_delta = cpu_stats['system_cpu_usage'] - precpu_
    stats['system_ cpu_usage']

    cpu_percent = round((cpu_delta / system_delta) * 100.0, 2)
    return cpu_percent


def get_memory_usage(stats):
    memory_stats = stats['memory_stats']

    memory_usage = memory_stats['usage'] / (1024 ** 2)
    memory_limit = memory_stats['limit'] / (1024 ** 2)
```

```python
    memory_percent = round((memory_usage / memory_limit) *
    100.0, 2)
    return memory_percent


def get_network_io(stats):

    network_stats = stats['networks']

    rx_bytes = network_stats['eth0']['rx_bytes']
    tx_bytes = network_stats['eth0']['tx_bytes']
    return (rx_bytes, tx_bytes)


# Example usage
container_id = 'your-container-id-here'


while True:


    stats = get_container_stats(container_id)
    cpu_usage = get_cpu_usage(stats)
    memory_usage = get_memory_usage(stats)

    rx_bytes, tx_bytes = get_network_io(stats)


    print(f'CPU Usage: {cpu_usage}%')
    print(f'Memory Usage: {memory_usage}%')
    print(f'Network In: {rx_bytes} bytes')
    print(f'Network Out: {tx_bytes} bytes')


    time.sleep(1)
```

Since containers literally can come and go in cloud environments and are continuously updated, it is essential to have real-time monitoring in place. It is necessary to know what is always happening in containers to identify issues and troubleshoot problems. This means that tools must be chosen that provide real-time monitoring and alerting to ensure that there is always awareness of what is happening in the containers. Examples of such tools are Prometheus, Grafana, New Relic, Datadog, and Sysdig.

If operations are being run in multi-cloud, the user as an administrator does not want to get into various dashboards to monitor containers. The use of a centralized dashboard is therefore highly recommended to keep track of all the containers in one place. It allows the user to see the status of all the containers briefly and quickly identify any issues that need attention. Use a dashboard that integrates with the monitoring tools to make it easy to monitor and manage containers.

Metrics have been discussed, but then it is necessary to have alerts if metrics are not met. Hence, alerts need to be set up to notify when there is an issue that needs attention, allowing a quick response to resolve the problem. Alerts must be set up for important metrics such as CPU usage and memory usage, as well as for critical events like container crashes.

After the relevant KPIs have been determined, thresholds and alerting rules need to be defined for each metric. This means setting limits for acceptable levels of each metric and configuring the monitoring system to send an alert when these limits are exceeded. For example, a threshold can be set for CPU usage at 80% and an alert can be sent when CPU usage exceeds this threshold.

Now that metrics, thresholds, and alerting rules have been set, it is necessary to be able to continuously monitor the application and adjust the metrics as needed. This means regularly reviewing the defined metrics and thresholds to ensure that they are still relevant and effective. Failing the regular review is probably the most common mistake in monitoring containers, but there are more pitfalls.

It is possible, for instance, to define too many metrics. This is over-monitoring. Monitoring too many metrics can lead to information overload and make it difficult to identify the most important issues. Metrics must be chosen that are most important for the application, and the focus should be on those.

A lack of integration between monitoring tools and container orchestration tools can make it difficult to get a complete view of the containers. Make sure that monitoring tools integrate with the chosen container orchestration tools to ensure a complete view of the containers and the applications running in these containers.

The last major pitfall may seem obvious, but it happens all the time: alerts that are not followed up. Alerts are useless if they are not acted upon. Make sure that there is a plan in place for responding to alerts and resolving issues quickly. Assign responsibilities to team members and make sure that everyone knows what to do when an alert is triggered.

Collecting and Analyzing Logs

Logs are a crucial source of information when it comes to monitoring containerized applications. They provide insights into the behavior of the applications, thus helping to identify potential issues and troubleshoot problems when they occur. Collecting and analyzing logs helps to gain a better understanding of the application's performance and usage patterns, as well as detect security threats and other issues.

The first task at hand is to set a logging strategy before starting to collect logs. This includes identifying which logs to collect, how frequently to collect them, and where to store them. A place is also needed to store the logs. A centralized logging solution is preferred and a best practice in container monitoring. This enables the collection and storing of logs from all the containers in a single location, making it easier to analyze and troubleshoot issues.

Logfiles only make sense if they are well-structured. Structured logging involves adding additional metadata to logs, making it easier to analyze and search for specific information. Using structured logging improves the accuracy of your monitoring and troubleshooting efforts. This also means that it might be necessary to remove information that is not required to keep in logs. With log rotation, old logs can automatically be deleted or archived to free up storage space. This is essential for managing the large volumes of logs generated by containerized applications.

All of this must be done in real time to enable fast detection of and response to issues, reducing downtime and minimizing the impact on users. Some popular tools to facilitate this are as follows:

- Elasticsearch and Kibana are open-source tools for log collection and analysis. Elasticsearch provides a powerful search engine for storing and indexing logs, while Kibana offers a graphical interface for visualizing and analyzing log data.
- Fluentd is an open-source log collector that supports a wide range of log formats and provides flexible routing and filtering options. It is highly

customizable, making it an ideal tool for managing complex containerized applications.

- Logstash is another open-source log collection and processing tool that is highly customizable. It supports a wide range of input and output plugins, making it easy to integrate with other tools and platforms.

What do these tools collect in terms of logs and events? There might be differences, but in general, these tools collect logs of the following events:

- Real-time logs of container events, including container creation, start, stop, and deletion. These logs can be used to monitor the container lifecycle and troubleshoot issues.

- Logs are generated by applications running in containers. This can include log files generated by Web servers, databases, and other application components.

- Network traffic logs, including logs of inbound and outbound traffic, as well as traffic between containers and other network resources.

- Security logs about security-related events in containers, such as failed login attempts, suspicious network traffic, and other security-related events.

- Performance logs using container performance metrics such as CPU usage, memory usage, and disk I/O. This can help identify performance bottlenecks and optimize container performance.

These are just a few examples of the types of logs that tools can provide in containers. The specific logs available will depend on the configuration of the container environment and the logging options enabled. Containers generate a vast number of logs, including application logs, system logs, and container runtime logs. Correlating these logs allows a holistic view of the containerized application's behavior. Correlating logs is, therefore, essential for troubleshooting and debugging.

Now, the next question is how can the user ensure that logs are collected from the containers and shipped to a store that keeps the logs? The following example uses a script that tells Fluentd to collect logs from a Docker container and send them to a centralized logging environment.

First, make sure Fluentd is installed on the host where the Docker container is running. The installation instructions can be found at: *https://docs.fluentd. org/ installation/install-by-deb*.

Next is to create a Fluentd configuration file, for example, `/etc/fluentd/conf.d/`

`docker.conf`, with the following content:

```
<source>
  @type forward
  port 24224
</source>


<match docker.**>
@type copy
<store>
  @type elasticsearch
  hosts <elasticsearch_host>:<elasticsearch_port>
  logstash_format true
  flush_interval 10s
</store>
</match>
```

This configuration file sets up a Fluentd forward input plugin to receive logs from the Docker container on port 24224. It then sends the logs to Elasticsearch using the Elasticsearch output plugin.

Replace `<elasticsearch_host>` and `<elasticsearch_port>` with the hostname and port of the designated Elasticsearch instance.

Start Fluentd using the configuration file in a sudo command:

```
sudo fluentd -c /etc/fluentd/conf.d/docker.conf
```

Start the Docker container with the following additional flags:

```
docker run -d --log-driver=fluentd --log-opt fluentd-address=
<fluentd_ host>:24224 --log-opt tag=docker.<container_name>
<image_name>
```

This command tells Docker to use the Fluentd logging driver and specifies the address and tag for Fluentd to use. Replace `<fluentd_host>` with the hostname or IP address of the host where Fluentd is running, `<container_name>` with a name for the container, and `<image_name>` with the name of the Docker image to be run.

With these steps, the Docker container logs should now be sent to Elasticsearch via Fluentd. Kibana or another Elasticsearch client can be used to visualize and analyze the logs.

As with monitoring, there are pitfalls to avoid in collecting logs. One of the biggest pitfalls of log collection and analysis is the overwhelming amount of data that can be generated. This can lead to difficulties in managing and analyzing logs, as well as increased storage costs.

Another common pitfall is insufficient log retention, which can result in the loss of valuable data. It is important to establish a log retention policy that meets specific needs and ensures that logs are retained for a sufficient period.

Of course, security also plays a significant role in logs. Collecting and storing logs can create security risks, as logs may contain sensitive information that could be exploited by attackers. It is important to implement adequate security measures, such as encryption and access controls, to protect logs and prevent unauthorized access.

Collecting and analyzing logs is a critical part of container monitoring in the cloud. Following best practices and using the right tools allows valuable insights into the performance and behavior of containerized applications, enabling the user as administrator to identify and troubleshoot issues quickly and effectively. However, it is necessary to be aware of pitfalls, one of them doing too much. It is all about making the right choices.

This concludes the chapter about containers. The next cloud-native technology to be explored is the concept of serverless functions. It is the topic of the next chapter.

CONCLUSION

This chapter discussed the concepts of containers. It was learned how to use container technology to develop, provision, and manage applications in the cloud. The chapter first explained exactly what a container is and what the benefits of deploying applications using container technology are. Then the container offerings of the major cloud providers AWS, Azure, GCP, and Alibaba Cloud were examined. All of them offer both managed and unmanaged services to deploy and manage containers on their platforms. It was learned that a container orchestration platform is needed to run containers. Kubernetes has evolved to be the industry standard.

The DevSecOps process to build applications and deploy them using containers was looked at extensively. The chapter stressed that security best practices must be bolted into the container development process to ensure that security is not an afterthought but built into the entire process. This includes implementing security testing and scanning as part of the CI/CD pipeline and using automation to enforce security policies.

The final part of this chapter was about setting up monitoring and logging. It was learned that setting the right metrics in monitoring is crucial. When it comes to monitoring and logging, the biggest pitfall is to get swamped by data if there is not enough precision in setting the right metrics.

KEY POINTS

- Containers have unique properties that require careful consideration during the application design and deployment process. Think of microservices, resource allocation, and security settings. It is essential to take measures to secure containers, such as using secure container images, applying security patches, and limiting container privileges. A base image can help to keep container deployments consistent.

- Major cloud providers offer a variety of managed container services, but these might not fit the multi-cloud approach. A multi-cloud container management platform can be used. These platforms provide a unified view of container management across different clouds. A multi-cloud container management platform will allow the management of containers from a single interface, regardless of the cloud provider.

- Monitoring is essential in managing containers, but it must be ensured that the right metrics are set to prevent an overload of monitoring data and logs. Metrics like CPU usage, memory usage, and network traffic are all important, but other metrics like container restarts, container uptime, and resource limits should also be considered. These metrics can help in identifying potential issues.

QUESTIONS

1. An open-source project was discussed that defines standards for container formats and runtime. What is the name of that project?

2. What processes are recommended to include in DevSecOps?

3. What are Elasticsearch and Kibana?

Answers appear in the appendix.

## CHAPTER 9

BUILDING AND MANAGING SERVERLESS

INTRODUCTION

Pay only for what will really be used. Serverless does not mean that there are no servers involved, but that only server resources that are really needed are paid for, such as, typically, CPUs, memory, and disk space for storage. But how can apps and services be deployed on serverless infrastructure?

This chapter explains how to define the environments as functions that can be deployed and managed as serverless environments. It explains event-driven architectures and discusses the various serverless frameworks and technologies, including the offerings from major cloud providers. The final section extensively discusses defining metrics to monitor serverless environments in multi-cloud settings.

STRUCTURE

This chapter discusses the following topics:

- Understanding the serverless concept
- Developing and provisioning serverless functions from architecture
- Using CI/CD for serverless deployments
- Managing multi-cloud environments with serverless frameworks
- Following best practices in serverless
- Deep dive into monitoring serverless

UNDERSTANDING THE SERVERLESS CONCEPT

Serverless computing is rapidly gaining popularity due to its many benefits. This section discusses what serverless computing is and what benefits it offers. Serverless concepts in AWS, Azure, GCP, and Alibaba Cloud will also be explored.

The term *serverless* has gone through different meanings over time:

- *Early Web applications*: Described applications that didn't require dedicated servers, relying on client-side technologies and using server-side infrastructure for data storage.
- *Backend as a Service (BaaS)*: Refers to third-party cloud services handling common backend functionalities, relieving developers from managing servers.
- *Function as a Service (FaaS)*: Associated with the execution of individual functions triggered by events without the need to manage underlying server infrastructure.
- *Serverless architectures*: Encompassing a wider range of cloud services beyond functions, such as managed databases and other services that abstract away infrastructure management.

So, the first obvious question is: what is serverless computing? To answer that question, first, one misunderstanding must be solved. Serverless does not mean that there are no servers involved. It is still code, and it still needs to run on a machine. Serverless computing, or FaaS, is a cloud computing model that allows developers to create and run applications without the need to manage the machines, which are typically the virtual servers in the cloud. In this model, the cloud provider manages the infrastructure, including server management, scaling, and availability.

In a serverless architecture, developers write code in the form of functions that are triggered by events such as HTTP requests, database changes, or message queues.

Note that the following section explores this event-driven architecture in more detail. These functions run in a stateless environment, where the cloud provider manages the underlying infrastructure, and the developer is only charged for the execution time of the functions. This is the main difference between building and managing application code in a traditional way or the cloud-native way using containers and serverless functions.

Traditionally, building and managing applications required developers to focus on server management, infrastructure maintenance, and scaling. This process was time-consuming and required significant resources, including money and manpower. This can be clarified with an example. In developing and deploying applications, the infrastructure that the code required to run also needed to be defined. The network needed to be thought of as well as how the various components of the application—the webserver, database, and application server, for instance—would communicate with each other and how users would approach the server with the application. The capacity of the server needed to be specified: how much CPU and memory it would need to run the code and, at the same time, perform well enough. At some stage, the application code and the infrastructure would need to merge to create the desired environment.

But there was more to do. The infrastructure had to be managed from that point onward. If the application would grow due to usage, the server would need to be expanded or the database enlarged. All of this would consume a lot of time.

Serverless computing simplifies this process, allowing developers to focus on writing code and building applications. With serverless, developers do not need to worry about infrastructure management, scaling, and availability anymore. This approach significantly reduces development time, reduces costs, and allows developers to focus on building the applications. To summarize, the benefits of using cloud-native concepts such as serverless are:

- Serverless computing is cost-effective since developers only pay for the time their code runs. With traditional cloud computing, developers pay for the entire infrastructure, regardless of the actual usage.

- Serverless functions allow for the automatic scaling of applications in response to user demand. This allows developers to build applications that can handle high traffic without worrying about infrastructure management.

- Developers can focus on writing code and building applications without worrying about infrastructure management. This approach significantly reduces development time and increases productivity. This also means that the effort of managing resources is heavily reduced. Since the cloud provider manages the infrastructure, developers can reduce the time and resources spent on maintenance.

▪ In terms of security, there's no server to scan to gather vulnerabilities and exploit them. Basically, there is always a clean server without the need to patch.

All cloud providers offer a variety of services that provide serverless functions and computing. Here are the most used ones:

▪ *AWS Lambda* is Amazon's serverless computing service that allows developers to run code in response to events. Lambda supports several programming languages, including Java, Python, Node.js, and C#. Developers can create and deploy Lambda functions in minutes, and the service automatically scales applications in response to user demand.

Lambda functions can be triggered by various events, such as changes to data in an Amazon S3 bucket, updates to a database, or incoming messages from an Amazon *Simple Queue Service (SQS)* queue. This event-driven architecture enables us to build serverless applications that respond to events in real time.

Other use cases involve, for instance, the Internet of Things (IoT), where functions execute custom business logic based on the incoming sensor data, perform real-time analytics, and trigger actions or alerts. In other words, Lambda functions can be used for a lot of different cases.

• Lambda is likely the best-known AWS serverless service, but of course, AWS has more to offer. Amazon API Gateway is a fully managed service to create, deploy, and manage APIs at any scale. It provides features like throttling, caching, and security and integrates with other AWS services such as Lambda, DynamoDB, or S3.

• AWS Step Functions is worth mentioning too. This is a serverless workflow service that allows coordination of distributed applications and microservices using visual workflows. Workflows can be designed using AWS Step Functions state machines, which support multiple AWS services like Lambda, Fargate as a serverless service to orchestrate containers, or Glue for serverless data integration.

• One more popular service is Amazon *Simple Notification Service (SNS)*. This is a fully managed messaging service that can be used to send notifications from the cloud to mobile devices, email, or HTTP endpoints. It supports multiple protocols, such as SMS, email, or HTTPS, and integrates with other AWS services like Lambda or S3.

- *Azure Functions* is Microsoft's serverless computing service. Like Lambda, it supports several programming languages, including Java, Python, Node.js, and C#. Next to the basic Functions, a variety of serverless solutions can be used in Azure. This includes Azure Durable Functions as an extension of Azure Functions, which allows the creation of stateful workflows and long-running tasks. It defines and orchestrates workflows using a declarative programming model.
  - Other services are Azure Logic Apps and Event Grid. Logic Apps is a serverless workflow orchestration service that allows the creation and running of workflows that integrate with a wide range of services, including Office 365 and Salesforce. Pre-built connectors can be used or custom connectors can be created. Azure Event Grid is a serverless event routing service that allows users to subscribe to and react to events from various Azure services and third-party sources.
- The main serverless service of GCP is Google Cloud Functions, which is comparable to Lambda and Azure Functions, enabling event-driven architectures. Moreover, GCP offers some fully managed serverless services. A good example is Cloud Run: a fully managed serverless container platform to run stateless HTTP containers in a serverless environment. Containerized applications can be deployed while Cloud Run automatically scales the application based on traffic.
  - App Engine is a fully managed serverless platform to deploy and scale applications without worrying about infrastructure. It supports several programming languages, including Python, Java, Node.js, PHP, and Go.
  - A similar service to AWS SNS is Cloud Pub/Sub. It is a fully managed messaging service that enables sending and receiving messages between independent applications. It supports multiple protocols, like HTTP, gRPC, or Pub/Sub Lite, and integrates with other GCP services like Cloud Functions or Cloud Run.
- Alibaba Cloud offers very similar services to AWS. The main serverless proposition is Function Compute, which can be used to run code in response to events. Function Compute supports several programming languages, including Java, Python, Node.js, and C#. Alibaba Cloud also offers a serverless API Gateway and message service. Where AWS offers DynamoDB as a serverless NoSQL database, Alibaba Cloud provides a service called Table Store as a fully managed NoSQL database service that provides real-time data access and storage. It can handle large amounts of data with automatic scaling and disaster recovery.

With serverless, developers can build and deploy applications without worrying about infrastructure management, scaling, and availability. AWS Lambda, Azure Functions, Google Cloud Functions, and Alibaba Cloud Function Compute are all good examples of serverless options. But the question arises of where to start; how can these serverless services be *built* and deployed into cloud environments? This will be discussed in the next section.

DEVELOPING AND PROVISIONING SERVERLESS FUNCTIONS FROM ARCHITECTURE

Developing and deploying serverless applications in the cloud requires a different approach than traditional application development. This section discusses the steps involved in developing and deploying serverless applications in the cloud, from architecture to deployment. Obviously, this process starts with defining the architecture. It is a misunderstanding that when using serverless concepts, it is not necessary to bother about the architecture. Serverless options are often managed by the cloud provider, but it is necessary to make sure that these serverless components *fit* into the architecture.

Defining the architecture can be cumbersome. Serverless architecture is event-driven, which means that the code is executed in response to events. The architecture consists of a set of functions that are triggered by events. These functions can be written in different programming languages, depending on the cloud provider. *Event-driven architecture (EDA)* is an architectural pattern that emphasizes the production, detection, consumption, and reaction to events. What are the events in this case? Events are significant occurrences or changes in the system or the environment that may require action. In EDA, services or components communicate with each other by producing or consuming events. Figure 9.1 represents an event-driven architecture:

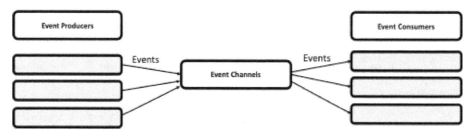

FIGURE 9.1 High-level presentation of an event-driven architecture.

EDA is often used in cloud computing environments as it provides an efficient and scalable way to build and operate complex distributed systems. But this leaves one question unanswered: what would EDA be used for? There are several use cases, such as:

- *IoT applications*: EDA is an ideal architecture for building Internet of Things (IoT) applications. IoT devices generate a vast amount of data and events, which can be challenging to manage and process in real time. With EDA, IoT devices can publish events to the cloud, which can be processed by serverless functions, triggering other events and actions in response. For example, an IoT-enabled smart home could use EDA to turn on the lights when a motion sensor detects movement or to alert the homeowner when a door is left open.

- *Financial services*: EDA is increasingly being used in the financial services industry to improve data processing and analysis, fraud detection, and real-time decision-making. Financial institutions can use EDA to consume events from multiple sources, including market data feeds, transaction systems, and customer interactions, to detect and prevent fraud, identify trading opportunities, and manage risk. A bank could use EDA to monitor transactions for suspicious activity, triggering an alert to the security team or temporarily blocking the account until the issue is resolved.

- *E-commerce*: EDA is also well-suited for e-commerce applications that require real-time processing of large volumes of data. EDA can be used to process events from multiple sources, including customer interactions, inventory systems, and payment gateways, to provide a seamless and personalized experience for customers. Think of an e-commerce site that uses EDA to trigger personalized recommendations for customers based on their browsing and purchase history or to update inventory levels and pricing in real time.

- *Healthcare*: In the healthcare industry, EDA is used to improve patient care and outcomes. EDA can be used to consume events from multiple sources, including medical devices, electronic health records, and patient interactions, to provide real-time monitoring, diagnosis, and treatment. An example is the hospital that uses EDA to monitor patients in real time, triggering alerts to medical staff when a patient's vital signs fall outside of normal parameters.

EDA is a powerful and flexible architecture pattern that is well-suited to many business cases. EDA enables organizations to process, analyze, and act on large volumes of data and events in real time, providing significant benefits for businesses and their customers. But it all starts with a well-defined architecture.

Next, a cloud provider has to be chosen. There are several cloud providers to choose from, including AWS, Azure, Google Cloud, and Alibaba Cloud. As explained in the previous section, each cloud provider has its own set of services, pricing models, and programming languages. It is important to choose a cloud provider that meets the specific requirements of the project. In fact, this is not different from anything else that is done in the cloud. With IaaS and containers, it is necessary to verify and validate if services are the right fit for the needs and requirements.

After defining the architecture and the selection of the cloud provider, it is possible to really start to create and test the functions. Each function is a piece of code that performs a specific task. Functions can be written in different programming languages, depending on the cloud provider. It is essential to keep the functions small and stateless, as this makes them easier to manage and scale. An e-commerce site can be used as an example, where the customer buys a good and automatically triggers the creation of an invoice that has to be sent to the customer. In this example, Azure Functions is used to create that function.

The code in C#—be aware that this is just an example—creates an Azure Function called CreateInvoice that is triggered by an HTTP POST request. When a customer buys a good, the e-commerce site sends an HTTP POST request to the Azure Function with the order information in the request body. The Azure Function then generates an invoice based on the order information and adds it to a queue for processing:

```
using System;
using System.IO;
using System.Net;
using System.Net.Http;
using System.Threading.Tasks;
using Microsoft.AspNetCore.Mvc;
using Microsoft.Azure.WebJobs;
using Microsoft.Extensions.Logging;
using Newtonsoft.Json;
```

```csharp
public static class CreateInvoice
{

    [FunctionName("CreateInvoice")]

    public static async Task<IActionResult> Run(

        [HttpTrigger(AuthorizationLevel.Function, "post",
        Route = null)]
        HttpRequestMessage req,
        [Queue("invoices")] IAsyncCollector<string>
        invoiceQueue,
        ILogger log)
    {

        log.LogInformation("Creating invoice...");

        // Deserialize the request body to get the order
        information
        string requestBody = await req.Content.
        ReadAsStringAsync();
        dynamic data = JsonConvert.
        DeserializeObject(requestBody);

        // Generate the invoice

        string invoice = GenerateInvoice(data);

        // Add the invoice to a queue for processing
        await invoiceQueue.AddAsync(invoice);

        log.LogInformation("Invoice created and added to the
        queue.");
```

```
        return new OkResult();



    }


    private static string GenerateInvoice(dynamic data)
    {

        // Generate the invoice using the order information
        string invoice = "Invoice for order #" + data.
        orderId + ":\n";
        invoice += "Item: " + data.itemName + "\n";
        invoice += "Price: $" + data.itemPrice + "\n";
        invoice += "Quantity: " + data.quantity + "\n";
        invoice += "Total: $" + (data.itemPrice * data.
        quantity) + "\n";
        // TODO: Add logic to send the invoice to the customer


        return invoice;



    }



}
```

Note that it is necessary to add logic to send the invoice to the customer, which could be done using Azure Logic Apps or SendGrid. This also makes clear that it is necessary to test the function in its entire setting. Testing is a critical step in the development process, as it ensures that the functions are working as intended. Each function should be tested in isolation as well as in the context of the entire application.

The final step is the actual deployment to the cloud. This involves uploading the code to the cloud provider and configuring the triggers. Triggers can be configured to respond to events such as HTTP requests, database changes, or message queues.

USING CI/CD FOR SERVERLESS DEPLOYMENTS

Typically, developers will integrate the development and deployment of functions into CI/CD pipelines. Serverless functions are designed to be highly scalable and flexible, which makes them a great choice for CI/CD pipelines. For instance, Azure DevOps can be used to deploy Azure Functions to different environments such as development, staging, and production. This can be done by creating a release pipeline that packages the Azure Functions code and deploys it to the appropriate environment. Of course, Azure DevOps can also be used to manage the CI/CD pipeline and trigger deployments automatically when code changes are made.

Testing is more convenient in CI/CD too. Before deployment, unit testing should be performed, for example, with unit testing frameworks such as NUnit or xUnit. This can help to catch bugs and ensure that serverless functions are working correctly before deploying them to production. Next, integration testing has to be executed since the function will be part of an entire environment. For this, popular tools such as Postman or Selenium can be used.

Once the functions have been deployed, it is essential to monitor them. Monitoring ensures that the functions are running correctly and that there are no issues. It is also essential to scale the functions as needed. Serverless applications are designed to scale automatically in response to user demand. This ensures that the application can handle high traffic without any issues. The final section of this chapter will extensively discuss how to monitor serverless components in cloud environments.

MANAGING MULTI-CLOUD ENVIRONMENTS WITH SERVERLESS FRAMEWORKS

This book is about multi-cloud and assumes that applications are developed, deployed, and run in multi-cloud settings. How would that work with serverless concepts? It is possible to use serverless concepts in a multi-cloud environment, although it can introduce some additional complexities and challenges.

Using a framework is a common approach to working with serverless concepts in a multi-cloud environment. A framework can help abstract away the underlying infrastructure and provide a consistent interface to deploy and manage serverless functions across multiple cloud providers. There are multiple frameworks that will help in architecting, deploying, and managing serverless concepts in multi-cloud. This section lists the most important ones:

▪ *Serverless framework*: This is a popular open-source framework that supports multiple cloud providers, including AWS, Azure, and Google Cloud. It provides a simple and consistent way to define and deploy serverless functions, as well as manage other related resources, such as APIs, databases, and event sources. An example of a multi-cloud solution using the Serverless Framework is provided in Figure 9.2:

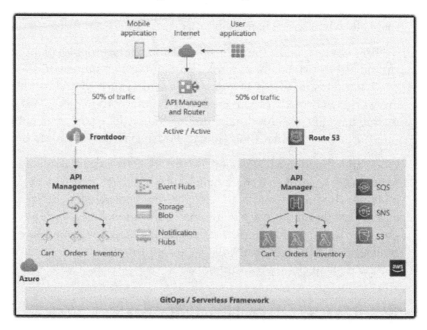

FIGURE 9.2 Example of working with serverless functions using the Serverless Framework.

The example from the Serverless Framework shows that traffic to order something in a webshop is split into two streams. Fifty percent is sent to Azure, and the other half to AWS. Orders can be made either using a mobile app or through a browser via the Internet. Both architectures use the same format; in Azure, we see Azure Functions that pick up the order from the cart and next check the inventory. In AWS Lambda, functions are used to execute the same tasks.

▧ *Open Functions as a Service (OpenFaaS)*: This is another open-source framework that supports multiple cloud providers, as well as on-premises environments. It has become very popular over the past years. It provides a platform for building and deploying serverless functions using Docker containers deploying to Kubernetes and supports a wide range of programming languages: Go, Java, Python, C#, Ruby, Node.js, and PHP. Existing microservices written with custom frameworks like Express.js, Vert.x, Flask, ASP.NET Core, FastAPI, and Django can also be brought. This makes OpenFaaS very powerful.

OpenFaaS allows for invoking functions through events from Apache Kafka, AWS *Simple Que Service (SQS)*, PostgreSQL, Cron, and *Message Queuing Telemetry Transport (MQTT)* as the standard for IoT messaging.

Figure 9.3 shows a conceptual design for deploying OpenFaaS functions. Each function is built into an immutable Docker image before being deployed:

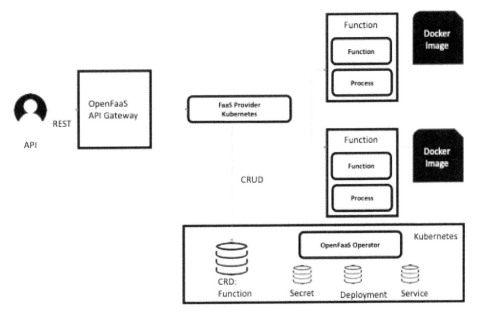

FIGURE 9.3 Conceptual design for OpenFaaS using Docker images.

■ Apache Kafka deserves a bit more explanation since it has gained popularity in defining and designing event-driven architectures in the cloud. Apache Kafka is an open-source distributed event streaming platform that provides a highly scalable, fault-tolerant, and reliable way of processing and storing real-time data streams. It was initially developed by LinkedIn and later donated to the Apache Software Foundation. Kafka is based on the publish-subscribe messaging model, where data is sent from producers to Kafka topics, and consumers subscribe to these topics to receive data. It is designed to handle large amounts of data and can process millions of messages per second. The power of Kafka lies in the fact that it can process data streams in real time, which is essential in EDA. Thanks to the increasing popularity of OpenFaasS, there is a very active community that posts developments and best practices in open-source repositories on GitHub. Find everything about OpenFaaS, including templates and scripts in various languages, at *https:// github.com/openfaas*.

Two other serverless frameworks that are worth mentioning are Apache OpenWhisk and Kubeless:

■ *Apache OpenWhisk*: Like the Serverless Framework and OpenFaaS, OpenWhisk is an open-source serverless platform that supports multiple cloud providers, including IBM Cloud, AWS, and Google Cloud. It provides a flexible and extensible architecture for building and deploying serverless functions, as well as event-driven workflows and APIs. The principle of OpenWhisk is shown in Figure 9.4:

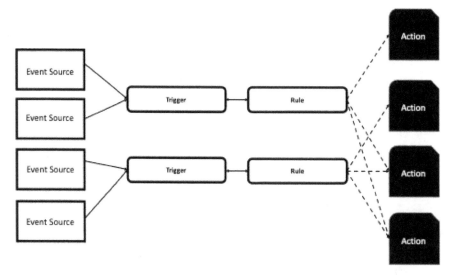

FIGURE 9.4 Architectural overview of Apache OpenWhisk.

OpenWhisk is a loosely coupled architecture that makes OpenWhisk scalable. Each layer is designed to scale independently. Actions, rules, and triggers are created and managed through REST endpoints. To invoke an action, the event source needs to call the trigger REST API. One of the building blocks in OpenWhisk is Kafka, which handles the events streaming.

Since OpenWhisk is open source, documentation and templates can be found at *https://github.com/apache/openwhisk*.

▫ *Kubeless*: This serverless framework runs on top of Kubernetes and supports multiple cloud providers, including AWS, Azure, and Google Cloud. It provides a platform for building and deploying serverless functions using Docker containers. The architecture for Kubeless is shown in Figure 9.5:

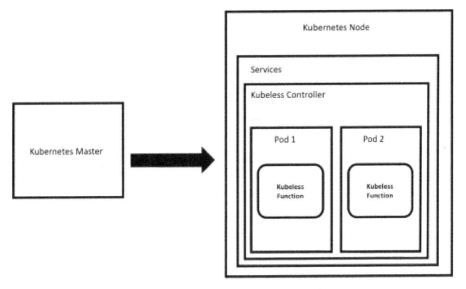

FIGURE 9.5 Architectural overview of Kubeless.

Using a framework will help abstract away the differences between different cloud providers and provide a consistent way to develop and deploy serverless functions. However, it is important to choose a framework that supports the cloud providers and programming languages that have been chosen to build and run the environments. Next, it is strongly recommended to follow best practices for secure coding, monitoring, and management. Now some of these best practices will be reviewed.

FOLLOWING BEST PRACTICES IN SERVERLESS

The serverless frameworks that were discussed in the previous section help in creating and deploying functions that are *agnostic* to a specific cloud provider, preventing a lock-in. To avoid being locked into a specific cloud provider, it is important to use cloud-agnostic serverless technologies and frameworks. This means choosing tools and services that are compatible with multiple cloud providers, such as Kubernetes, Docker, and Apache OpenWhisk.

By using cloud-agnostic tools, applications and services can easily be moved between cloud providers as required. This is enabled by common standards. Using common standards and protocols can help ensure compatibility and interoperability between cloud providers. For example, using APIs that conform to RESTful architecture principles can make it easier to integrate with different cloud providers. Also, using common languages and frameworks, such as Python or Node.js, can help ensure that serverless functions are portable across cloud providers.

Although monitoring will be discussed extensively in the final section of this chapter, the need to implement monitoring and logging that is capable of monitoring serverless functions is already emphasized. Monitoring and logging are essential to detect and diagnose issues in serverless applications. It is recommended to use a centralized monitoring and logging platform that can work across multiple cloud providers. Tools such as Prometheus, Grafana, and ELK Stack can help to monitor and troubleshoot serverless functions across different clouds.

When talking about best practices, security must be addressed, which is paramount in serverless environments. Proper security measures must be implemented, such as authentication, access control, and encryption, to protect data and applications. Best practices include secure coding and deployment and regularly scanning applications for vulnerabilities. In event-driven architecture and serverless environments, data is transmitted between services, and if proper security measures are not implemented, there is a risk of data breaches or unauthorized access. Attackers can exploit vulnerabilities in serverless functions or event streams to gain access to sensitive data or execute malicious code.

As event-driven architectures and serverless computing rely on third-party services, there is always a risk of service outages, which can cause downtime and loss of revenue. It is crucial to have a backup plan or failover strategy in place to ensure high availability. This can involve replicating data and functions across different cloud providers, implementing automated failover mechanisms, and regularly testing backup and recovery procedures.

To simplify the management of serverless applications in a multi-cloud environment, consider using a cloud management platform that can provide a unified view and control of the applications across different cloud providers. Platforms such as VMWare's CloudHealth and RightScale can help manage serverless functions, as well as other cloud services, across multiple clouds.

Serverless functions are very powerful, but deploying and managing these environments requires careful consideration and implementation of best practices. To conclude this section, these practices will be summarized briefly:

- *Set up monitoring and logging*: Serverless environments generate a lot of data, and it is important to set up monitoring and logging to track performance, identify issues, and debug problems. Cloud providers offer native services with the required capabilities. Think of AWS CloudWatch and X-Ray. In multi-cloud settings, third-party solutions to monitor and log serverless functions might be preferred.

- *Optimize function performance*: Since serverless functions are billed based on usage, it is important to optimize their performance to minimize costs. Use techniques such as function caching, code optimization, and event-driven architectures to improve performance.

- *Use security best practices*: Serverless environments can be vulnerable to security threats, so it is important to use security best practices like network isolation, encryption, and least privilege access controls. As always, *Identity and Access Management (IAM)* must be considered and implemented to manage access to serverless resources. Remember that everything in the cloud is an identity, and thus it is necessary to define what an identity is allowed to do and where it has access to it. This includes serverless functions.

- *Implement scaling strategies*: Serverless environments are designed to automatically scale based on usage, but it is still important to implement scaling strategies to ensure optimal performance. Use techniques such as autoscaling, sharding, and load balancing to ensure that the serverless functions can handle any level of traffic.

- *Test thoroughly*: Serverless environments can be complex, so it is important to thoroughly test code before deploying it to production. Cloud providers like AWS provide tools such as Lambda Layers to manage dependencies and ensure consistent environments across development, testing, and production. For testing serverless in multi-cloud environments, Selenium might be a good option. Be aware that only a few tools are mentioned. Obviously, there are many more. Selecting the right one that fits the requirements will take time.

- *Use version control*: Serverless environments can be highly dynamic, so it is important to use version control to manage changes to the code and configuration. Git and GitHub are likely the most popular tools to utilize as repositories with version control. Many companies, especially the larger ones, use Innersource, a software development approach that brings open-source development practices and methodologies inside an organization's boundaries. Innersource enables internal teams to collaborate and share code across teams and business units, using the same principles as open-source development. It is a way to promote transparency, reuse, and knowledge sharing within an organization.

When it comes to security, other best practices can be added. Think of:

- *Monorepos*: A monorepo, short for *monolithic repository*, is a software development approach where multiple projects or applications are stored within a single version control repository. In the context of serverless, a monorepo can be used to manage multiple Lambda functions or serverless applications within a single repository. This approach simplifies code sharing, dependency management, and deployment processes, as all the related serverless components are kept together.

- *Choke points or functions*: In serverless architectures, choke points or functions refer to the components or services that handle a large portion of the workload or act as the central processing hub. These functions typically have higher computational requirements or are responsible for coordinating and orchestrating other serverless functions. Choke points should be carefully designed and optimized to ensure they can handle the anticipated load without becoming a bottleneck.

- *Granule policies*: Granule policies, also known as granular access policies, refer to fine-grained permissions that can be assigned to serverless functions or resources within a serverless architecture. With granule policies, the actions that individual functions or resources can perform can be controlled and restricted. This allows for precise access control, enhancing security and minimizing the risk of unauthorized or unintended operations.

Serverless functions should be designed and optimized to execute quickly and efficiently. Techniques such as reducing unnecessary dependencies, optimizing resource utilization, and implementing caching mechanisms can help improve performance and reduce execution time.

Implementing these best practices can effectively manage serverless environments in the cloud and ensure optimal performance, scalability, and security.

However, it was promised that monitoring would be looked at in more detail as a critical component of the architecture. That is the topic of the final section.

DEEP DIVE INTO MONITORING SERVERLESS

Monitoring serverless functions in a multi-cloud environment requires a different approach than monitoring in a single-cloud environment. This section discusses the preferred approach and how to set metrics for monitoring. While working in a multi-cloud setting, a multi-cloud monitoring solution will be needed. Multi-cloud monitoring solutions such as Datadog or Dynatrace enable monitoring serverless functions across multiple clouds from a single dashboard. These solutions can provide insights into metrics like latency, error rate, and invocation count. However, whatever tool is used, the metrics must be specified first.

Custom metrics are important for monitoring serverless functions in a multi-cloud environment. Metrics provide visibility into the behavior and performance of the application, helping to identify and diagnose issues before they become critical problems. These metrics should be relevant to the application and help measure the performance and behavior of the application. For example, if the application is processing orders, the choice may be made to monitor the number of orders processed per second, the average processing time per order, and the number of failed orders. Metrics related to resource utilization might also be monitored, such as CPU usage and memory usage. The following are the most important metrics:

- Invocation metrics are used to track the number of times a serverless function is invoked, as well as the duration of each invocation. These metrics can help to identify potential bottlenecks and optimize the performance of serverless functions. Some invocation metrics to monitor include:
  - *Invocation count*: The number of times a function is invoked.
  - *Invocation duration*: The amount of time it takes for a function to complete an invocation.

- *Error rate*: The percentage of invocations that result in errors.
- *Cold start rate*: The percentage of invocations that require a cold start, which can impact the latency of the first request.

■ Resource metrics track the utilization of serverless resources such as memory, CPU, and network bandwidth. These metrics help to optimize resource usage and ensure that enough resources have been allocated to handle the workload of the application. Some resource metrics to monitor include:

- *Memory usage*: The amount of memory used by a function during an invocation.
- *CPU usage*: The amount of CPU time used by a function during an invocation.
- *Network usage*: The amount of network bandwidth used by a function during an invocation.

■ Error metrics track the occurrence and frequency of errors in serverless functions. These metrics are essential to troubleshoot issues that may be impacting the performance and reliability of the application. Some error metrics to monitor include:

- *Error rate*: The percentage of invocations that result in errors.
- *Error type*: The type of errors that occur, such as timeouts or memory errors.
- *Error message*: The specific error message associated with each error.

■ Cold start metrics track the time it takes for a serverless function to initialize and execute its first request. Cold starts can impact the latency and performance of an application, so it is important to monitor and optimize them. Some cold start metrics to monitor include:

- *Cold start time*: The amount of time it takes for a function to initialize and execute its first request.
- *Cold start frequency*: The percentage of invocations that require a cold start.

■ Cost metrics track the cost of running serverless functions. These metrics will help to identify cost optimizations and ensure that costs are not exceeding the allocated budgets. Some cost metrics to monitor include:

- *Execution time*: The amount of time a function is executed, which impacts the cost of running the function.

- *Memory usage*: The amount of memory used by a function, which impacts the cost of running the function.
- *Invocation count*: The number of times a function is invoked, which impacts the cost of running the function.

Once the key metrics that we want to monitor have been identified, the next step is to choose a monitoring solution. There are several monitoring solutions available, including open-source tools like Prometheus, commercial tools like Datadog and New Relic, and cloud-native tools like AWS CloudWatch and Google Cloud Operations. When choosing a monitoring solution, consider factors like cost, ease of use, scalability, and integration with the existing toolchain.

The metrics have been defined and the monitoring tooling has been selected. The next step is to set up metrics collection. This involves instrumenting code to emit metrics and sending those metrics to the monitoring solution. Most monitoring solutions provide libraries and SDKs for various programming languages that make it easy to install the code. For example, CloudWatch provides the CloudWatch Logs Agent for collecting logs and metrics from Amazon EC2 instances; remember that serverless does not mean that there are no servers involved, and on-premises servers, while Google Cloud Operations provides an SDK for collecting metrics from Google Cloud Functions.

In addition to monitoring metrics, it is also important to log events and errors in the application. Logging provides a record of what happened in the application, making it easier to diagnose issues and troubleshoot problems.

Alarms and alerts must be defined at this stage. Alarms and alerts notify when a metric exceeds a certain threshold or when a specific event occurs. For instance, an alarm may be set when the number of failed orders exceeds a certain threshold or when CPU usage exceeds a certain percentage.

After defining the metrics and configuring monitoring and logging, the final step is to monitor and analyze the collected metrics and logs. It is recommended to define log filters: allowing to search and filter through logs to find specific events or errors. By analyzing metrics and logs, issues can be identified and diagnosed before they become critical problems. Most monitoring solutions provide dashboards and visualization tools to make the life of an administrator easier.

Some other best practices also include using distributed tracing and log aggregation. Distributed tracing will help to track requests as they move through multiple services and clouds. This is important for identifying bottlenecks and issues in complex, distributed systems. With Log aggregation, logs can be collected from multiple sources and stored in a single location.

By implementing these best practices and setting up relevant metrics, serverless functions will be monitored in an effective way, identifying issues before they impact the application and, with that, the end user. This concludes the part about creating the interoperable multi-cloud. The next part of this book will be about securing the multi-cloud, starting with identity and access management.

CONCLUSION

This chapter discussed serverless concepts that can be used in multi-cloud. It has been explained that in serverless concepts, the user typically only pays for server resources that are really needed, such as CPUs, memory, and disk space for storage. It was discovered that serverless functions are important components in event-driven architectures where an event triggers an action that must be executed. An example is a user who buys something in a webshop: the purchase triggers the action to verify if the purchased item is in stock, next picks it up for delivery, and prepares the invoice to the customer. All these actions can be performed by functions.

Major cloud providers offer a variety of serverless options, such as Azure Functions and AWS Lambda. It was also learned that serverless concepts could be cloud-agnostic, operated across multiple cloud platforms. Serverless frameworks are a good help to guide in architecture, developing, and deploying event-driven environments in multi-cloud. OpenFaaS has gained a lot of popularity as a framework. Most frameworks use serverless functions in combination with containers.

The final part of this chapter was about setting up monitoring and logging. The required metrics to monitor serverless functions, such as invocation metrics, were examined. Defining these metrics, tracking the number of times a serverless function is invoked, as well as the duration of each invocation, is crucial in serverless and event-driven architecture. These metrics can help to identify potential bottlenecks and optimize the performance of serverless functions.

Serverless is a fast-evolving technology. As more businesses recognize the cost-saving and efficiency benefits of serverless architectures, it is expected to have increased adoption across various industries. Security was also intensively discussed as a major concern in serverless computing. Future developments might focus on enhancing security measures, such as better isolation of functions, improved access controls, and advanced threat detection mechanisms.

Remember that serverless computing doesn't exist in a vacuum. It's often used in conjunction with other technologies like containers, microservices, and machine learning.

This chapter concludes the section about cloud-native technologies. The next section will discuss implementing and managing security in multi-cloud.

KEY POINTS

- The most important point to remember is that being serverless does not mean that there are no servers involved. There is still infrastructure that must be managed. In serverless concepts, the infrastructure, such as servers and networks, is typically managed by the cloud provider.
- Serverless architecture is typically event-driven, which means that the code is executed in response to events. The architecture consists of a set of functions that are triggered by events.
- Major cloud providers offer a variety of serverless functions. Serverless frameworks will help to define the architecture and enable portability in multi-cloud settings. A popular framework is OpenFaaS, which is open-source. It provides a platform for building and deploying serverless functions using Docker containers deploying to Kubernetes and supports a wide range of programming languages. A very active community manages a vast library of templates to get started with OpenFaaS in a fast yet very comprehensive way.
- As with everything, proper monitoring is essential. Specific metrics for monitoring serverless functions in the event-driven architecture are invocation metrics, measuring how often functions are invoked and how they perform.
- Remember the first point: There is still infrastructure and, thus, resources involved. Resources invoke costs. Part of monitoring serverless functions is monitoring costs and optimizing the performance of serverless functions.

QUESTIONS

1. Name two other serverless offerings in Azure.

2. What would Apache Kafka be used for?

3. What does OpenFaaS stand for, and what is it?

4. What is measured with *cold start time*?

Answers appear in the appendix.

MANAGING ACCESS MANAGEMENT

INTRODUCTION

The previous chapters discussed various cloud infrastructure concepts with IaaS, containers, and serverless. Whatever is chosen as infrastructure, it must be kept in mind that data and applications are being hosted on this infrastructure. Not just anyone should be able to access that data and the applications. Hence, access management is necessary, which is a complicated topic in multi-cloud. This will be discussed in this chapter, exploring identities, how to define roles and permissions using role-based access, and how to control access to the resources in the cloud.

STRUCTURE

This chapter discusses the following topics:

- Exploring the basics of access management
- Using cloud tools for access management
- Understanding and working with PAM
- Creating and storing secrets
- Defining, implementing, and managing role-based access control
- Monitoring access control

EXPLORING THE BASICS OF ACCESS MANAGEMENT

Access management plays a vital role in ensuring security and protecting sensitive data across multiple cloud platforms. In such an environment where organizations utilize different cloud service providers simultaneously, managing access becomes complex due to the diverse set of resources, applications, and users involved.

Access management provides a centralized control mechanism for managing user identities, permissions, and access rights across multiple cloud platforms. It allows the enforcement of consistent security policies, ensuring that only authorized users can access specific resources or perform certain actions. Centralized control simplifies administration, reduces the risk of misconfigurations, and enhances security posture.

Users are required to authenticate themselves before accessing cloud resources, typically through username-password combinations, multifactor authentication, or even biometrics. Strong authentication mechanisms prevent unauthorized access attempts and protect against password-related attacks, such as brute-forcing or credential stuffing.

Access management typically enables fine-grained authorization and follows the principle of least privilege, granting users only the permissions necessary to perform their tasks. But access management also involves segmentation and isolation. Multi-cloud environments often involve multiple tenants or business units within an organization. Access management allows for the segmentation and isolation of resources and data between different tenants, preventing unauthorized access or data leakage between them. This isolation is critical for maintaining data confidentiality, integrity, and regulatory compliance.

It will be no surprise that access management in multi-cloud environments is complex. By adopting best practices such as using a unified identity management system, implementing a *Role-Based Access Control (RBAC)* model, and using a *Cloud Access Security Broker (CASB)*, organizations can simplify access management and reduce the risk of unauthorized access, data breaches, and compliance violations. This chapter will extensively discuss all these topics. The final section will be about monitoring access management.

First is a recap of the definition of multi-cloud: multi-cloud refers to the use of multiple cloud computing services from different vendors or providers. In a multi-cloud environment, organizations can select different cloud services based on specific requirements, such as cost, performance, availability, and geographic location. As already discussed in the first chapter of this book, multi-cloud offers several advantages, such as the ability to avoid vendor lock-in, reduce single-point-of-failure risks, and optimize workload placement. However, managing access to cloud resources across multiple clouds can be challenging, as each cloud provider has its own access management tools and policies.

Understanding Managed Identities

Before starting to explore access management, identities in the cloud must be studied. More specifically: managed identity. After all, access to resources will be provided in the clouds, and access is provided to identities. What is meant by managed identity?

A managed identity is a feature provided by cloud service providers that enables applications running in the cloud to authenticate and access cloud resources without the need for explicit credentials. In essence, a managed identity is a virtual identity associated with a specific resource, such as a virtual machine or a container instance. The cloud service provider manages the identity and provides it with credentials that can be used to access cloud resources. When an application needs to access a resource, it uses the managed identity to authenticate and access the resource.

Managed identities are important in the cloud because they help to simplify authentication and access management. Instead of managing explicit credentials for each application, managed identities can be used to grant permissions to specific resources. This reduces the risk of credential theft and makes it easier to manage access to cloud resources.

Another important benefit of managed identities is that they are automatically rotated and renewed by the cloud service provider, reducing the risk of credential theft or misuse. This helps to ensure the security and compliance of cloud resources. Later in this chapter, secrets that are related to managed identities will be studied.

Challenges in Access Management

Now to start talking about providing and managing access. The following are some of the challenges that are faced when managing access to cloud resources in a multi-cloud environment:

- Each cloud provider offers its own access management tools, which can be different in terms of syntax, semantics, and capabilities. This can make it difficult to develop consistent access policies and enforce them across multiple clouds.

- In a multi-cloud environment, user identities and access privileges need to be managed across multiple cloud providers, as well as on-premises and legacy systems. This requires a unified identity management approach that can synchronize identities, roles, and permissions across multiple clouds.

- Managing compliance and audibility across multiple clouds can be challenging, as different cloud providers may have different compliance requirements and audit trails. Organizations need to develop a unified compliance and audibility framework that can provide visibility and control across multiple clouds.

In the previous chapters, cloud-native services such as containers and serverless options were studied. Access management is a critical aspect of securing cloud-native services, as these services often involve multiple components, and the management of access to each component needs to be properly controlled.

To address these challenges, it is best to adopt best practices for multi-cloud access management. Some of them are as follows:

- First and most important of all is to use a centralized identity management system that can synchronize user identities, roles, and permissions across multiple clouds. This can help ensure consistent access policies and reduce the risk of unauthorized access.

- An RBAC model should be developed and adopted in which roles are assigned to users based on their job functions and responsibilities. This can help simplify access management and reduce the risk of human errors.

- The least privilege must be the default. Users are only granted the minimum level of access needed to perform their job duties. This will reduce the risk of data breaches and limit the scope of potential damage.

- A unified policy management system must be used that can provide a single view of access policies across multiple clouds. This is to ensure consistent access policies and to simplify compliance and auditability.

- Finally, a CASB is a security tool that can provide visibility and control over cloud usage and enforce security policies across multiple clouds. CASBs help to detect and prevent security threats, monitor compliance, and provide audibility across multiple clouds.

Basically, a CASB is a tool that supports the user in keeping the clouds secure. The next section will explore various tools that can be used for access management.

USING CLOUD TOOLS FOR ACCESS MANAGEMENT

Access management is about granting access to identities. Hence, identities also need to be managed in our cloud environments. Before getting into tools to manage identities, an important principle must be underpinned. The tools that cloud service providers offer can be used. But be aware that a cloud provider is typically only responsible for the security of the cloud, while the customer is responsible for security in the cloud, including access.

A solution to manage identities is *Identity as a Service (IDaaS)*, which is something different than CASB. The difference will be explained, making clear why both are needed. This is very helpful if a user needs to have access to multiple systems that are hosted in different environments, which is typically the case in multi-cloud.

IDaaS solutions provide a centralized platform for managing user identities, access controls, and authentication across multiple cloud services and applications. Some popular IDaaS solutions include Okta, Microsoft Azure Active Directory, and Google Cloud Identity. These solutions provide a range of features, such as *single sign-on (SSO)*, *multifactor authentication (MFA)*, and user provisioning and de-provisioning. A reference architecture for IDaaS is shown in Figure 10.1:

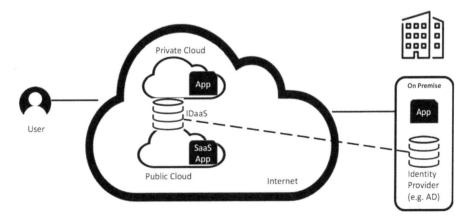

FIGURE 10.1 High-level example architecture for IDaaS using AD as identity provider.

CASB solutions, on the other hand, provide a layer of security and access control between cloud services and end-users. CASB solutions can be used to monitor and control user access to cloud services, enforce security policies, and provide visibility into user activities. Some popular CASB solutions include Netskope, McAfee Skyhigh, and Symantec CloudSOC. These solutions can provide features such as *Data Loss Prevention (DLP)*, threat detection and response, and granular access controls. A high-level reference architecture for a CASB solution is shown in Figure 10.2:

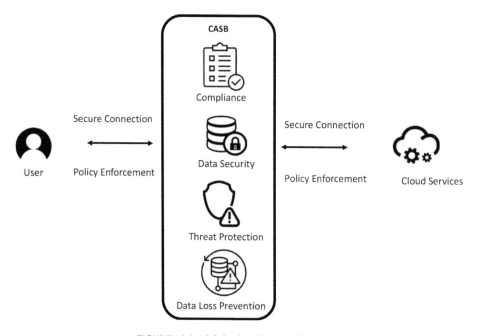

FIGURE 10.2 High-level architecture for CASB.

When it comes to multi-cloud environments, IDaaS and CASB solutions can help organizations manage user identities and access controls across multiple cloud services and applications. This can help improve security and compliance, as well as simplify the management of user access.

In addition to IDaaS and CASB solutions, there are also other cloud tools and services that can be used for access management in multi-cloud environments. For example, cloud-native *Identity and Access Management (IAM)* services such as AWS IAM and Google Cloud IAM can be used to manage access to cloud resources and services within their respective cloud environments.

These services can provide features such as fine-grained access controls, identity federation, and audit logging.

Implementing IDaaS and CASB solutions involves several key steps:

1. The first step is to define the requirements for the solution, including the scope of the cloud services and applications to be covered, the types of access controls and policies needed, and the user groups to be managed.

2. Once the requirements are defined, the next step is to evaluate different IDaaS and CASB solutions based on features, scalability, cost, and ease of integration with existing systems.

3. Next, a detailed implementation plan should be developed that includes timelines, resource requirements, and integration points with existing systems.

4. After the implementation plan is in place, the solution can be configured according to the requirements defined earlier. This involves setting up policies, access controls, and authentication mechanisms and integrating the solution with existing user directories.

5. The solution must be tested thoroughly to ensure it is working as expected. After testing is complete, the solution can be deployed in production.

Managing IDaaS and CASB solutions requires ongoing monitoring and maintenance.

Some key points to consider include:

- *Regular review of policies*: Access policies should be reviewed periodically to ensure they remain relevant and effective.

- *Monitoring user activity*: User activity should be monitored to detect and respond to suspicious behavior or policy violations.

- *Continuous improvement*: The solution should be continuously improved based on user feedback, changing requirements, and emerging threats.

- *Integration with other systems*: The solution should be integrated with other security and management systems, such as SIEM and ITSM tools, to ensure a holistic view of security and compliance across the organization.

- *Training and awareness*: Users must be trained on the use of the IDaaS and CASB solutions and made aware of policies and controls to ensure compliance and reduce risk.

This final step may look obvious, but it will take some time to train users to adopt standards in access management, especially when the principle of least privilege has been applied. In some cases, this means that users cannot do everything that they were used to. They will only be granted access to the activities they need to perform for their job. There might be exceptions where user rights have to be elevated. Moreover, in that case, full control is necessary. That is the essence of privileged access management, the topic of the next section.

UNDERSTANDING AND WORKING WITH PAM

Privileged Access Management (PAM) is a security practice that involves controlling and monitoring the access of privileged users to critical systems and data. Privileged users are individuals or accounts that have elevated access privileges, such as system administrators, database administrators, and application developers.

Before starting to explore the details of PAM, it's good to have a deeper understanding of the Zero Trust concept as a major trend in IAM and PAM. Zero Trust is a security framework that assumes no inherent trust in any user or device, whether inside or outside the network perimeter. It emphasizes the principle of *never trust, always verify*. In a Zero Trust model, every user, device, and network component must be authenticated and authorized before accessing resources, regardless of their location or network segment. IAM solutions ensure that the right individuals have appropriate access to the right resources at the right time, whereas PAM focuses specifically on managing and securing privileged accounts, which have elevated access rights and permissions.

In a Zero Trust model, IAM plays a crucial role in implementing strong authentication and authorization mechanisms. IAM solutions ensure that users are properly identified, authenticated, and authorized before accessing resources, regardless of their location or network segment. IAM helps enforce the Zero Trust principle by consistently verifying user identities and access privileges throughout the organization's infrastructure.

Zero Trust frameworks often incorporate privileged access controls as a critical component. Privileged accounts pose a higher risk due to their extensive access rights. Zero Trust principles demand that even privileged users or accounts should not be automatically trusted, and their access must be continuously verified and authorized based on contextual factors. PAM solutions provide the necessary controls to secure and manage privileged access, aligning with the Zero Trust philosophy of never assuming trust and constantly validating access.

To summarize: PAM solutions are needed to elevate the rights of users and systems in a controlled manner. Implementing PAM will reduce the risk of insider threats, external attacks, and accidental or intentional data breaches by controlling access to privileged accounts and monitoring user activity. It also is a tool to meet regulatory compliance requirements by providing audit trails and documentation of privileged user activity. With PAM in place, administrators can manage the process of granting and revoking access privileges, ensuring that access is provided only when needed and revoked promptly when no longer required.

With the increasing adoption of multi-cloud environments, PAM has become even more critical. Organizations must manage multiple cloud services and platforms, each with its own privileged access management mechanisms. Without a centralized approach to PAM, organizations face the risk of inconsistent access controls, a lack of visibility into privileged user activity, and potential security breaches.

There are several tools available for PAM in cloud environments, including:

- CASBs provide a centralized approach to managing access controls across multiple cloud services and platforms. They enable organizations to define policies and access controls and enforce them consistently across different cloud environments.
- IAM solutions support centralized management of user identities and access privileges across multiple cloud services and platforms. IAM is needed to manage access controls, enforce policies, and monitor user activity.
- Lastly, specific PAM solutions can be used, providing a centralized approach to managing privileged access across multiple cloud services and platforms. These tools help in managing and controlling access to privileged accounts, enforce policies, and monitor user activity.

There are several risks associated with PAM, including the risk of insider threats, external attacks, and data breaches. These risks can be mitigated by implementing a robust PAM program that includes access controls, monitoring of user activity, and regular audits. PAM solutions must comply with regulatory requirements and industry standards. Some of the regulations and standards include the *Payment Card Industry Data Security Standard (PCI-DSS)*, the *Health Insurance Portability and Accountability Act (HIPAA)*, and the *General Data Protection Regulation (GDPR)*. Naturally, PAM solutions must also adhere to specific organizational policies and guidelines.

All cloud providers offer their own native PAM solutions. The most common ones are as follows:

- Azure
  - *Azure Active Directory Privileged Identity Management (PIM)*: Azure PIM enables organizations to manage and control access to privileged resources in Azure AD and other Azure services. It provides just-in-time access, role-based access control, and privileged access approval workflows.
  - *Azure AD Identity Protection*: Azure AD Identity Protection provides real-time detection and remediation of identity-based risks, including compromised accounts, suspicious sign-in activity, and risk events.
  - More information about Azure identity and access solutions can be found at *https://azure.microsoft.com/en-us/products/category/identity*.

- AWS
  - *AWS Identity and Access Management (IAM)*: AWS IAM enables organizations to manage access to AWS services and resources. It provides fine-grained access control, centralized user management, and policy-based access.
  - *AWS Secrets Manager*: AWS Secrets Manager helps organizations to manage and secure secrets such as database credentials, API keys, and encryption keys. It provides automated secret rotation, encryption at rest, and fine-grained access control.
  - More information about AWS identity and access solutions can be found at *https://aws.amazon.com/iam/*.

- GCP
  - *GCP Identity and Access Management (IAM)*: GCP IAM enables organizations to manage access to GCP services and resources. It provides fine-grained access control, centralized user management, and policy-based access.

- *GCP Cloud Identity-Aware Proxy (IAP)*: GCP IAP provides secure access to applications running on GCP. It provides context-aware access control, multifactor authentication, and secure remote access.
- More information about GCP's identity and access solutions can be found at *https://cloud.google.com/iam*.

- Alibaba Cloud
  - *Resource Access Management (RAM)*: RAM is a centralized access control service that enables organizations to manage access to Alibaba Cloud resources. It provides fine-grained access control, centralized user management, and policy-based access.
  - More information about Alibaba Cloud's identity and access solutions can be found at *https://www.alibabacloud.com/product/identity-as-a-service-idaas*.

In addition to these native PAM solutions, there are also third-party PAM solutions available for Azure, AWS, and GCP, such as CyberArk, BeyondTrust, and Thycotic. These solutions offer more advanced features and functionality for managing privileged access in the cloud.

PRIVILEGED SESSION AND PRIVILEGED BEHAVIOR ANALYTICS

IAM, PAM, and Zero Trust have been discussed, but there are two more concepts that will help in managing identities and access: *Privileged Session Management (PSM)* and *Privileged Behavior Analytics (PBA)*.

PSM focuses on securing and monitoring privileged user sessions when accessing critical systems, applications, or sensitive data. The main components of PSM are:

- *Secure access*: PSM solutions enforce secure access controls by acting as intermediaries between privileged users and target systems. They establish a secure session through a proxy or gateway, often employing techniques like protocol isolation, session isolation, and application-level encryption. This ensures that privileged access is protected against interception, unauthorized access, or tampering.
- *Just-in-Time privilege*: PSM implements the concept of just-in-time privilege, where users are granted temporary elevated access only for the duration of their specific task or session. This minimizes the exposure of

privileged credentials and reduces the risk of misuse or compromise of privileged accounts.

▓ *Session monitoring and recording*: PSM solutions enable comprehensive monitoring and recording of privileged sessions. They capture detailed logs of all activities performed during the session, including commands executed, files accessed, and changes made. Session recordings serve as valuable audit trails for forensic analysis, compliance reporting, and post-incident investigations.

▓ *Session termination and access revocation*: PSM solutions facilitate the automatic termination of privileged sessions once the authorized task is completed or after a predefined period of inactivity. This ensures that access is promptly revoked, reducing the risk of unauthorized access to critical resources.

With PBA, the behavior and activities of privileged users can be analyzed to detect anomalous or suspicious actions that may indicate insider threats, compromised accounts, or malicious activities. PBA solutions leverage machine learning algorithms and advanced analytics techniques to identify patterns and deviations from normal privileged user behavior. Typically, PBA involves the following components:

▓ *Baseline profiling*: PBA solutions establish a baseline profile of normal privileged user behavior by analyzing historical data, including user activity, access patterns, and usage patterns. This baseline is continuously updated and refined over time.

▓ *Anomaly detection*: PBA solutions monitor privileged user activities in real time and compare them against the established baseline. They look for deviations, outliers, or unusual behavior that may indicate potential security threats, such as unusual access attempts, unauthorized system changes, or suspicious data transfers.

▓ *Risk scoring and alerts*: PBA solutions assign risk scores to detected anomalies based on their severity and contextual factors. High-risk activities trigger alerts or notifications to security teams, enabling them to investigate and respond to potential security incidents promptly.

▓ *Behavioral profiling and adaptive learning*: PBA solutions employ adaptive learning techniques to enhance the accuracy of anomaly detection. They continuously update behavioral profiles based on new data and feedback, adapting to evolving privileged user behavior patterns and improving the effectiveness of threat detection.

By integrating PSM and PBA into the PAM solution, the security posture can be strengthened by securing privileged sessions, reducing the attack surface, and proactively detecting and mitigating potential insider threats or unauthorized activities by privileged users. These components work together to provide granular control, real-time monitoring, and behavior-based insights into privileged access, ensuring the confidentiality, integrity, and accountability of critical systems and data.

So far, identities and granting access to these identities in a controlled way has been discussed. To ensure that identities and access to these identities are protected, secrets must be attached to these identities and their access tokens. The next section will examine how to implement secrets and keys.

CREATING AND STORING SECRETS

One of the most important aspects of security in cloud computing is managing access to resources. This requires careful management of secrets—any sensitive information such as passwords, API keys, or access tokens that can grant access to systems or services.

Here is a recap of what was learned so far. Access management is about controlling who can access cloud resources and what actions they can perform on those resources. To enable this, secrets and keys are needed to authenticate users and applications, encrypt data in transit and at rest, and establish secure connections between cloud resources. If secrets and keys are not properly managed, it can lead to unauthorized access to sensitive information, data breaches, and other security incidents.

For example, if a user's password is compromised, an attacker could use that password to gain access to cloud resources and potentially steal sensitive data. Similarly, if encryption keys are not properly protected, an attacker could potentially decrypt sensitive data that is being transmitted or stored in the cloud.

Proper secrets and key management help prevent these types of security incidents by ensuring that secrets are properly protected and access is tightly controlled. This includes generating keys securely, rotating them on a regular basis, and properly destroying them when they are no longer needed. It also involves monitoring access to secrets and auditing usage to identify potential security issues. Most important: don't store secrets in code repositories. This common mistake often leads to security breaches.

The following sections will briefly discuss the various key management offerings of AWS, Azure, GCP, and Alibaba Cloud. Most services include the creation of keys, adding cryptographic parameters, storing the keys in a protected vault, and using automation to rotate the keys in regular intervals.

Although the focus will be on the native tools to store secrets in the various clouds, Hashicorp Vault must be mentioned as a widely used open-source tool for secrets management that can be used across various platforms, including AWS, Azure, GCP, and Alibaba Cloud.

Managing Secrets and Keys in AWS and Azure

In AWS, there are a few different services that can be used for managing secrets. The most commonly used service to store and manage secrets is AWS Secrets Manager. This service also automatically rotates secrets on a regular basis.

To use AWS Secrets Manager, the following steps must be taken:

1. A secret can be created using the AWS Management Console, AWS CLI, or AWS SDK. When creating a secret, the type of secret needs to be specified, for instance, a database password. Next, the value of the secret must be specified and any additional metadata that should be associated with the secret.

2. Now access can be granted to the secret. Controlling access to secrets is done through AWS *Identity and Access Management (IAM)* policies. It is recommended to create policies that grant specific permissions to users or roles, such as the ability to retrieve a secret or rotate it.

3. AWS Secrets Manager can automatically rotate secrets on a schedule that the user defines. Scheduling is the best practice, but secrets can also be manually rotated using the AWS Management Console, AWS CLI, or AWS SDK.

   The code is an example in Python to demonstrate how we create a secret using a Boto3 SDK. It should be noted that Boto3 is used since it makes it easy to integrate a Python application, library, or script with AWS services:

```
import boto3

from botocore.exceptions import ClientError
```

```
def create_secret(secret_name, secret_value):
    """

    Creates a new secret in AWS Secrets Manager.


    :param secret_name: The name of the secret.

    :param secret_value: The value of the secret.

    :return: The ARN of the created secret.
    """
    # Create a Secrets Manager client
    client = boto3.client('secretsmanager')


    # Create the secret
    try:
        response = client.create_secret(
            Name=secret_name,
            SecretString=secret_value
        )

        return response['ARN']
    except ClientError as e:
        print(f"Error creating secret: {e}")
        raise
```

Now the function can be called with the desired name and value of the secret:

```
arn = create_secret('my-secret', 'my-secret-value')
print(f"Created secret with ARN: {arn}")
```

This will create a new secret in AWS Secrets Manager with the name my-secret and value my-secret-value and return the ARN of the created secret. It should be kept in mind that the appropriate IAM permissions will be needed to create secrets in AWS Secrets Manager in order to use this code.

More information on AWS Secrets Manager can be found at *https://aws. amazon.com/secrets-manager/*.

The way of working in Azure is comparable to the example that was discussed in AWS. The most commonly used service for storing and managing secrets is Azure Key Vault. Like AWS Secrets Manager, Key Vault automatically rotates secrets on a regular basis.

4. Creating a secret in Key Vault is done through the Azure Portal, Azure CLI, or by using Azure PowerShell. A name, subscription, resource group, and location will need to be specified. Next, the type of secret is specified, the value of the secret, and any additional metadata that should be associated with the secret.

The PowerShell code will look like this:

```
# Connect to Azure using Azure PowerShell module
Connect-AzAccount


# Define the name of the Key Vault and the secret to be
created

$keyVaultName = "my-key-vault"

$secretName = "my-secret"

$secretValue = "my-secret-value"


# Get the Key Vault

$keyVault = Get-AzKeyVault -VaultName $keyVaultName


# Create the secret

$secret = Set-AzKeyVaultSecret -VaultName $keyVaultName -Name

$secretName -SecretValue $secretValue


# Output the secret ID

Write-Output "Created secret with ID $($secret.id)"
```

It is only necessary to replace the values for `$keyVaultName`, `$secret-Name`, and `$secretValue` with the desired values and then run the script. The script will connect to Azure using the Azure PowerShell module, get the key vault with the specified name, create a new secret with the specified name and value, and then output the ID of the created secret.

5. Controlling access to secrets is done through *Azure Active Directory (AAD)* policies.

6. Azure Key Vault will automatically rotate secrets on a schedule that the user defines. There is an option to do this manually, but it is strongly advised to automate this as it will increase the level of security.

One remark: the script assumes that the Key Vault already exists, so do make sure that a Key Vault is available to use:

```
az keyvault create --name <key_vault_name> --resource-group
<resource_group_name> --location <location>
```

More information on the service Azure Key Vault can be found at *https://azure.microsoft.com/en-us/products/key-vault*.

Managing Secrets and Keys in GCP and Alibaba Cloud

In GCP, the primary service used for managing secrets is Google Cloud *Key Management Service (KMS)*. Google Cloud KMS allows the creation and management of cryptographic keys for use in encrypting data, as well as storing and managing secrets. To manage secrets in GCP, the follow steps should be taken:

1. First, a key ring, a container for cryptographic keys, must be created, which can be used to encrypt and decrypt data. A key ring is created using the GCP console or the Cloud SDK.

2. Within a key ring, one or more keys can be created. A key is a named object that represents a cryptographic key. A key can be created using the GCP console or the Cloud SDK. This may sound more complex than in AWS and Azure, but it is not very hard, as will be learned in the example. The code using the GCP SDK is written in Python. It will create a key ring and then create a key in KMS:

```
from google.cloud import kms_v1

# Set the parameters for the new key ring and key

project_id = "your-project-id"

location_id = "us-central1" key_ring_id = "my-key-ring" key_
id = "my-key"

purpose = kms_v1.CryptoKey.CryptoKeyPurpose.ENCRYPT_DECRYPT
```

```
# Create a new key ring

client = kms_v1.KeyManagementServiceClient()

key_ring_parent = f"projects/{project_id}/locations/
{location_id}"

key_ring = client.create_key_ring(request={"parent": key_
ring_ parent, "key_ring_id": key_ring_id})


# Create a new key in the key ring
key_parent = f"{key_ring.name}/cryptoKeys"

key = client.create_crypto_key(request={"parent": key_parent,
"crypto_key_id": key_id, "purpose": purpose})


# Print the details of the new key

print(f"Created key {key.name} with purpose {key.purpose}")
```

The placeholders your-project-id, my-key-ring, and my-key must be replaced with the desired values. Note that the appropriate permissions are necessary to create key rings and keys in KMS. This code creates a new key ring in the specified project and location and then creates a new key in the key ring with the specified ID and purpose (in this case, ENCRYPT_DECRYPT). Finally, it prints the details of the new key, including its name and purpose.

3. Once a key has been created, it can be used to encrypt and decrypt secrets. When creating a secret, the key to use for encryption must be specified.

4. Access to secrets is controlled by using *Identity and Access Management (IAM)* policies.

5. Google Cloud KMS can automatically rotate secrets on a schedule. These schedules should also be defined as part of the process. An alternative to KMS is Google Secret Manager.

It is important to ensure that the GCP IAM policies are properly configured to control access to secrets. Additionally, the cryptographic keys must be properly protected and a process must be in place for rotating keys on a regular basis.

More information on GCP KMS can be found at *https://cloud.google.com/ security-key-management*.

Last is an examination of Alibaba Cloud. Like GCP, the primary service used for managing secrets is Alibaba Cloud KMS. To manage secrets in Alibaba Cloud, the follow steps must be taken, that by now will be recognized:

1. Create a key using the Alibaba Cloud console or API. When creating a key, specify the type of key and the key size.

2. Once the key has been created, it can be used to encrypt and decrypt secrets using the Alibaba Cloud console or API.

3. Access is controlled through policies in *Resource Access Management (RAM)*.

4. Alibaba Cloud KMS can automatically rotate secrets on a schedule.

Please note that in Alibaba Cloud, KMS is mainly used for key management rather than secrets. A more suitable service for managing secrets would be Alibaba Cloud *Resource Access Management (RAM)*.

More information about Alibaba Cloud's KMS can be found at *https://www. alibabacloud.com/product/kms*.

Avoiding Pitfalls in Managing Secrets and Keys

Now that a good overview has been given of the various services that cloud providers offer, one must also realize that managing secrets in the cloud can be a complex task. There are several common pitfalls that organizations should be aware of to ensure that their secrets are properly managed and protected.

One of the most critical aspects of managing secrets is ensuring that access to those secrets is properly controlled. Organizations should use IAM policies or similar tools to ensure that only authorized users or systems can access secrets. Failure to properly control access can result in unauthorized access to sensitive information. However, there is much more that is needed to do to keep secrets really secrets.

Secrets should be encrypted both in transit and at rest to protect against interception and unauthorized access. It is important to ensure that encryption is properly implemented and that keys are properly protected. Weak encryption can allow attackers to easily access secrets, even if access controls are properly configured. It is all part of proper key management. Keys should be generated securely, rotated on a regular basis, and properly destroyed when no longer needed. It has been stressed a couple of times that rules must be defined to rotate secrets and keys automatically. Secrets should be rotated on a regular basis to reduce the risk of unauthorized access. Failure to properly rotate secrets can result in an attacker being able to access a secret for an extended period, even if access controls are properly configured.

The various services that cloud providers offer have been discussed. These services do not take away the responsibility of having processes in place for key management. Many cloud services offer default configurations that may not be appropriate for all use cases. It is important to carefully review and customize default configurations to ensure that they meet the specific needs of the organization.

Be aware that storing and managing keys is an important part of audit controls. Monitoring and auditing are critical components of any secret management strategy. Organizations should monitor access to secrets and audit usage to identify potential security issues. This will be talked about extensively in the final section of this chapter. But first, there is one more task to fulfill as administrators: a proper RBAC model must be created.

DEFINING, IMPLEMENTING, AND MANAGING ROLE BASED ACCESS CONTROL

Role-Based Access Control (RBAC) is a widely used access control mechanism that restricts system access based on the roles or positions of individual users within an organization. RBAC helps organizations to manage access to critical resources, applications, and systems, thus preventing unauthorized access and reducing the risk of data breaches. It is an essential step in identity and access management.

RBAC defines the roles, privileges, and permissions that are associated with each role in an organization. These roles are then assigned to users, who are granted access to the resources and applications that they need to perform their jobs. RBAC typically involves three components: roles, permissions, and users. Roles are defined based on the job functions, positions, or responsibilities within the organization. Permissions are the actions that users are allowed to perform, and users are the individuals who are assigned to specific roles.

Implementing RBAC involves several steps, including identifying the roles and permissions needed for each role, defining the rules and policies that govern access control, and implementing the RBAC model into the organization's systems and applications. The following steps can be followed to implement RBAC:

1. Identify the roles that are necessary for the organization and define the job functions and responsibilities associated with each role.

2. Define the permissions that are required for each role, including the actions that users are allowed to perform.

3. Assign roles to users based on their job functions and responsibilities.

4. Implement the RBAC model into the organization's systems and applications, including access control policies and rules.

Be aware that RBAC policies can vary greatly among different cloud providers. Also, RBAC policies can be applied at different levels, including at the management group, subscription, resource group, and resource levels.

Once the model has been implemented, user activity must be monitored, access rights reviewed, and access policies updated as needed. This includes managing user accounts, reviewing user activity logs, and modifying user access permissions as necessary. The principle of least privilege should always be followed. Of course, it's crucial to perform continuous reviews and updates of roles and permissions as a part of security hygiene.

Least privilege is the concept of granting users and applications only the minimum level of access necessary to perform their required functions. In a multi-cloud environment, where data and applications are distributed across multiple clouds and providers, applying the principle of least privilege is essential to ensure the security and integrity of the organization's data and resources.

Multi-cloud environments can be complex and challenging to manage, and the risk of security breaches and data loss is high. Access controls are essential to limit the exposure of sensitive data and applications to unauthorized access, and the principle of least privilege provides an effective approach to achieving this goal. By granting users and applications only the permissions they need, the risk of malicious activities and unauthorized access is significantly reduced.

Implementing the least privilege in multi-cloud environments requires careful planning and attention to detail. It involves identifying and documenting the different levels of access required by users and applications and defining policies and procedures for granting and revoking access. Additionally, it involves regularly monitoring and reviewing access logs to ensure compliance and identify any potential security threats.

To ensure that the RBAC model and least privilege are safeguarded, follow these steps:

1. Monitor user activity to identify any potential security risks or unauthorized access attempts.

2. Regularly review user access rights and permissions to ensure that they are appropriate for the user's job function and responsibilities.

3. Update access policies as needed to reflect changes in the organization's structure, job functions, or security requirements.

RBAC is an effective access control mechanism that can help organizations to manage access to critical resources, applications, and systems. Defining, implementing, and managing RBAC involves identifying roles and permissions, defining access control policies and rules, and monitoring user activity to ensure that access rights are appropriate and secure. However, as has been concluded, proper monitoring is critical. That is the topic of the last section.

MONITORING ACCESS CONTROL

Multi-cloud environments can present unique challenges when it comes to monitoring access control. With multiple cloud providers, each with its own access control mechanisms, it can be difficult to get a comprehensive view of who has access to what resources. It requires a comprehensive approach that includes centralized IAM systems, RBAC, access control logging and monitoring, regular policy reviews, and automation. By implementing these best practices, organizations can ensure that access to critical resources is properly managed and monitored and that security risks are identified and addressed in a timely manner.

First, keys and secrets must be monitored. Keys and secrets are used to authenticate and authorize access to resources, applications, and services in the cloud. As such, monitoring and securing these keys and secrets is critical to maintaining the security of the entire environment. Some specific requirements for monitoring keys and secrets in multi-cloud environments include:

- Implementing a centralized key and secret management system can help to ensure that keys and secrets are properly managed and secured across all cloud environments. This can also provide a single point of control for monitoring and auditing access to keys and secrets.

- Keys and secrets should be encrypted and stored securely using industry-standard encryption algorithms and secure storage systems. This will prevent unauthorized access and ensure that keys and secrets are only accessible to authorized users.

- Access to keys and secrets should be controlled and monitored, with access granted only to authorized users and roles. The principle of least privilege must be adhered to. Access rights may be elevated following a strict process and using PAM. Access should be monitored and audited to ensure that any unauthorized access attempts are quickly detected and addressed.

- Keys and secrets should be rotated regularly, with new keys and secrets generated and old ones revoked or retired. Unauthorized access will be avoided by ensuring that keys and secrets are not compromised due to long-term use.

- Keys and secrets management in multi-cloud environments should comply with regulatory and compliance requirements, such as PCI-DSS, HIPAA, and GDPR. This can help to ensure that the organization meets its legal and regulatory obligations.

By implementing these requirements, organizations can ensure that keys and secrets are properly secured and managed across all cloud environments. But this is only about the keys and secrets. Obviously, resources and access to these resources themselves must be monitored.

Implementing a centralized IAM system that can manage access across multiple cloud environments can help to simplify access control and reduce the risk of unauthorized access. This can also provide a single point of control for monitoring access across all cloud environments. Other topics to be addressed are:

- RBAC can help to ensure that users have only the necessary access permissions for their job functions and responsibilities.

▪ Implementing logging and monitoring of access control events will help to detect and respond to unauthorized access attempts. Any security incidents must be quickly identified and addressed.

▪ Regularly reviewing access policies and permissions can help to ensure that they are up-to-date and aligned with the organization's security policies and compliance requirements.

▪ It is strongly recommended to simplify access control through automation. For example, automation can be used to automatically provision and de-provision access permissions, ensuring that access is properly managed and controlled.

What is needed to manage and monitor access control? The various tools have already been discussed with IAM, PAM, and CASB solutions. Additionally, organizations implement SIEM solutions: Security Information and Event Management. SIEM systems are designed to collect, analyze, and correlate security events and alerts across multiple sources, including cloud services. They can provide visibility into access control events and help detect and respond to security incidents.

While SIEM systems can provide valuable insights into access control events in multi-cloud environments, they may not be the best option for managing access control directly. SIEM systems are typically used for security monitoring and incident response and may not provide the granular control required for access management. Instead, IAM and PAM solutions are better suited for managing access control in multi-cloud environments.

Monitoring has been discussed a lot in the past chapters. Using centralized systems for this is almost a necessity in multi-cloud environments. A popular word to describe this centralized monitoring is a *single pane of glass view*. In multi-cloud, this single pane has become crucial to have one integrated view of all the resources in various clouds. That is the topic of the next chapter.

CONCLUSION

This chapter illustrated that access management in multi-cloud environments can be challenging. Proper access management is crucial for ensuring the security of sensitive data and resources. It requires the use of various tools and techniques, including IAM, PAM, and CASB.

IAM is essential for managing user identities and controlling access to cloud resources. IAM enables organizations to define user roles and permissions and ensure that access is granted only to authorized users. PAM is important for managing access to administrative accounts and other high-risk areas. PAM enables organizations to enforce tighter controls around privileged access, reducing the risk of data breaches. In addition, organizations should use secrets and keys to further secure access to cloud resources. Secrets and keys can be used to authenticate users, applications, and devices accessing cloud resources. This helps to prevent unauthorized access and reduce the risk of data breaches.

Cloud Access Security Broker (CASB) is a security solution that sits between an organization's on-premises infrastructure and cloud provider to provide visibility, control, and protection of cloud resources. CASB solutions can monitor access and usage of cloud resources and enforce policies to ensure compliance with security regulations.

The final section was about monitoring, which is critical to detect and respond to security incidents. Organizations must monitor access to cloud resources to ensure that only authorized users are accessing them. This includes tracking access attempts, identifying failed login attempts and suspicious activity, and analyzing access logs for potential security incidents.

KEY POINTS

- Access management in multi-cloud environments is complex but critical for ensuring the security and integrity of cloud resources. Organizations should adopt best practices such as using a unified identity management system, implementing a *Role-Based Access Control (RBAC)* Model, and using a *Cloud Access Security Broker (CASB)*.

- Be aware that access control is a critical component in audits. Access management should comply with regulatory and compliance requirements, such as PCI-DSS, HIPAA, and GDPR.

- The least privilege must be the default. Access rights might be elevated using a strict process with *Privileged Access Management (PAM)*. Privileged users are individuals or accounts that have elevated access privileges, such as system administrators, database administrators, and application developers.

- One of the most important aspects of security in cloud computing is managing access to resources. This requires careful management of secrets—any sensitive information such as passwords, API keys, or access tokens that can grant access to systems or services. Cloud providers offer services for key management that must be explored and implemented to protect resources in cloud environments.

- The best practice is to have keys automatically rotated. All key management offerings of cloud providers include automatic rotation of keys and secrets.

- Organizations must develop an RBAC, including the definition of roles and permissions that are needed for each role.

QUESTIONS

1. What are the typical services that are captured in a CASB system?

2. What does the least privilege mean?

3. What are keys and secrets used for?

Answers appear in the appendix.

Managing Security

INTRODUCTION

When environments, data, and apps are distributed in various clouds, including on-premises-private clouds, security must be in place. Security is not on the menu, though. It is either done or not, but there is nothing in between. With distributed environments, frameworks must be used that cover the various cloud technologies and tools that can handle various clouds, and a single pane glass of view is needed to keep track of it all. That is the topic of this chapter.

STRUCTURE

This chapter discusses the following topics:

- Working with cloud security frameworks
- Choosing the security tools
- Managing security through one lens
- Keeping track and up to date with security trends

WORKING WITH CLOUD SECURITY FRAMEWORKS

As demonstrated in this book, organizations are increasingly adopting cloud computing to harness its scalability, flexibility, and cost-efficiency. As businesses evolve, they often find themselves relying on multiple cloud service providers simultaneously, giving rise to the concept of a multi-cloud environment. While this approach offers numerous advantages, it also introduces unique security challenges that must be effectively managed. With multiple cloud providers involved, each with its own security frameworks and practices, ensuring a cohesive and robust security posture becomes a complex task.

Each cloud service provider has its own set of security tools, configurations, and access controls, making it challenging to establish a unified security strategy. Moreover, ensuring compliance with various regulatory requirements across different cloud platforms adds another layer of complexity, not to mention the criticality of the secure exchange of data and information between different cloud providers and on-premises systems. Establishing secure communication channels and implementing encryption mechanisms becomes crucial to protect sensitive data from unauthorized access and interception.

Furthermore, managing identity and access control across multiple clouds poses a significant challenge. Maintaining a central identity management system that seamlessly integrates with various cloud platforms while maintaining strong authentication and authorization mechanisms becomes essential to prevent unauthorized access and data breaches.

Additionally, monitoring and detecting security incidents across multiple clouds can be intricate. The ability to have centralized visibility and threat intelligence across the entire multi-cloud environment is crucial for early detection and prompt response to potential security breaches. Security frameworks will help in setting up comprehensive security management.

Before diving into the cloud security frameworks, it is necessary to learn what the most common frameworks are that can or even must be used in the cloud. Moreover, just as important is the question: why is it necessary to adhere to the principles and guidelines in these frameworks? The most common frameworks are:

- *Cloud Security Alliance (CSA) security guidance*: CSA provides a comprehensive framework for secure cloud computing. It covers a wide range of security domains, including governance, risk management, data protection, and compliance.

- *National Institute of Standards and Technology (NIST) cybersecurity framework*: NIST's framework provides guidelines for managing and improving cybersecurity risk. While not specific to cloud computing, it can be applied to secure cloud environments effectively.

- *ISO/IEC 27001*: This international standard outlines the requirements for establishing, implementing, maintaining, and continually improving an *Information Security Management System (ISMS)*. It includes specific controls and practices for cloud security.

- *Payment Card Industry Data Security Standard (PCI DSS)*: PCI DSS is a set of security standards designed to protect credit card data. It includes requirements for securing cardholder data in cloud environments that handle payment card information.

- *FedRAMP: The Federal Risk and Authorization Management Program (FedRAMP)* is a U.S. government program that provides a standardized approach to security assessment, authorization, and continuous monitoring of cloud services. It is primarily used for federal agency cloud deployments.

- *CIS controls:* The *Center for Internet Security (CIS)* controls provide a set of best practices for cybersecurity. While not specific to the cloud, it includes guidelines that can be applied to secure cloud environments effectively.

- *GDPR*: The *General Data Protection Regulation (GDPR)* is a European Union regulation that sets rules for the protection of personal data. It includes requirements for the secure processing and storage of data in the cloud.

These frameworks and standards provide organizations with guidelines, controls, and best practices to ensure the security of cloud computing environments. The choice of framework depends on factors such as industry regulations, compliance requirements, and specific security needs of the organization. Failing to be compliant with mandatory security guidelines and frameworks will definitively lead to severe consequences. These consequences can vary depending on the specific regulations and the jurisdiction in which the organization operates. Think of:

- Noncompliance with security regulations can result in legal penalties, fines, or sanctions imposed by regulatory bodies or government agencies. The severity of the penalties can vary, but they can be substantial, especially for major breaches or repeated noncompliance.

- Failure to comply with security regulations can expose organizations to lawsuits from affected individuals, customers, or business partners. This can lead to legal damages, settlements, or other financial liabilities. The consequences can be severe. Think of data breaches, fines, penalties, and lawsuits, but also disruption of business and loss of market access. As an example, the European Union's GDPR requires companies to meet certain data protection standards to operate within the EU. Noncompliant companies may face restrictions in accessing the EU market, limiting their growth opportunities and putting them at a competitive disadvantage compared to compliant competitors.

- Security breaches or noncompliance can result in significant reputational damage to an organization. News of a breach or failure to protect sensitive data can erode customer trust, lead to loss of business, and damage the company's brand image.

- Noncompliance with security regulations can disqualify organizations from participating in certain contracts, partnerships, or business opportunities. Many clients and partners require proof of compliance as a prerequisite for engagement.

- In the event of noncompliance, organizations may incur significant costs to investigate and address the issues, implement security improvements, and demonstrate compliance. This can involve investing in new technologies, hiring external experts, or conducting audits.

- Failure to comply with security regulations can result in increased regulatory scrutiny, including audits and inspections. This can be a time-consuming and resource-intensive process, diverting attention and resources from core business operations.

Considering all of this, it is highly recommended to understand and adhere to the relevant security regulations and compliance requirements to mitigate these risks. Having said that, it is apparent that this is not an easy task. How can one determine to what frameworks the organization should adhere, and how should the guidelines from the relevant frameworks be implemented?

First, it is necessary to analyze what frameworks are relevant by following these crucial steps:

1. The first step is to identify the relevant industry-specific regulations and legal requirements that the organization must comply with. For example, if our organization handles payment card information, PCI DSS compliance is necessary. Similarly, if our organization operates in the healthcare industry, HIPAA compliance will almost certainly be applicable. This step helps narrow down the frameworks that align with the industry's specific requirements.

2. Next, the security needs, objectives, and risk tolerance have to be evaluated. Consider factors such as the type of data handled, the cloud infrastructure, the sensitivity of the information, and also the security budget. This assessment will help to understand the unique security requirements and prioritize the frameworks that align with the organization's goals. Be careful, though, with the budget allocation: security is not something that can be done afterward. It has to be top of mind, and that will require investments. Breaches are way more expensive than taking accurate security measures.

3. The best practices in the organization's industry should be considered. Hence, industry best practices and standards must be reviewed to identify frameworks that are widely accepted and recognized. Look for frameworks developed by reputable organizations such as the CSA, NIST, or ISO. Figure 11.1 shows an overview of a lot of security and compliance frameworks which cloud providers such as AWS and Azure are compliant with. In this case, the frameworks that Azure listed to be compliant with are shown. The differences between global standards, industry standards, and national standards such as U.S. Government and more regional frameworks can be observed.

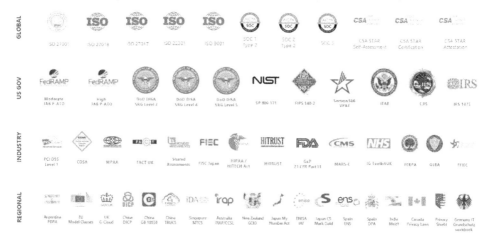

FIGURE 11.1 Compliance framework overview for Azure.

For an overview of the compliance programs of the various providers, visit *https://aws.amazon.com/compliance/programs/* for AWS, *https://azure.microsoft.com/en-us/explore/trusted-cloud/compliance* for Azure, *https://cloud.google.com/security/compliance* for GCP, and *https://www.alibabacloud.com/trust-center* for Alibaba Cloud.

The next and final chapter of this book will study compliance in the cloud in more detail, but here is a brief overview:

- We cannot be all specialists. It is advised to consult with security and compliance professionals who have expertise in the industry. They can provide valuable insights and guidance based on their knowledge and experience. These professionals can help to understand the specific frameworks that are commonly adopted in the industry and can offer recommendations based on the organization's needs.

- Assess the regulatory compliance requirements for the organization. Determine the specific controls, certifications, or attestations needed to meet those requirements. This evaluation will help to identify frameworks that provide the necessary controls and guidelines for compliance.

- Based on the previous steps, prioritize the frameworks that align with the industry requirements, organizational needs, and compliance obligations. Consider the maturity, comprehensiveness, and practicality of each framework. It may be necessary to adopt multiple frameworks to address various aspects of security.

- Keep in mind that the security landscape and regulatory environment evolve over time and at a mind-blowing pace. Regularly review the framework selection to ensure they remain up to date with the latest industry practices and regulations. Periodically reassess the organization's needs and revise the framework selection as necessary.

Remember that selecting the appropriate frameworks requires careful consideration of the specific organizational context and compliance obligations. It is necessary to involve relevant stakeholders, such as IT, legal, and compliance teams, in the decision-making process to ensure a comprehensive and well-informed approach.

Example of Implementing CIS Guidelines for Azure

The relevant frameworks have been selected, but that is only half of the work. Now the guidelines coming from these frameworks need to be implemented. Taking CIS as an example, CIS separates the controls into three categories: basic, foundational, and organizational, as shown in Figure 11.2:

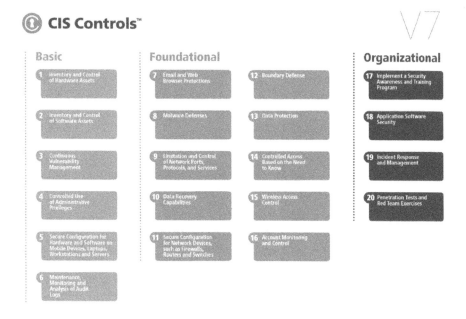

FIGURE 11.2 The CIS Framework, version 7 (taken from *https://www.cisecurity.org/insights/blog/cis-controls-version-7-whats-old-whats-new*).

Next, the CIS framework provides a set of security controls and recommendations per platform to enhance the security posture of the Azure infrastructure. For this, CIS Benchmarks are used. Some key steps and best practices for implementing the CIS benchmark guidelines in Azure would, for example, include:

- Identity and Access Management (IAM):
  - Enforce strong password policies and multi-factor authentication (MFA) for user accounts.
  - Implement *Azure Active Directory (Azure AD) Privileged Identity Management (PIM)* to manage privileged access.

- Follow the principle of least privilege by assigning permissions based on the user's roles and responsibilities.
- Regularly review and update access controls to ensure only authorized individuals have access to resources.

- Configuration and vulnerability management:
  - Continuously monitor and enforce compliance with Azure Defender for Cloud Security Policies to detect and remediate misconfigurations.
  - Regularly apply security updates and patches to virtual machines and Azure services using Azure Defender for Cloud or Azure Update Management.
  - Enable vulnerability assessment and integrate it with Azure Defender for Cloud to identify and remediate security vulnerabilities in the environment.

- Monitoring and logging:
  - Enable Azure Monitor and configure logging and alerting for critical resources and security-related events.
  - Centralize logs using Azure Monitor Log Analytics and leverage Azure Sentinel for advanced threat detection and response.
  - Regularly review logs, investigate security events, and establish incident response processes.

- Networking:
  - Implement *Network Security Groups (NSG)* and Azure Firewall to control inbound and outbound traffic at the network level.
  - Utilize Azure Virtual Network Service Endpoints and Private Link to secure access to Azure services.
  - Configure Azure DDoS Protection Standard to mitigate *Distributed Denial of Service (DDoS)* attacks.
  - Implement Azure Bastion for secure remote access to virtual machines.

- Data protection:
  - Implement encryption for data at rest and in transit using Azure Disk Encryption, Azure Storage Service Encryption, and Azure VPN Gateway.
  - Utilize Azure Key Vault to securely store and manage cryptographic keys, secrets, and certificates.

- Implement backup and disaster recovery strategies for critical data using Azure Backup and Azure Site Recovery.
- Application security:
  - Follow secure coding practices and regularly update and patch applications running on Azure.
  - Utilize Azure *Web Application Firewall (WAF)* or Azure Front Door to protect Web applications from common attacks.
  - Implement Azure API Management to secure and manage APIs.

- Incident response:
  - Establish an incident response plan that outlines roles, responsibilities, and procedures for responding to security incidents.
  - Test and simulate incident response scenarios to ensure readiness.
  - Leverage Azure Defender for Cloud threat intelligence and automated response capabilities.

The CIS framework provides detailed guidelines for specific controls, configurations, and security measures. It is advisable to review the complete CIS Azure Foundations Benchmark and consult Azure documentation and resources for step-by-step implementation guidance tailored to the organization's specific Azure environment.

Obviously, if workloads are run in AWS, GCP, and Alibaba Cloud, too, or on on-premises stacks, then the exact same exercise must be done for these clouds. The benchmarks for all platforms can be found at *https://www.cisecurity.org/cis-benchmarks*.

Now the frameworks have been selected and the guidelines implemented, and tools are needed to manage security. That is the topic of the next section.

CHOOSING THE SECURITY TOOLS

This section aims to provide a method to select tools and discusses some best practices in multi-cloud. However, it does not aim to dive deep or provide a comprehensive overview of all tools that are available. While cloud providers such as Azure, AWS, and GCP offer built-in security features, organizations must take a proactive role in enhancing security. It's about the data of the organization and that of its customers. Cloud providers will provide a toolbox, but it's up to the organization to use these tools or choose differently.

First of all, it is important to understand the concept of shared responsibility. The components of this concept are:

- *Infrastructure security*: Cloud providers are responsible for the security of the underlying infrastructure, including data centers, networks, and hardware. They implement physical security measures, network isolation, and protection against external threats, such as DDoS attacks. Additionally, they ensure the availability and reliability of their cloud services.

- *Platform security*: Providers offer security features and controls within their cloud platforms, including IAM, authentication mechanisms, and encryption services. They secure the platform components, such as virtual machines, containers, and databases, to protect against common vulnerabilities and exploits.

- *Compliance and certifications*: Cloud providers adhere to industry standards and regulations, obtaining certifications like ISO 27001, SOC 2, and PCI DSS. They offer compliance frameworks, security audits, and reporting capabilities, ensuring their platforms meet the required security and privacy standards.

Customers of these providers, organizations that host their workloads and data in the cloud, have their own responsibility to enhance the security that cloud providers offer. As said at the beginning of this section, providers such as AWS, Azure, GCP, and Alibaba Cloud offer giant toolboxes with a lot of security tools. It is up to the organizations to use these tools, use different tools, or not use security tools at all. To be very clear about this: security is intrinsic and should never be neglected. In general, it means that organizations will have to collaborate closely with their provider:

- Understand the organization's security requirements, data sensitivity, and compliance obligations. Perform a comprehensive risk assessment to identify potential threats and vulnerabilities specific to the organization's multi-cloud environment.

- Select security tools that can provide centralized visibility and control across multiple cloud platforms. Look for solutions that integrate with APIs provided by Azure, AWS, and GCP, allowing management and monitoring of security configurations, access controls, and compliance policies from a single interface.

- Implement robust IAM practices across all cloud platforms. Utilize RBAC, enforce strong authentication mechanisms (for example, multifactor authentication), and regularly review and audit user access privileges.

- Leverage encryption mechanisms provided by cloud providers, such as Azure Key Vault, AWS KMS, and Google Cloud KMS. Encrypt sensitive data at rest and in transit, both within and between cloud providers.

- Deploy network security tools, such as firewalls, intrusion detection/prevention systems, and Virtual Private Networks (VPN), to safeguard network traffic between on-premises systems and the multi-cloud environment. Implement network segmentation and monitor network activities for anomalous behavior.

- Utilize threat intelligence feeds and *Security Information and Event Management (SIEM)* solutions to detect and respond to security incidents. Implement continuous monitoring, log analysis, and real-time alerts to identify potential threats and intrusions across multiple cloud platforms.

- Conduct periodic security audits and vulnerability assessments to identify and remediate any weaknesses. Monitor compliance with industry regulations and standards applicable to the organization, such as GDPR, HIPAA, or PCI DSS.

- Educate employees on cloud security best practices, social engineering risks, and data handling policies. Promote a security-conscious culture within the organization and encourage reporting of potential security incidents or breaches.

The security tool landscape is continually evolving, so it would be extremely challenging to provide an exhaustive list. Organizations should review their security landscape very frequently, recommended every quarter. Specific security requirements, industry regulations, and cloud provider integrations must be evaluated to choose the most suitable security tools for the multi-cloud environment. The following are some key security tools, including SIEM and *Security Orchestration, Automation, and Response (SOAR)*.

SIEM tools collect, correlate, and analyze security event logs and data from various sources across cloud environments. They provide centralized visibility into security events, helping identify potential threats, detect anomalies, and respond to security incidents. SIEM tools enable real-time monitoring, log management, and advanced analytics to support proactive threat detection and incident response. Popular tools are Splunk, IBM QRadar, LogRhythm,

McAfee Enterprise Security Manager, and Elastic. Some cloud providers offer native SIEM. Azure Sentinel is a good example of this.

SOAR platforms combine security orchestration, automation, and incident response capabilities. They streamline and automate security processes, allowing organizations to respond rapidly and effectively to security incidents across multi-cloud environments. SOAR tools integrate with various security systems and technologies, facilitating automated incident investigation, response coordination, and remediation workflows. Some popular products on the market are Demisto (Palo Alto), Swimlane, and Splunk Phantom.

Cloud Security Posture Management (CSPM) should also be mentioned. CSPM tools enable organizations to assess and manage their cloud security posture by continuously monitoring cloud configurations and detecting misconfigurations or security gaps. These tools provide insights into compliance violations, insecure configurations, and potential risks, helping organizations maintain a strong security posture across multiple cloud platforms. Palo Alto Networks Prisma Cloud, Dome9 (now part of Check Point Software Technologies), and Rapid7 are examples of popular CSPM tools. Native environments such as AWS Security Hub also include CSPM capabilities.

When containerization is used in cloud environments, specific security tools must be considered for containers. Container security tools focus on securing containerized environments, such as those based on Docker or Kubernetes. These tools ensure container image integrity, vulnerability scanning, runtime protection, and compliance enforcement. They help organizations secure applications and data running in containers across multi-cloud deployments. Aqua Security, Sysdig Secure, and Twistlock by Palo Alto are a few examples. Google Cloud Security Command Center includes capabilities specifically for container security.

One of the most critical aspects of cloud security is observability, which makes sense: one needs to be able to "see" before something can be spotted. Observability provides real-time visibility and insights into the behavior and state of cloud environments. It will help to detect, investigate, and respond to security threats, incidents, and vulnerabilities effectively.

Observability enables proactive threat detection by continuously monitoring and analyzing cloud infrastructure, applications, and user activities. It helps identify security incidents, such as unauthorized access attempts, abnormal behavior, or indicators of compromise, allowing organizations to respond promptly and mitigate potential risks. How would that work in practice?

Think of the security team that uses observability tools to monitor network traffic, log events, and user access patterns across multiple cloud providers. They detect a sudden spike in network traffic to a critical server and investigate the incident promptly, discovering a potential Distributed Denial of Service (DDoS) attack and taking necessary measures to mitigate the threat.

Some popular tools for observability that are not platform specific include:

- *Sysdig Secure*: Provides container and cloud-native security with built-in observability and threat detection capabilities.
- *Datadog*: Offers cloud monitoring and observability solutions to gain visibility into cloud infrastructure, applications, and security metrics.
- *Dynatrace*: Provides AI-driven observability and Application Performance Monitoring (APM) for cloud environments.
- *New Relic*: Offers observability and monitoring solutions to gain insights into cloud infrastructure, applications, and user experience.
- *Google Cloud Operations*: Provides a suite of observability tools, including monitoring, logging, and tracing, to enhance visibility in *Google Cloud Platform (GCP)*.

Observability allows organizations to conduct in-depth incident investigations and root cause analyses by capturing and correlating relevant data from different cloud sources. The security team will use the tools to analyze access logs, authentication events, and user activity data. This will help to identify the compromised user account and trace the attack's origin, helping them patch the vulnerability, revoke unauthorized access, and implement additional security measures. Tools they can use for this are:

- *Elastic Observability (ELK Stack)*: Provides log management, monitoring, and APM capabilities for cloud environments, enabling comprehensive observability and analysis.
- *AWS CloudTrail*: Offers visibility into user activity and API usage in AWS, facilitating incident investigation and auditing.
- *Azure Monitor*: Provides monitoring and observability capabilities for Azure resources, including logs, metrics, and diagnostics.
- *GCP Cloud Logging and Cloud Monitoring*: Enables log management, monitoring, and observability in the Google Cloud Platform.

Lastly, observability supports compliance requirements by providing visibility into cloud configurations, access controls, and data handling practices. It allows organizations to monitor adherence to security policies, regulatory frameworks, and industry standards, ensuring continuous compliance and simplifying audit processes.

In highly regulated industries like healthcare and finance, compliance with industry-specific regulations and standards is of utmost importance. Maintaining compliance ensures the protection of sensitive information, promotes transparency, and helps prevent fraudulent activities. Observability plays a vital role in supporting and enhancing compliance efforts in these industries.

An example is the financial institution that utilizes observability tools to monitor access controls, encryption settings, and data handling practices across their multi-cloud infrastructure. They ensure compliance with regulations like PCI DSS by actively monitoring and auditing cloud environments and promptly addressing any noncompliant configurations.

This section discussed a lot of different tools with different focus areas. Many organizations will use a set of tools to cover their security needs and requirements. This will bring some serious challenges for administrators: how can they keep track of it all, especially in multi-cloud settings? The next topic discusses the concept of the single pane-of-glass view, managing security through one lens.

MANAGING SECURITY THROUGH ONE LENS

With organizations increasingly adopting multiple cloud providers to leverage different services and capabilities, it becomes crucial to have a unified view of security across all cloud environments. The principle of a single pane glass view provides a comprehensive and centralized approach to managing security in a multi-cloud environment. This section explores how this principle can be implemented, the tools that can be used, and the benefits it offers. How AI can help in this will also be discussed.

First, the following are the different layers of defense that must be implemented. It is shown in Figure 11.3:

FIGURE 11.3 Layers of defense in the cloud.

The concept of a single pane glass view entails having a centralized security management platform that aggregates and correlates security information from various cloud providers. It allows security teams to monitor, analyze, and enforce security policies consistently across all cloud environments, regardless of the underlying cloud service providers. This approach enables organizations to gain better visibility, control, and compliance while minimizing complexities and ensuring a holistic security posture.

To implement the single pane glass view principle, organizations can utilize cloud-native security tools or adopt third-party security platforms that offer multi-cloud management capabilities. These tools typically provide features such as:

- *Cloud security monitoring*: Tools that enable continuous monitoring of cloud environments, collecting logs, events, and metrics from multiple cloud providers. This allows security teams to detect and respond to security incidents promptly.

- *Centralized policy management*: Platforms that offer a unified interface for defining and managing security policies across multiple cloud environments. This ensures consistent application of security controls, reducing the risk of misconfigurations or security gaps.

- *Threat intelligence integration*: Integrating threat intelligence feeds into the security management platform enhances the ability to detect and respond to emerging threats across all cloud environments. This ensures proactive threat hunting and faster incident response.

- *Compliance and audit support*: Tools that provide automated compliance checks against industry standards and regulations, enabling organizations to maintain regulatory compliance across multiple cloud environments. They can generate comprehensive reports for audits and streamline compliance processes.

- *Identity and access management*: A centralized identity and access management solution that integrates with different cloud providers' identity services, allowing organizations to enforce uniform access controls and user authentication mechanisms across all clouds.

It's good to realize the pros and cons of both cloud-native and third-party tools when implementing security in the cloud. Pros of cloud-native could be integration and native insights. Cloud-native security tools are designed specifically for the cloud environment and seamlessly integrate with native cloud services and infrastructure. They often provide out-of-the-box compatibility with cloud platforms, simplifying deployment and management. Native tools offer native visibility and insights into the cloud environment, providing deep integration with cloud-specific APIs and telemetry data. They can leverage platform-specific features and capabilities, enabling organizations to gain granular visibility and control over their cloud assets.

The cons might be limited functionality, lack of possibilities for customization, and vendor lock-in. Third-party security tools are often designed to address a wide range of security challenges across different cloud platforms. They may offer advanced features, such as threat intelligence, advanced analytics, or specialized compliance modules, providing comprehensive security coverage. In addition, these tools are typically designed to work across multiple cloud environments, offering flexibility and compatibility for organizations adopting multi-cloud or hybrid cloud architectures. They can integrate with various cloud platforms and provide centralized management and visibility.

Also, third-party tools offer more customization options, allowing organizations to adapt the tools to their specific security requirements. They may provide APIs and extensions for integration with existing security infrastructure, enabling seamless workflows and custom integrations.

Next to integration challenges, a downside of this might be the costs. Third-party security tools often come with additional licensing or subscription costs. By adopting a single pane glass view approach to multi-cloud security, organizations can reap several benefits:

- A unified view of security across multiple clouds provides a holistic understanding of the organization's security posture, enabling proactive identification and mitigation of risks.

- With centralized security policy management, organizations can streamline security operations, reducing complexity and eliminating the need for disparate tools and processes for each cloud provider.

- The ability to enforce consistent security policies and controls ensures that security standards are uniformly applied across all cloud environments, reducing the likelihood of misconfigurations and vulnerabilities.

- Centralized security monitoring and incident management enable quick detection, analysis, and response to security incidents, regardless of the cloud provider involved.

- Organizations can maintain regulatory compliance more efficiently by having a centralized platform that helps automate compliance checks, generate reports, and streamline auditing processes.

Introducing Cloud Security Posture Management

Cloud Security Posture Management (CSPM) can help with security challenges in multi-cloud. CSPM refers to the practices, tools, and technologies used to continuously assess, monitor, and manage the security posture of cloud environments. It focuses on identifying misconfigurations, vulnerabilities, and compliance violations within cloud infrastructure, applications, and services. CSPM helps organizations ensure that their cloud deployments adhere to security best practices, industry standards, and regulatory requirements.

CSPM tools scan cloud environments, including *infrastructure-as-a-service (IaaS)*, *platform-as-a-service (PaaS)*, and *software-as-a-service (SaaS)*, to identify misconfigurations in security settings. This includes analyzing network configurations, access controls, encryption settings, storage configurations, and more. By identifying and remediating misconfigurations, organizations can reduce the risk of security incidents. Examples of such tools are Check Point, Aqua Security, Fugue, and Palo Alto, but there are many more. The basic capabilities of CSPM are shown in Figure 11.4:

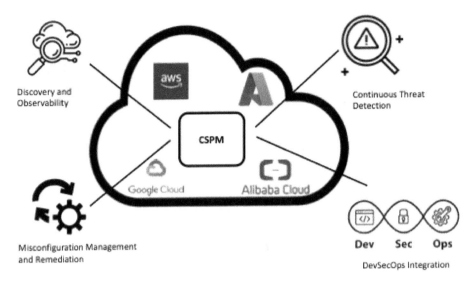

FIGURE 11.4 Basic capabilities of CSPM.

CSPM tools assess cloud environments against regulatory requirements, industry standards, and security best practices. They provide automated checks to ensure that configurations align with specific compliance frameworks such as PCI DSS, HIPAA, GDPR, and CIS benchmarks. Compliance monitoring helps organizations maintain a strong security posture and demonstrate adherence to regulatory obligations.

With CSPM, vulnerability scanning can be performed within cloud environments to identify security weaknesses and potential entry points for attackers. They analyze cloud infrastructure, applications, and services for known vulnerabilities and provide recommendations for remediation. Regular vulnerability assessments are essential to proactively address security risks and protect against exploits.

Lastly, CSPM enables continuous monitoring of cloud environments, collecting logs, events, and metrics from various cloud service providers. They leverage machine learning and behavioral analysis techniques to detect anomalous activities, potential threats, and security incidents. Continuous monitoring ensures timely detection and response to security events, enhancing overall cloud security.

Good tools will not only identify security issues but also provide remediation recommendations. They offer guidance and automation capabilities to help organizations fix misconfigurations, apply security patches, and enforce security policies consistently across cloud deployments. Remediation workflows streamline the process of addressing security gaps and reducing the attack surface.

Using ML and AI, CSPM tools will assess and quantify the risks associated with identified security issues. They prioritize vulnerabilities and misconfigurations based on their potential impact, severity, and exploitability. Risk assessment enables organizations to allocate resources effectively and prioritize remediation efforts for the most critical security issues. How can ML contribute to this?

ML algorithms can analyze data and detect security threats through a process known as anomaly detection. It does so by following a number of steps:

1. *Training phase*: ML algorithms require a training phase where they learn from historical or labeled data. In the context of security threat detection, this training data typically consists of examples of normal, legitimate behavior and known security threats. The algorithm analyzes the data to identify patterns, correlations, and features that distinguish normal behavior from anomalous or malicious activities.

2. *Feature extraction*: once the training data is collected, ML algorithms extract relevant features from the data. These features are specific attributes or characteristics that help describe the data and provide useful information for the algorithm to make predictions. In security threat detection, features can include network traffic patterns, system log events, user behavior, or application usage statistics.

3. *Model creation*: based on the extracted features, ML algorithms create a model that represents the learned patterns and relationships between normal and malicious behavior. The model can take various forms, such as decision trees, neural networks, or support vector machines, depending on the specific algorithm used.

4. *Real-time analysis*: once the model is created, it can be deployed to analyze real-time or streaming data. Incoming data is fed into the ML algorithm, which compares the observed patterns and features against the learned model. The algorithm then assigns a probability or score to each data point, indicating the likelihood of it being a security threat or an anomaly.

5. *Anomaly detection*: ML algorithms excel at identifying deviations from normal behavior. If the algorithm detects data points that significantly deviate from the learned patterns, it flags them as potential security threats or anomalies. These anomalies could indicate malicious activities, such as unauthorized access attempts, unusual network traffic, or abnormal user behavior.

6. *Feedback loop*: ML algorithms continuously improve their performance by incorporating feedback. When security analysts or domain experts review and validate the algorithm's detections, they can provide feedback on misclassified instances. This feedback is used to refine and update the model, making it more accurate over time.

ML algorithms will adapt and learn from new data over time. As the threat landscape evolves, the algorithm can be retrained with updated datasets to account for emerging threats or changes in normal behavior. This adaptive learning allows the algorithm to stay effective and up to date in detecting evolving security threats.

But it is not only tools and technology. It is a culture. A way of thinking. It is important to involve all relevant stakeholders, such as IT and security teams, as well as business leaders and end users, in order to ensure the success of the program. All of these stakeholders must be aware of the threats, the risk, and the potential damage that breaches will cause. It is essential to regularly review and update posture management policies and procedures in order to stay ahead of evolving threats and compliance requirements. It means that it is a serious task keeping up with the security trends, the topic of the final section of this chapter.

KEEPING TRACK AND UP TO DATE WITH SECURITY TRENDS

It is extremely hard to keep up with trends when it comes to security in multi-cloud. To understand this, it must first be acknowledged that types of attacks in the cloud are rapidly evolving. Yet, some common types of attacks can be identified that very often start with misconfigurations as a cause of security breaches in multi-cloud environments. Attackers often exploit misconfigured access controls, insecure default configurations, or inadequate security settings.

Misconfigurations can lead to data breaches due to vulnerabilities in cloud services, weak authentication mechanisms, or compromised credentials.

Attackers may target sensitive data stored in multi-cloud environments, such as *Personally Identifiable Information (PII)* or intellectual property. There are many ways to exploit these vulnerabilities, for instance, through insider threats where malicious or compromised insiders with legitimate access can abuse their privileges to steal or manipulate data, disrupt services, or perform unauthorized actions.

These are just examples. But how can vulnerabilities be recognized, and more important, how can environments be protected from breaches? Tools have been extensively discussed, but it is also necessary to have knowledge of how attacks work. TTP is a process that helps to understand tactics, techniques, and procedures. A TTP analysis will help security teams detect and mitigate attacks by understanding the way threat actors operate. A framework that certainly helps in keeping track of identifying threat actors is Mitre ATT&CK, which can be found at *https://attack.mitre.org/*.

TTPs, as presented in Mitre ATT&CK, are an essential framework for identifying and understanding security threats in multi-cloud environments. They provide a structured approach to analyzing and categorizing the methods employed by attackers, enabling security teams to effectively detect, prevent, and respond to threats. Additional information is as follows:

- Tactics refer to the high-level objectives or goals that attackers aim to achieve. Understanding the tactics employed by threat actors helps security teams anticipate potential attacks and develop appropriate defensive measures. Some common tactics in multi-cloud security include unauthorized access, data exfiltration, privilege escalation, lateral movement, and denial of service.

- Techniques describe the specific methods and tools used by attackers to execute their tactics. By studying the techniques employed in past attacks or known attack patterns, security teams can recognize similar activities or behaviors within their multi-cloud environments. Techniques may include exploiting misconfigurations, conducting phishing campaigns, using malware, leveraging insider access, or exploiting vulnerabilities in cloud services.

- Procedures outline the step-by-step processes or sequences of actions followed by attackers to achieve their objectives. Procedures encompass the tools, infrastructure, and actions taken by threat actors during an attack. Understanding the procedures helps security teams identify the *Indicators of Compromise (IOC)* associated with specific attack campaigns, enabling early detection and response. Procedures may involve reconnaissance, initial compromise, persistence, lateral movement, data exfiltration, or covering tracks.

By analyzing and mapping TTPs, security teams can identify patterns, signatures, or anomalies indicative of potential threats or ongoing attacks in multi-cloud environments. Some examples of ways that TTPs help in threat identification are listed as follows:

- *Signature-based detection*: TTPs enable the creation of signatures or rules that match known attack patterns. Security tools can then use these signatures to identify and alert malicious activities that align with specific TTPs.

- *Anomaly detection*: By understanding the expected behavior and TTPs associated with various threats, security systems can detect anomalies or deviations from the norm. Unusual network traffic, abnormal user behaviors, or unauthorized actions can be flagged as potential threats.

- *Threat intelligence*: TTPs serve as valuable information for threat intelligence gathering. Security teams can leverage public or private sources to gather insights on known TTPs associated with specific threat actors or campaigns. This intelligence helps in proactively identifying emerging threats and taking appropriate preventive measures.

- *Security incident response*: During incident response, understanding the TTPs associated with an attack can help security teams investigate, contain, and remediate the incident effectively. TTPs provide valuable context, allowing analysts to trace the attack chain, identify affected systems, and develop appropriate response actions.

It is important to note that TTPs alone may not provide complete protection against evolving threats. Regular updates to TTP knowledge, continuous monitoring, and a multilayered security approach that combines TTP analysis with other security measures are crucial for effective threat identification and mitigation in multi-cloud environments.

Now, imagine that all of this has to be done manually. With a rapidly evolving landscape and an increasing number of attacks, there is simply no way to keep track of all security breaches manually. A way is needed to automate to keep the environments continuously protected and, by doing so, compliant. That is the topic of the final chapter.

CONCLUSION

Managing security in a multi-cloud environment presents numerous challenges due to the complex nature of distributed systems and the diverse set of cloud service providers, such as AWS, Azure, GCP, and Alibaba Cloud. This chapter explained how these challenges can be addressed effectively, for instance, by leveraging security frameworks such as the Center for Internet Security (CIS) benchmarks, along with appropriate tool selection and the implementation of a single pane glass view. Additionally, Cloud Security Posture Management (CSPM) solutions can play a crucial role in managing security across multiple cloud platforms.

The single pane of glass concept was extensively discussed, which is crucial in multi-cloud. This refers to a unified dashboard or interface that provides a centralized view of the security posture across all the cloud environments being used. A single-pane glass view helps security teams gain visibility into the overall security landscape, identify potential vulnerabilities or misconfigurations, and respond swiftly to emerging threats.

The final section examined the concept tactics, techniques, and procedures to understand how to identify possible new threats. A closer look at the Mitre ATT&CK framework was taken to help us in keeping up with security trends.

KEY POINTS

- The first step is to understand what security frameworks apply to the business, industry, or geographical location where the business resides. It is necessary to learn what the most common frameworks are that must be used in the cloud and to which principles and guidelines the organization must adhere.

- The CIS benchmarks provide guidelines and guardrails for various cloud platforms. They are a great help in defining the security policies in an organization that uses the cloud.

- Cloud platforms are very well protected, yet organizations are still responsible for how they protect their own workloads when they use cloud technology. Azure, AWS, GCP, and Alibaba Cloud offer built-in security features and tools, but organizations must take a proactive role in enhancing security.

- In multi-cloud, the principle of a single pane glass view should be adopted: a centralized security management platform that aggregates and correlates security information from various cloud providers. It allows security teams to monitor, analyze, and enforce security policies consistently across all cloud environments, regardless of the underlying cloud service providers.

- To understand security threats, it is necessary to understand how attacks work by learning Tactics, Techniques, and Procedures (TTP). The Mitre ATT&CK is a good framework that will help in this.

QUESTIONS

1. What are the key capabilities of CSPM?

2. Name three popular tools for observability.

3. What are CIS Benchmarks?

Answers appear in the appendix.

AUTOMATING COMPLIANCY

INTRODUCTION

Part of security is compliancy, which has become a very important topic for almost every organization entering the cloud. Governmental bodies, certification authorities, and auditors are setting compliancy guardrails to allow usage of major cloud providers. These guardrails tend to change every now and then, leaving organizations with tasks to stay compliant with their environments, including data and apps. A recent example of this is the implementation of the *Software Bill of Materials (SBOM)* by the U.S. government. Automating compliancy can be a way to keep in control of these developments, keeping track of all environments on multi-cloud platforms.

STRUCTURE

This chapter will discuss the following topics:

- Understanding compliance in multi-cloud
- Automating governance
- Using RPA for automating compliance
- The next step: using AI for compliance checking

UNDERSTANDING COMPLIANCE IN MULTI-CLOUD

The previous chapter already discussed some elements of compliance. This will be discussed a bit further in this section before starting to think of automating cloud environments to ensure compliancy.

As learned in the previous chapter, compliance is a critical concern for organizations operating in regulated industries such as healthcare, finance, and government. Meeting compliance requirements across multiple cloud providers poses unique challenges due to variations in regulatory frameworks, audit procedures, and data protection laws. However, automation can play a pivotal role in ensuring compliance in multi-cloud environments by streamlining and enhancing governance practices. The following are some key topics when it comes to compliance.

The first step toward compliance is to identify the applicable regulatory requirements that govern the organization's operations. The specific compliance standards, industry regulations, and data protection laws that pertain to the business must be understood. Examples include HIPAA, GDPR, PCI-DSS, and ISO 27001. From these frameworks, a comprehensive set of governance policies and controls need to be established that align with the identified regulatory requirements. These policies should cover areas such as data privacy, access controls, encryption, incident response, and audit trails. Now, these may vary between cloud providers, which makes it a bit more complex in multi-cloud settings. Be sure to clearly define and document the expectations for each cloud provider regarding compliance obligations.

It's crucial to keep in mind the ever-changing nature of the regulatory landscape. A periodic review of this content might be necessary to ensure it stays up to date with any changes in regulations.

Automation can significantly streamline the enforcement of governance policies and controls across multiple cloud providers. The advantages of automation versus manual are significant. By implementing policy-driven automation tools, organizations can continuously evaluate the compliance status of their cloud resources and automatically remediate any noncompliant configurations. This reduces manual effort, minimizes human error, and ensures consistent adherence to compliance requirements. The following is a closer look at the main benefits of automation:

■ Automation allows for the execution of repetitive tasks and processes with minimal human intervention. It enables the cloud infrastructure to perform actions quickly and consistently, reducing the time required to complete tasks. In contrast, manual actions may involve human errors, delays, and inefficiencies.

- Automation facilitates the scaling of cloud resources, such as virtual machines, storage, and networking. With automation, rules and triggers can be defined that automatically adjust resources based on demand. Manual actions can be time-consuming and error-prone when it comes to scaling resources effectively.

- Automation ensures consistent deployment and configuration of cloud resources, following predefined templates and best practices. By eliminating manual intervention, the risk of configuration errors or inconsistencies is reduced. Manual actions, on the other hand, rely on human interpretation and may lead to inconsistencies and nonstandard configurations.

- Automation helps in ensuring the high availability and reliability of cloud services. It enables proactive monitoring, automatic fault detection, and recovery mechanisms. Manual actions may lack the ability to respond quickly to issues and may require human intervention, resulting in potential downtime or reduced service availability.

- Automation can contribute to cost optimization by enabling the efficient utilization of cloud resources. It allows for automated scheduling, resource allocation, and cost monitoring, leading to better cost management and optimization. Manual actions may overlook cost-saving opportunities or may not be as effective in resource optimization.

The following sections study more closely how governance policies can be automated and, with that, ensure compliance. The benefits of automation are clear:

- Automated monitoring solutions enable continuous compliance checking in multi-cloud environments. These tools can proactively scan the cloud infrastructure, identify potential compliance violations, and trigger alerts or automated remediation actions. By continuously monitoring the compliance posture of cloud resources, organizations can address issues promptly and maintain a robust compliance framework.

- Automation simplifies the auditing and reporting processes required for compliance. Instead of manually gathering data and generating compliance reports, organizations can leverage automation tools to collect and consolidate information from different cloud providers. This enables faster and more accurate audits, as well as the ability to produce comprehensive compliance reports in a timely manner.

▣ Automation facilitates effective change management and documentation, which are crucial for maintaining compliance in dynamic multi-cloud environments. By automating the provisioning and configuration of cloud resources, organizations can ensure that changes are tracked, documented, and auditable. Additionally, automation can enforce approval workflows and maintain a history of all modifications, simplifying compliance assessments and demonstrating compliance to auditors.

▣ Automation provides the scalability and flexibility needed to adapt to evolving compliance requirements in multi-cloud settings. As regulations change or new compliance standards emerge, organizations can update their automated governance workflows and policies accordingly. Automation allows for swift and efficient adjustments, ensuring that compliance measures remain up to date across all cloud providers.

So, by harnessing automation in multi-cloud environments, organizations can achieve and maintain compliance with greater ease, efficiency, and accuracy. Automation not only streamlines governance practices but also enhances the organization's ability to respond to regulatory changes, mitigate risks, and demonstrate a strong commitment to compliance.

One topic that has not been addressed yet, in terms of compliance, is SBOM. The U.S. government introduced the concept of SBOM through an executive order for the purpose of improving cybersecurity in the software supply chain. The specific executive order is *Executive Order (EO)* 14028, titled *Improving the Nation's Cybersecurity*, signed by President Joe Biden on May 12, 2021.

The primary motivations behind the introduction of SBOM as an act by the U.S. government include:

▣ *Supply chain security*: With the rise of sophisticated cyber threats, the software supply chain has become a potential target for attackers to infiltrate and compromise critical systems. SBOM aims to enhance the security of the software supply chain by increasing transparency and visibility into the components and dependencies used in software applications.

▣ SBOM enables organizations to track and monitor the software components they use, including known vulnerabilities associated with those components. This helps in prioritizing patching and mitigation efforts, reducing the risk of exploitation through vulnerable components.

▣ SBOM facilitates effective incident response and remediation processes. In the event of a security incident or vulnerability disclosure, having an accurate and up-to-date SBOM enables organizations to quickly identify and address affected software components. It streamlines the process of understanding the potential impact and applying necessary fixes or mitigations.

▦ SBOM aims to establish accountability and compliance requirements for software vendors and suppliers. The government can set standards and guidelines regarding SBOM inclusion and accuracy, ensuring that software providers take responsibility for the components they incorporate into their products. This encourages a culture of transparency, accountability, and security throughout the software supply chain.

SBOM almost forces organizations to automate compliance checking, in this specific case, for all the software that is used. Be aware that this applies to all software, regardless of if it is used in the cloud or not. Figure 12.1 shows all the aspects of SBOM:

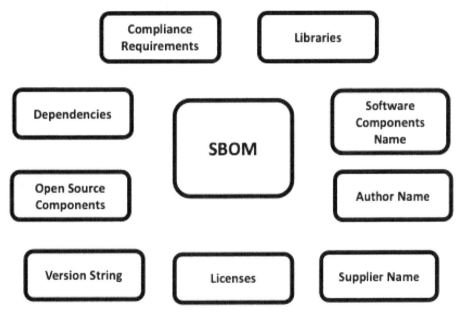

FIGURE 12.1 Components for SBOM.

It might be surprising that it is important to discuss SBOM at this place. The relationship between SBOM and compliance in the cloud is closely tied to transparency, security, and risk management. SBOM is a detailed inventory that lists all the components and dependencies of a software application or system. It provides comprehensive visibility into the software supply chain, including open-source libraries, third-party components, and their associated vulnerabilities.

When it comes to compliance in the cloud, SBOM plays a crucial role in several areas:

- *Vulnerability management*: SBOM enables organizations to identify known vulnerabilities in their software components. By maintaining an up-to-date SBOM, organizations can assess the compliance of their cloud infrastructure with vulnerability management standards and guidelines. This allows them to proactively address vulnerabilities, apply patches, or implement compensating controls to reduce security risks and maintain compliance.

- *Open source*: Many cloud applications and services rely on open-source software components. Complying with open-source licenses and obligations is essential to avoid legal and compliance issues. SBOM provides visibility into the open-source components used in the cloud infrastructure, allowing organizations to track licenses, verify compliance, and ensure adherence to license obligations.

- *Supply chain*: The cloud ecosystem involves multiple vendors, suppliers, and partners. Assessing the security posture of these entities is crucial to maintain compliance. SBOM helps in mapping the software supply chain, allowing organizations to identify potential security risks or vulnerabilities introduced by third-party components. This enables organizations to assess the compliance and security practices of their suppliers and make informed decisions about their cloud service providers.

- *Risk assessment and audits*: SBOM assists in risk assessments and compliance audits by providing a comprehensive overview of the software components and their associated risks. Auditors can review the SBOM to evaluate compliance with regulatory requirements, security standards, and industry best practices. The detailed information in the SBOM helps auditors assess the effectiveness of vulnerability management, security controls, and risk mitigation strategies.

- *Incident response and remediation*: In the event of a security incident or data breach, having an up-to-date SBOM can significantly aid incident response and remediation efforts. It allows organizations to quickly identify and assess the impact of the incident on the affected software components. With this information, organizations can take appropriate actions to remediate the issue, update the SBOM, and demonstrate compliance with incident response requirements.

Overall, SBOM provides essential transparency and visibility into the software supply chain, which is crucial for maintaining compliance in the cloud. It helps organizations manage vulnerabilities, ensure open-source compliance, assess supply chain security, facilitate risk assessments and audits, and improve incident response capabilities.

Now having a deep understanding of what compliance is and what benefits can be gained by automation, automation can really start to be implemented. But where and how to start? That is the topic of the next section.

AUTOMATING GOVERNANCE

If there is one thing that is apparent throughout this book, it is that traditional governance practices struggle to keep pace with the dynamic and complex nature of multi-cloud environments. However, through the application of automation, organizations can streamline governance processes, improve compliance, enhance security, and maximize operational efficiency. This section will explore the challenges associated with governance in multi-cloud settings, discuss potential approaches to automate governance, and outline best practices for successful implementation.

Governance in multi-cloud settings introduces several challenges that need to be addressed to ensure effective management and control:

- Multi-cloud environments consist of different cloud providers, each with its own set of policies, APIs, and interfaces. Coordinating governance across these diverse, heterogenous platforms can be complex and time-consuming.

- The distributed nature of multi-cloud deployments often leads to a lack of visibility into resource utilization, security posture, and compliance status. Without proper monitoring and control mechanisms, organizations face increased risks.

- Organizations operating in industries with strict regulatory requirements face the challenge of ensuring compliance across multiple clouds, each with its own compliance frameworks and standards.

- Maintaining consistent governance policies and controls across different cloud providers is difficult due to variations in service offerings, capabilities, and configurations.

To overcome the challenges associated with multi-cloud governance, best practices should be implemented, starting with *Infrastructure-as-Code (IaC)*. Implementing IaC allows the user to define and manage the cloud infrastructure using machine-readable configuration files. By codifying governance policies and controls, the deployment and management of cloud resources can be automated across multiple clouds. This is what is called a declarative way of working, and this includes policy-driven automation: leveraging policy-driven automation tools, organizations can define and enforce governance policies consistently across different cloud providers. These tools continuously evaluate cloud resources against predefined policies and automatically remediate any noncompliant configurations.

The previous chapter stressed the importance of the single pane of glass view. This is absolutely crucial in enforcing and maintaining compliance. Implementing a centralized monitoring and management platform provides a holistic view of the multi-cloud environment. By aggregating data from various cloud providers, organizations can gain insights into resource utilization, security vulnerabilities, and compliance status, enabling proactive governance.

However, this is just the beginning. To successfully automate governance in multi-cloud settings, it is necessary to have a governance strategy that aligns with business objectives, regulatory requirements, and cloud provider capabilities. Identify key stakeholders and establish clear governance policies and controls. The steps that are crucial in defining the governance strategy are as follows:

1. *Objectives*: Start by clearly defining the governance objectives. Identify the specific compliance, security, and operational requirements that need to be met across the multi-cloud environment. Consider factors such as data protection, access controls, resource allocation, cost management, and regulatory compliance.

2. *Policies*: Develop a set of governance policies that align with the organization's objectives. These policies should outline rules, standards, and best practices for managing the multi-cloud environment. Consider aspects such as security controls, data classification, encryption standards, user access management, *Service-Level Agreements (SLA)*, and incident response protocols.

3. *Roles and responsibilities*: Determine the roles and responsibilities of individuals or teams responsible for implementing and enforcing governance policies. This may include cloud architects, security teams, compliance officers, and operations personnel. Clearly define the scope of each role and establish communication channels for collaboration.

4. *Standardization*: Standardize governance practices, naming conventions, and resource configurations across different cloud providers. This ensures consistency and simplifies automation efforts. Utilize cloud-native automation tools and services provided by cloud providers. These tools are specifically designed to integrate seamlessly with the underlying infrastructure and offer built-in governance capabilities.

5. *Monitor*: Implement continuous monitoring and compliance checking mechanisms to proactively identify and remediate any violations. Leverage automation to trigger alerts, perform remediation actions, and maintain compliance posture.

6. *Review*: Conduct regular audits and reviews to assess the effectiveness of governance automation. Evaluate the accuracy of policies, identify areas for improvement, and adjust automation workflows as necessary.

This is a full cycle, as shown in Figure 12.2. From the review, it might be necessary to adjust policies and even reconsider strategy:

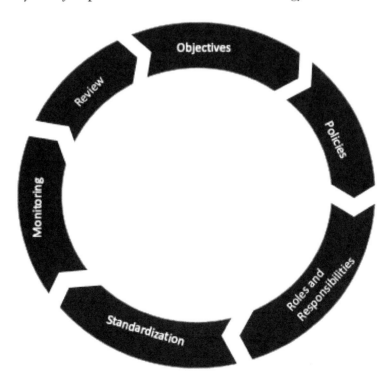

FIGURE 12.2 Governance cycle.

A final or additional step might be continuous learning and adaptation. With cloud technologies evolving rapidly, it's crucial for organizations to keep learning and adapting their strategies to stay ahead.

Can all of this be automated? Not everything, but enforcing that policies are followed, and roles and actions are monitored, can definitively be automated. By leveraging approaches such as Infrastructure as Code, policy-driven automation, and centralized monitoring, organizations can enhance governance practices, improve compliance, and optimize operational efficiency. The principles of *Robotic Process Automation (RPA)* can be used to do so, as is explained in the next section.

USING RPA FOR AUTOMATING COMPLIANCE

The rapid adoption of cloud technology has revolutionized the way businesses operate, providing flexibility, scalability, and cost-effectiveness. However, as organizations transition their operations to the cloud, ensuring compliance with industry regulations and internal policies becomes increasingly complex. Manual compliance monitoring processes often fall short of keeping up with the dynamic nature of cloud environments. To address this challenge, many organizations are turning to RPA as a powerful tool to automate compliance monitoring in the cloud.

One might wonder how RPA can be used for automating compliance in multi-cloud. Compliance monitoring in the cloud involves tracking, validating, and reporting adherence to regulations, policies, and security controls. It encompasses various aspects such as data privacy, access controls, encryption, and auditing. Manual monitoring can be time-consuming, error-prone, and costly. RPA can help overcome these challenges by automating routine tasks, data collection, analysis, and reporting.

What would be the benefits of using RPA in compliance monitoring? To start with, it will increase accuracy. RPA bots perform repetitive tasks with precision, reducing the risk of human error in compliance monitoring. They can gather data from multiple cloud platforms, databases, and applications, ensuring accurate and consistent monitoring across the organization.

RPA eliminates the need for manual data collection, validation, and analysis, enabling faster and more efficient compliance monitoring. Bots can work 24/7, ensuring continuous monitoring without the limitations of human resources, thereby improving overall efficiency. This efficiency is increased through scalability: RPA allows organizations to scale compliance monitoring efforts easily. As the cloud environment grows, RPA bots can be deployed to handle increased data volume, monitor additional systems, and adapt to evolving compliance requirements without significant effort.

Of course, there is a cost element as well. By automating compliance monitoring, organizations can reduce labor costs associated with manual efforts. RPA bots can perform monitoring tasks at a fraction of the time and cost required by human resources, allowing employees to focus on higher-value activities.

RPA bots can automatically extract and analyze audit logs from various cloud platforms, detecting unauthorized access attempts, unusual activities, and potential compliance violations. Alerts can be generated for further investigation or corrective actions. One example is of an RPA bot collecting logs in Azure using Logic Apps. Azure Logic Apps, in this case, is used to build an RPA bot that automatically extracts log files from Azure workloads. Logic Apps provide a visual designer and a wide range of connectors to automate workflows and integrate with various services, including Azure. Of course, there are other ways to do this; Azure Logic Apps is just one option for building RPA bots in Azure. Other tools like Azure Automation, Power Automate, or even Azure Functions may be considered, depending on requirements and preferences.

In this very basic example, a Logic App workflow is used that extracts log files from Azure Blob Storage and saves them to a designated location:

1. A new Logic App is created in the Azure portal.

2. Next, add a trigger to start the workflow. In this case, use the *When a blob is added or modified (properties only)* trigger from the Azure Blob Storage connector. Select the storage account and container where the log files are stored.

3. Add an action to retrieve the log file contents. Use the *Get blob content* action from the Azure Blob Storage connector. Provide the storage account and container information, as well as the blob path from the trigger output.

4. Add any necessary actions to analyze or process the log file contents. Various connectors and actions can be used based on the requirements. For example, the *Extract text from PDF* action could be used if the logs are in PDF format or custom analysis could be performed using Azure Cognitive Services or Azure Functions.

5. Finally, add an action to save the log file to a designated location. Use the *Create file* action from the Azure Blob Storage connector or choose a different connector based on the desired destination. Provide the necessary information, such as the destination folder and file name.

6. Once the Logic App workflow has been defined, it will automatically trigger whenever a new log file is added or modified in the specified Azure Blob Storage container. The bot will then retrieve the log file, perform any required analysis, and save it to the designated location.

In code, using the Python SDK, it will look like this:

```
from azure.identity import DefaultAzureCredential
from azure.storage.blob import BlobServiceClient


# Configure the storage account connection string and container
name storage_connection_string = "<your_storage_connection_
string>" container_name = "<your_container_name>"


# Initialize the BlobServiceClient using the connection string

blob_service_client = BlobServiceClient.from_connection_
string(storage_ connection_string)


# Get a list of blobs in the container

container_client = blob_service_client.get_container_client(con-
tainer_ name)

blobs = container_client.list_blobs()


# Iterate over the blobs and download them
for blob in blobs:

    # Download the blob contents

    blob_client = container_client.get_blob_client(blob.name)
    blob_content = blob_client.download_blob().readall()
```

```
# Perform analysis or processing on the log file contents

# For example, you can use regular expressions, data
parsing, or any required analysis logic


# Save the log file to a designated location
save_location = "<your_save_location>"

with open(f"{save_location}/{blob.name}", "wb") as file:
    file.write(blob_content)
```

In this code, `<your_storage_connection_string>` needs to be replaced with the connection string of the Azure Storage account and `<your_container_name>` with the name of the container where the log files are stored. Provide the `<your_save_ location>` with the desired folder where the log files should be saved. Moreover, it is necessary to make sure that the required dependencies are installed. It is recommended to install them using pip.

In AWS, AWS Lambda and AWS SDKs can be used to automate the extraction of log files from AWS workloads, using Python and AWS SDK for Python (Boto3). In GCP, the best options are Google Cloud Functions and Google Cloud Storage Client Libraries to automate log file extraction.

This is just a basic example of the usage of RPA bots. This section discussed the native technology of cloud providers, but a lot of organizations might choose to use third-party tools to automate compliance. Examples are Cloud Custodian, Dome9, or Prisma Cloud. The primary functions of these tools include:

- *Cloud security and compliance monitoring*: These tools continuously monitor cloud infrastructure, services, and resources to identify security vulnerabilities, misconfigurations, and compliance violations. They provide real-time visibility into the security posture of cloud environments, helping organizations proactively address risks and ensure compliance with industry standards and regulatory requirements.

- *Automated policy enforcement*: Tools like Cloud Custodian, Dome9, and Prisma Cloud allow organizations to define and enforce security policies and best practices across their cloud deployments. They enable the automation of policy enforcement, ensuring that cloud resources adhere to specific security guidelines and configurations. This helps prevent security incidents and maintain a secure cloud environment.

- *Threat detection and incident response*: These tools employ advanced threat detection techniques and machine learning algorithms to identify suspicious activities, indicators of compromise, and potential security breaches within cloud environments. They provide alerts, notifications, and actionable insights to security teams, enabling them to respond quickly to security incidents and mitigate threats.

- *Compliance reporting and auditing*: Tools like Cloud Custodian, Dome9, and Prisma Cloud assist organizations in generating compliance reports and conducting audits. They provide predefined compliance frameworks and standards, enabling organizations to assess their cloud environments against specific regulatory requirements. These tools simplify the process of preparing for audits and demonstrate compliance with regulatory bodies.

- *Security automation and remediation*: These tools offer automation capabilities to streamline security tasks and remediation processes. They can automatically fix misconfigurations, apply security patches, and remediate security issues identified within cloud environments. This helps organizations improve operational efficiency and reduce the manual effort required for security management.

As seen from this brief overview of the capabilities that these third-party tools have, RPA can be utilized for a lot more. For instance, to run user access reviews: RPA can automate the process of reviewing user access privileges in the cloud. Bots can collect user access data, compare it against defined roles and policies, identify any discrepancies, and generate reports for management and compliance teams. Overall, RPA is a good practice to streamline the generation of compliance reports by automatically collecting data from different sources, formatting it, and generating comprehensive reports. This reduces the time and effort required for manual report generation and ensures accuracy and consistency. As previously illustrated, consistency is key to compliance. RPA bots can enforce compliance policies by monitoring cloud resources and configurations. They can identify deviations from defined policies, trigger remedial actions, or generate alerts for the IT or compliance teams to take appropriate measures.

There are some important considerations to take into account. First and most important of all, it is necessary to make sure—as with anything—that security measures are in place to protect RPA bots and the data they handle. Access controls, encryption, and secure communication protocols should be implemented to prevent unauthorized access or data breaches. Next, RPA bots should be regularly updated to accommodate changes in compliance requirements, cloud platforms, and regulations. Maintenance tasks, such as patching and monitoring, should be performed to ensure the bots' effectiveness and reliability.

While RPA can automate many compliance monitoring tasks, human oversight and governance remain crucial. Organizations should establish clear guidelines, policies, and processes for managing RPA bots, reviewing their output, and addressing exceptions or complex scenarios.

Automating compliance monitoring in the cloud using RPA offers numerous benefits to organizations, including enhanced accuracy, improved efficiency, scalability, and cost reduction. It is essential to carefully plan and implement RPA solutions while considering security, maintenance, and human oversight aspects. By embracing RPA in compliance monitoring, organizations can achieve higher levels of compliance and governance in their cloud environments. The final section explains how AI and machine learning can be a great aid in this.

THE NEXT STEP: USING AI FOR COMPLIANCE CHECKING

No modern book about cloud technology can do without discussing how AI could help in managing environments in the cloud. So, the final section of this book looks at the possibilities that AI will bring to multi-cloud management, especially in ensuring compliance. AI can certainly play a significant role in managing and controlling compliance in multi-cloud environments by providing automated and intelligent solutions.

Most chapters in this book ended with a section about monitoring. With multi-cloud environments can become very complex, and solid monitoring will be needed to know the actual status of the workloads and what possible consequences there might be if one of the workloads, connections, databases, or APIs fails. AI algorithms can continuously monitor various data sources, including logs, configurations, and user activities across multiple cloud platforms. By analyzing this data, AI can identify any noncompliant actions, policy violations, or security breaches in real time. It can generate alerts and notifications for immediate action, enabling organizations to proactively address compliance issues.

Before having a closer look at AI, it's good to explore emerging trends in cloud compliance.

- There is expected to be an increase in regulations specific to cloud computing, addressing data privacy, security, cross-border data transfers, and vendor accountability. Compliance frameworks, such as GDPR and CCPA, are likely to evolve and become more cloud-centric.

- Data residency and sovereignty concerns are gaining prominence as organizations grapple with cross-border data transfers and conflicting jurisdictional requirements. Compliance regulations may address the storage and processing of data within specific geographic boundaries, leading to the development of cloud solutions that offer localized data centers or mechanisms to control data residency.

- With the increased reliance on cloud service providers, there is a growing demand for transparency and accountability from *cloud service providers (CSPs)* regarding their compliance practices. Organizations are seeking assurance that CSPs adhere to stringent compliance requirements and follow best practices for data security, privacy, and governance. More rigorous audits, certifications, and third-party assessments of CSPs can be anticipated.

- As organizations adopt multi-cloud and hybrid cloud strategies, compliance challenges become more complex. Compliance frameworks will need to address the unique considerations associated with managing compliance across multiple cloud providers and on-premises infrastructure. Standards for interoperability, data portability, and consistent compliance controls are expected to evolve.

- Of course, automation will play a crucial role in ensuring cloud compliance. Organizations will increasingly leverage technologies such as IaC and Continuous Compliance to automate the deployment, configuration, and enforcement of compliance controls. Integrating compliance into DevOps and adopting DevSecOps practices will become essential for maintaining compliance in highly dynamic cloud environments.

- As cloud-native architectures, such as containers and serverless computing, gain wider adoption, compliance frameworks will need to adapt accordingly. Regulations will likely include specific guidelines for securing cloud-native applications and microservices architectures, addressing container security, secrets management, and secure development practices.

⬛ The need for real-time compliance monitoring and continuous assessment will grow. Tools and technologies that provide real-time visibility into compliance posture, automated scanning for misconfigurations, and monitoring of cloud environments for policy violations will become increasingly important.

As AI and machine learning applications become more prevalent in the cloud, compliance frameworks will evolve to address the ethical and responsible use of AI. Regulations may include guidelines on transparency, explainability, fairness, and accountability in AI algorithms and models deployed in the cloud.

AI can assist in enforcing compliance policies by automatically evaluating cloud resources and configurations against predefined compliance rules and standards. It can identify any deviations and suggest appropriate remedial actions to bring the environment back into compliance. This will help in maintaining a consistent and secure configuration across their multi-cloud infrastructure. AI can also perform automated risk assessments by analyzing the security posture of different cloud providers and identifying potential vulnerabilities or weaknesses in the infrastructure. It can evaluate factors such as encryption practices, access controls, data privacy measures, and regulatory compliance. This helps organizations identify areas of improvement and ensure adherence to compliance requirements.

However, the best part about AI is that it learns, and by doing so, it can become predictive. AI can leverage historical compliance data and patterns to perform predictive analytics. By analyzing past compliance violations and incidents, it can identify potential future risks and provide recommendations to mitigate them. This proactive approach allows organizations to anticipate compliance challenges and take preventive measures in advance.

Most monitoring systems in the cloud already work with AI. Examples are Azure's Sentinel, AWS GuardDuty, and Google *Cloud Security Command Center (Cloud SCC)*. They all use AI and machine learning techniques to enhance security operations, detect and respond to threats, and provide actionable insights:

⬛ *Threat detection*: Employing AI algorithms to analyze large volumes of security event data in real time. Sentinel, GuardDuty, and Cloud SCC can automatically identify patterns, anomalies, and suspicious activities that may indicate a potential security breach. AI-powered threat detection helps in discovering both known and unknown threats, including sophisticated and evolving attack techniques.

- *Behavioral analytics*: By applying machine learning, these systems create baselines of normal behavior for users, devices, and applications in the environment. They then compare ongoing activities against these baselines to identify deviations that could indicate malicious behavior. AI algorithms help in detecting unusual patterns, privileged access abuse, insider threats, and other anomalous activities. This can be very simple: if someone, for example, logs in from London at 10:00 AM, this person cannot log in to systems from the other side of the world at 10:05 AM. Systems will detect and flag this.

- *Anomaly detection*: Sentinel, GuardDuty, and Cloud SCC utilize AI-based anomaly detection techniques to identify abnormal events or deviations from expected behavior. It can detect anomalies in user behavior, network traffic, application usage, system logs, and more. By continuously learning from data patterns, these systems improve their anomaly detection capabilities over time, making them more accurate in recognizing potential threats.

- *Automated threat response*: With AI integration, these systems enable automated threat response actions. It can trigger automatic remediation actions or orchestrate security workflows based on predefined playbooks. For example, if a specific threat is detected, Sentinel or one of the other systems can automatically block an IP address, quarantine a compromised device, or initiate incident response procedures.

- *Threat intelligence and hunting*: This one specifically applies to Azure Sentinel, which integrates with threat intelligence feeds, both from Microsoft and third-party sources. AI algorithms analyze and correlate this information with real-time security events to provide context and prioritize threats effectively. It helps security analysts in threat-hunting activities by surfacing relevant indicators of compromise and supporting proactive detection of emerging threats.

- *Data analysis and visualization*: AI-powered data analysis and visualization techniques provide meaningful insights into security events. It can automatically categorize and tag security events, perform entity extraction, and identify relationships between various entities. This helps analysts quickly identify important security events and investigate incidents more efficiently.

Sentinel, GuardDuty, and Cloud SCC certainly share capabilities, but keep in mind that each service has its own unique features and integrations specific to their respective cloud platforms.

Overall, AI brings automation, scalability, and intelligence to compliance management in multi-cloud environments. It enhances the ability to monitor, enforce, and report compliance, thereby reducing human effort, improving accuracy, and ensuring a higher level of security and adherence to regulatory requirements.

This is the end of this chapter and this book. By now, there should be a good understanding of managing multi-cloud environments, the challenges that multi-cloud brings along, and how these challenges could be overcome.

CONCLUSION

The most important lesson from this chapter is that compliance is a critical concern for organizations operating in almost every industry, but especially in healthcare, finance, and government. Meeting compliance requirements across multiple cloud providers poses unique challenges due to variations in regulatory frameworks, audit procedures, and data protection laws that vary from continent to continent and even from country to country. Compliance frameworks will offer guidance in applying the right policies. Next, it was explained how automation can be used to enforce and monitor these policies.

It was shown that *Infrastructure as Code (IaC)*, policy-driven automation, and centralized monitoring organizations can help with governance practices and improve compliance and how the principles of RPA can be used to do so. Examples of automated bots in Azure, AWS, and GCP were studied.

The final section discussed the possibilities of integrating AI and machine learning to help in managing compliance by providing automated and intelligent solutions. Most major cloud providers already offer sophisticated solutions, such as Azure Sentinel, AWS GuardDuty, and GCP Security Command Center, that all utilize AI to monitor workloads on their platforms.

KEY POINTS

- Although this chapter focused on automation, the most important first step in managing compliance is identifying the applicable regulatory requirements that govern the organization's operations. The specific compliance standards, industry regulations, and data protection laws that pertain to the business must be understood. Examples include HIPAA, GDPR, PCI-DSS, and ISO 27001.

- Since monitoring compliance can become extremely complex, automation becomes key. By implementing policy-driven automation tools, organizations can continuously evaluate the compliance status of their cloud resources and automatically remediate any noncompliant configurations.

- SBOM is, or will be, a mandatory document in many industries.

- Keep in mind that not everything can be automated (yet). However, enforcing that policies are followed and roles and actions are monitored can definitively be automated.

- The principles of RPA are good guidance in automating security and compliance. RPA can be used for tracking, validating, and reporting adherence to regulations, policies, and security controls. RPA can help by automating routine tasks, data collection, analysis, and reporting.

- On top of RPA, AI and machine learning are recent developments that are great enhancements in monitoring, including actioning of events, for instance, in threat detection. AI can trigger automatic remediation actions or orchestrate security workflows based on predefined playbooks. In this case, the work will have to be done with both RPA and AI. Major cloud providers offer already sophisticated tools to enable this.

QUESTIONS

1. What are GDPR, HIPAA, and PCI-DSS?

2. Six stages were discussed in the governance cycle. Name these six stages.

3. What are the security suites of cloud providers that offer AI capabilities?

4. Name three aspects of SBOM.

Answers appear in the appendix.

APPENDIX

ANSWER KEY FOR CHAPTER QUESTIONS

Chapter 1

1. Rehost.

2. Learn, lead, scale, and secure.

3. Configuration Management Database—a database holding all assets that IT has to manage.

Chapter 2

1. MPLS is considered to be a private network.

2. vNet.

3. Infrastructure, control, applications.

4. Direct Interconnect.

Chapter 3

1. Host based.

2. File, block, object.

3. Blob.

4. Glacier.

Chapter 4

1. Hypervisor.
2. True.
3. Outposts.
4. Virtual machines, containers, serverless.

Chapter 5

1. Kubernetes.
2. Sidecar.
3. Lightweight Kubernetes, for example, IoT.
4. Data gravity.

Chapter 6

1. Accuracy, completeness, consistency, timeliness, relevance, validity.
2. Snowball.
3. Data stewards are responsible for ensuring that data is accurate, complete, and available when needed.

Chapter 7

1. GraphQL, React, Apollo, Neo4j Database.
2. Canary release.
3. Build, test, and deploy new software, streamlining the release of software.

Chapter 8

1. OCI.
2. SCA, SAST. DAST, Pen testing.
3. Open-source tools for collecting and analyzing logs.

Chapter 9

1. Event Grid and Logic Apps.

2. Handling streaming events in real time.

3. Open Functions as a Service—open source serverless framework.

4. Amount of time it takes for a function to initialize and execute its first request.

Chapter 10

1. Compliance check, data security, threat protection, and data loss prevention.

2. Minimal rights that an identity needs to perform a job.

3. Keys and secrets are used to authenticate and authorize access to resources, applications, and services in the cloud.

Chapter 11

1. Discovery and observability, continuous threat detection, misconfiguration management and remediation, and devsecops integration.

2. Datadog, New Relic, Sysdig, Dynatrace.

3. Guidelines and guardrails to implement security policies in the cloud.

Chapter 12

1. Compliance frameworks.

2. Objectives, policies, roles and responsibilities, standardization, monitoring, review.

3. Azure Sentinel, AWS GuardDuty, GCP Security Command Center.

4. Software components, compliance requirements, libraries, author name, supplier name, open-source components, version string, licenses, dependencies.

INDEX

www.ingramcontent.com/pod-product-compliance
Lightning Source LLC
LaVergne TN
LVHW062306060326
832902LV00013B/2071